A CONVERSATION WITH THE WORLD

Human is at once a beginning and an end. It is the start of a worldwide conversation between people who do not yet know each other but who have a lot to say to one another. It is a conversation between people who hold more power than they think because we are all concerned, each and every one of us; we all have, in our own way, something to say about the world and we all have the capacity to transform it, at least in modest measure.

This is also the conclusion of several years of work: Human has its roots in the photographic project that I began twenty years ago with *Earth from Above*, a project that I expanded on in my film *Home*. As for the interviews, they stem from my series of photographic portraits and then from my interview project on humanism around the globe: a project named *6 Billion Others*, which became *7 Billion Others* with worldwide population growth.

With both *7 Billion Others* and *Human*, the goal is to give voice to people we don't usually hear: the voiceless, the nameless, people who don't make the cover of magazines but who are nevertheless exceptional. Often—although unknown, or rather because they are—they have messages of explosive power, proportionate to their authenticity; their words have not yet been eroded by the filter of media.

For these words not to be lost, they must find echo. You need to grab hold of the words that have impressed you, reflect upon them, repeat them, answer, and maybe counteract them.

And so, I would like these stories to mark the beginning of conversations, ones that you'll have with others around you, which, in the age of the Internet and social networks, means conversations with the whole planet: beyond oceans, time zones, cultures, and religions. That is why the film *Human* will be distributed for free as widely as possible throughout the world. For this, we can thank its patron the Fondation Bettencourt Schueller.

As a way to encourage these conversations, this book adds to the stories that only appear as short excerpts. It nourishes them with supplementary information, puts them into perspective with reportages on the areas they address, sheds light on them with the perspectives of some of the journalists on my team, expands on them with readings and films.

But I hope that you will expand on these conversations as well with action, by committing, each one of you in your own way, to make the world better. That is the profound challenge of the film *Human*, of the volunteering project I'm conducting with Google; it is also the goal of the GoodPlanet Foundation, which I've founded: living together.

Each and every one of you can do it in your own way: by smiling at strangers, by talking with senior neighbors or by bringing them groceries, by financially supporting a cause, by volunteering your time to an organization....More generally, you can do it by choosing to be happy and by avoiding the dark passageways of selfishness and fear.

All this is possible only if you open your heart, so that you can begin the conversation with the world, in other words, with all the people around you—and so that from this conversation is born a little more love.

—Yann Arthus-Bertrand

ABRAMS, NEW YORK

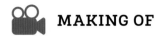
THE WORLD SEEN FROM THE SKY

LANDSCAPES AND MEN

The movie *Human* alternates between interview sequences and aerial footage. The latter, which represents about a third of the film, shows the beauty of our world: This is Yann Arthus-Bertrand's trademark. It also allows the viewer to situate the interviews within a larger context, a big city or farmland, for example. Yann wasn't alone behind the camera when these scenes were captured: *Human* was made by a team. The various camerapeople shot a total of some thirty landscapes in the course of two and a half years.

"As a general rule, we film from a helicopter as part of our artistic signature. You can't tell the same story from a plane and you can't get unique and wonderful images from one," explains Yazid Tizi, head of aerial filming, who for twenty years worked for the television program *Ushuaïa Nature*. But before you can film, there's a long scouting and preparation process, and you have to secure permissions. Sometimes you have to deal with a country's army, if that's the only body that can provide the necessary aerial means.

Once on site, Yazid, Bruno Cusa, the aerial photography manager, Stéphane Azouze, visual engineer, and Yann set to work on their mission to gather images. Bruno, who worked on the Tour de France, on the film *Planet Ocean*, and on the series *Vu du Ciel* for many years, explains his role: "As an aerial cameraman, I have to reproduce what Yann wants in cinematic images. When he sees a place, he immediately has an idea about what he wants to pull from it. I try to adapt to his very specific style, which makes you feel through image and beauty."

The film doesn't lack impressive images. Some appear in this book.

Yazid randomly cites the caravan of yaks in northern Pakistan (page 16), the stone trees of the Salar de Uyuni in Bolivia (page 86), the salt caravan and its camel convoy in Ethiopia (page 208), the human tower in Catalonia, and the untouched beauty of Mongolia (page 84).

Bruno Cusa was struck by the shots of a garbage sorter in Santo Domingo. "We were filming a man from behind, most likely a Haitian, who was walking in front of a mountain of moving garbage. Then he stops and glances at the camera. The pilot's skill was such that I could keep the frame on this man while tires, toys, and miscellaneous household garbage pour out like a permanent wave behind him. His momentary stare is overwhelming; it's one of the images that made the biggest impression on me while filming."

However, sometimes even powerful footage gets cut during editing. As an

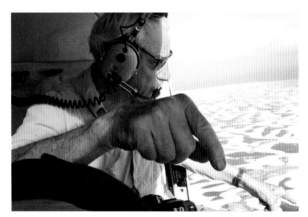

2

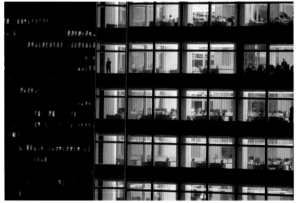

3

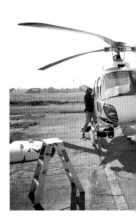

4

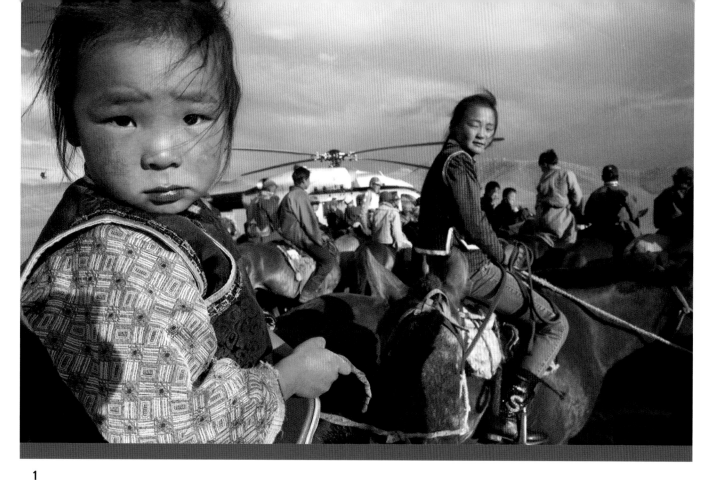

1

example, Bruno cites filming the ravages of Typhoon Haiyan in the Philippines in 2013. Despite the desolation, people smiled and kept hope alive. Bruno remembers, "We had filmed a close-up of a little girl. Then the camera pulled back and you gradually could see the extent of the destruction around her. But the scene didn't tie into the film or into any story. So it was cut during editing."

Because Yann and the editors constructed *Human* around strong stories and used aerial images as a way to create a pause, the sequences seen from the sky are conceived of both as moments of escape and as metaphors. As a result, the beauty of the world dazzles while the viewer is invited to confront the reality of what is expressed in the stories.

—Julien Leprovost

1. An Airbus EC 145 helicopter, in Mongolia, amid young seminomads preparing for a horserace.

2. Yann Arthus-Bertrand giving instructions while filming in Brazil, above the Lençóis Maranhenses National Park.

3. Working late at night in an office building in New York.

4. Helicopter preparation for filming in Cambodia.

5. In Mongolia, before the race.

6. Bruno Cusa filming from the helicopter.

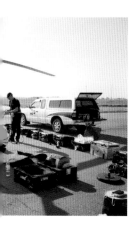

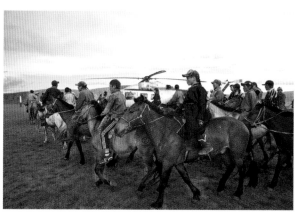

5

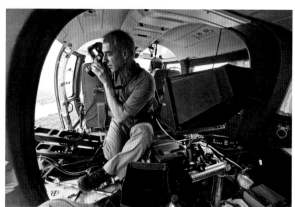

6

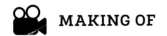

OTHER PEOPLE'S WORDS

A JOURNEY INTO THE PRIVATE LIVES OF STRANGERS

How do you get the mind-blowing interviews seen in the film *Human* and recorded in this book? The journalists and camerapeople who took part in more than two thousand interviews conducted for the movie each have their own opinion, way, and sensibility. And each interview is a unique encounter.

Another important role is that of the "fixer." In the world of the media, this is a "local" who helps the film crew: a man or a woman who knows the place and the people. Fixers get the permissions to film and take care of logistics. In *Human*, they often did a lot more: They helped find the people interviewed and also, most of the time, translated their words.

On specific sets, the fixer is a specialist in the area. For filming in American prisons, Isabelle Vayron chose an activist and a specialist on the subject, someone who knew the people, who could convince them to talk, and who also knew the laws specific to filming in prison. On other sets that didn't have a specific theme, finding the right fixer was a question of chemistry. The work is so specific that you have to spend a lot of time explaining what you want. But when it works, "there's a real trust and you become one," explains Anastasia Mikova, the head of interview filming for *Human*.

Once you find the right people, how do you get them to talk? How do you instill trust so that, for an hour or an hour and a half—the time it takes to do an interview—a stranger will tell you things he or she may never have told anyone, and in front of the camera?

There is no recipe. But sometimes it's easier to talk to someone you don't know, says Baptiste Rouget-Luchaire, who filmed numerous interviews and codirected the project *6 Billion Others*—in some ways, the forefather of *Human*. Sometimes, he continues, "you have to get out of questions and answers. You have to open a door to introspection." Mia Sfeir, a journalist on the *Human* team, explains, "If you start by talking about yourself, you make the other person want to share." Other times, she continues, "It's by starting with questions about childhood and the memories that go along with it," that you can head down the path of introspection.

Sometimes, nothing happens. But when it works, there's magic—and often an amazing energy that reaches everyone. It's even sometimes difficult to move on to something else. But, explains Anastasia, "After an interview that's gone well, people often say thank you; you're the first person who has listened to me, or, it's the first time I've ever said what I said. Despite the brevity of the meeting, you feel like you've made others feel good, and so, you feel good too. Also, often you keep in touch, you write, you find out what's new."

Months after an interview during which a woman spoke about very difficult things in her life, Hervé Kern, a journalist for *Human*, still wonders, "How was that woman able to go back to her life after telling such a heavy story? Will it take its toll or will it serve as a liberation?"

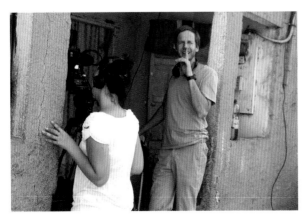

2

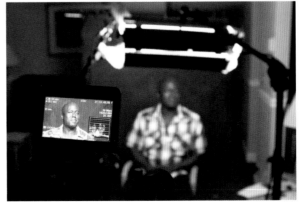

3

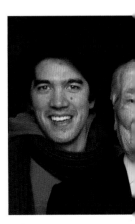

4

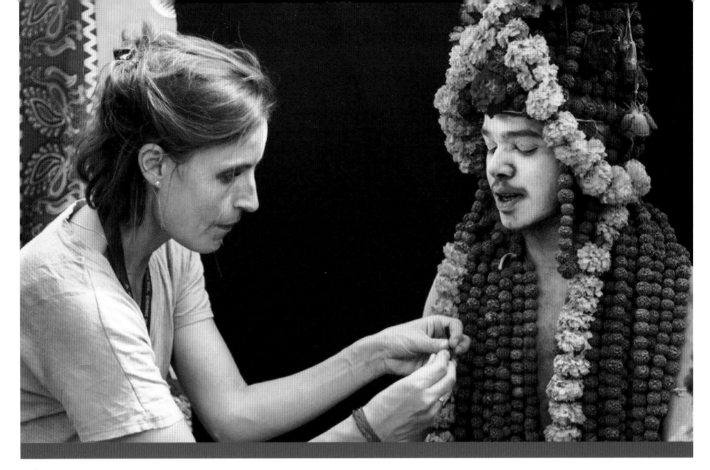

1

The journalists don't go unmarked by these encounters. When Hervé interviewed an atomic-bomb survivor in Hiroshima who at age eighty-nine continues fighting for peace, his stomach was in knots. He'll never forget those moments, or the sound of the peace bell, in the city's park.

For Mia, it was meeting a very poor Indian woman in Uttar Pradesh that left a mark on her. The woman was crying out her distress and her anger. "I didn't understand her language, but I could imagine what she was saying. And that woman was capable of transmitting a message so strong without me understanding her words! I felt the universality of her suffering and I broke down in tears. And then she took me in her arms, and I understood that she also was bearing a message of generosity." The film as a whole also bears this message, undoubtedly.

—Olivier Blond

1. Marie-France, a journalist on the *Human* team prepares for an interview during the massive Kumbh Mela: a Hindu pilgrimage that takes place every twelve years. This time, it brought together close to one hundred million faithful to the banks of the Ganges.

2. Baptiste and Anastasia in Senegal: "Quiet on the set!"

3. The *Human* team interviewing a former detainee in an American prison.

4. Hervé, a journalist for *Human*, with a Hiroshima survivor in Japan, and his cameraman, Jérémy.

5. Yann Arthus-Bertrand with José Mujica Cordano, president of Uruguay.

6. Portrait of Ekami, the Indian woman whose story left its mark on Mia.

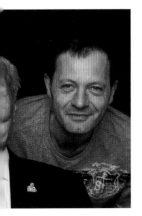

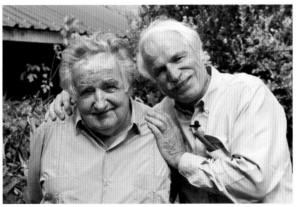

5

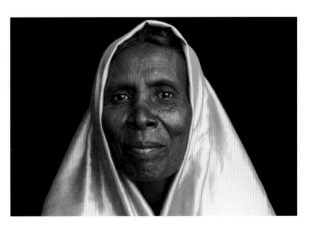

6

THOUSANDS OF HOURS OF VIDEO

THE MAKING OF A MONTAGE

How can you tell a story that combines two thousand interviews and aerial footage from thirty-two shoots that took place all over the world? *Human* is a significant cinematographic accomplishment because of the vastness of the project and the quantity of video rushes. The four-woman editing team spent two years bringing the film to light.

"We had to listen and verify the quality of images, catalog them, subtitle them, and then make a first selection," explains Maeva Issico, associate editor.

"We had the privilege of watching an uninterrupted flow of poetic and dreadful images and hundreds of hours of people talking, each one enriching," remembers Anne-Claire Decaus, assistant editor.

Why keep or reject a story? "Editing is about choosing and letting go.

Human was terribly frustrating because of the incredible number of stories we had available," says Anne-Marie Sangla, one of the two head editors.

There were obvious choices, like the story of Leonard, the first in the movie (see page 12). But aside from this extraordinary account, there were hundreds of others that deserved time in the film. The editors looked for "that little indescribable something, that ability some have to communicate something beyond their own story. This is something that happens with body language, attitude, and intonation…all subjective elements that touch us unconsciously and allow us to empathize and identify with the person, despite the language barrier," explains the other head editor, Françoise Bernard.

Once the interviews are selected, how do you weave the connections

between stories? How do you make it so that these men and women who don't know each other are telling one story together? "The difficulty was precisely finding that story, based on Yann's intention, which was to create a portrait of humanity," Sangla explains. "The film was to be universal, but also singular, it was to tell of our differences and also of what unites us, it was to tell the best and the worst, allow us to feel the complexity of the human soul. *Human* was meant to touch us and make us think."

Universal themes emerged naturally from the editing: love, family, the meaning of life, and war. Then there were others, more specific themes, but still fundamental for Yann: homosexuality, inequality, agriculture, and immigration. Engaging with all of these primary themes, the film became more political and engaged.

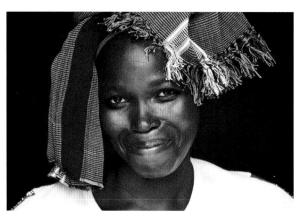

2

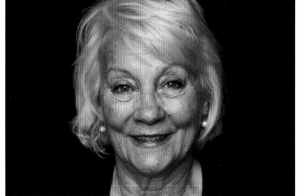

3

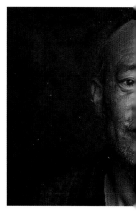

4

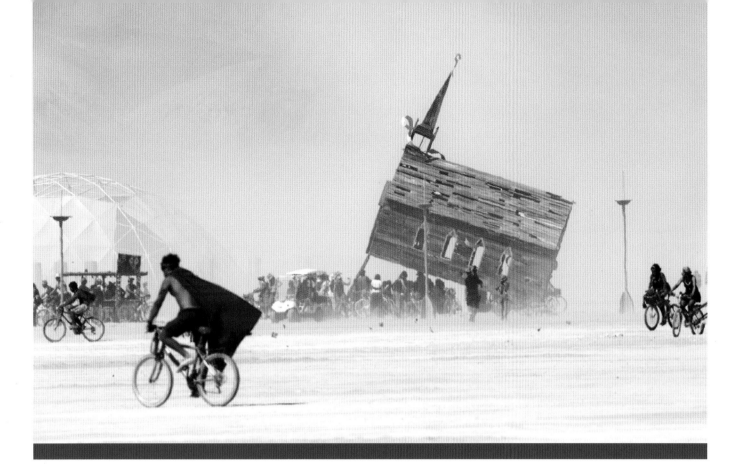

1

Once these large themes were identified, the other challenge was to pair them with aerial images. "Yann wanted the aerial sequences to be moments of contemplation that allowed you to think about the words you just heard. And at the same time, they were to show the world's beauty," Bernard explains.

"These images, accompanied by music composed by Armand Amar, take us elsewhere and tell a story themselves," she continues.

After several months of editing, once the rhythm of sequences was found, they had to be given an order.

But while each theme worked well separately, giving them a balance when put together was a challenge. Bernard remembers trying a huge number of different constructions with Sangla.

In the end, the editing led to a film that reflects the different facets of being human that are familiar to everyone. "To get there, the collaboration between Françoise and myself, with the help of Maeva and Anne-Claire, was essential," Sangla concludes, "because we all lent our sensibility to create a portrait of humanity with many voices."
—Julien Leprovost and Anastasia Mikova

1. Burning Man takes place every year in the Black Rock Desert of Nevada. It draws many tens of thousands of people for a huge celebration in an ephemeral city. This festival came into being in 1986, and includes the burning of a huge wooden effigy, the burning man.

2–6. Some of the two thousand people interviewed for *Human*.

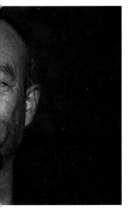

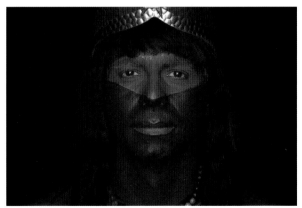

5

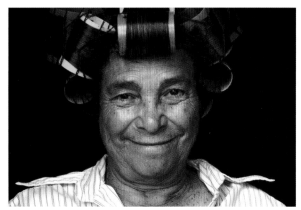

6

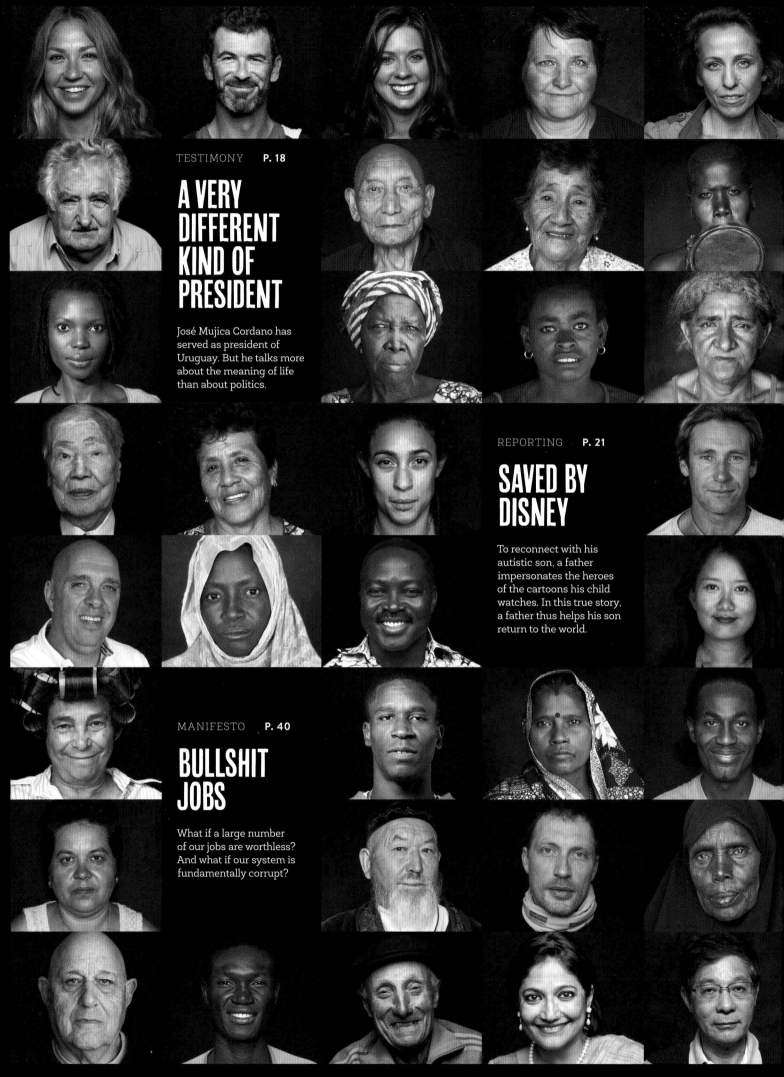

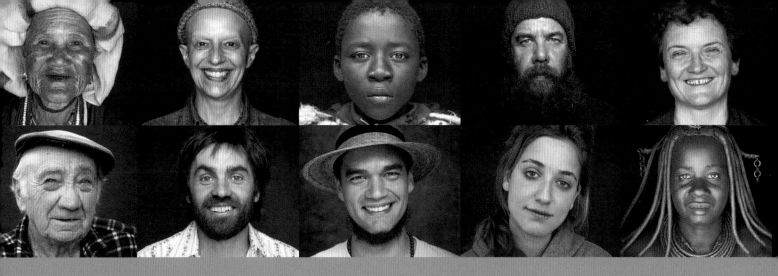

HAPPINESS

What is happiness? What is the meaning of life? None of humanity's great philosophers or thinkers have managed to provide universally accepted answers to these questions. Perhaps there aren't any answers, and each of us must stumble along to find the right path. In this adventure, the challenges we overcome are often the most precious.

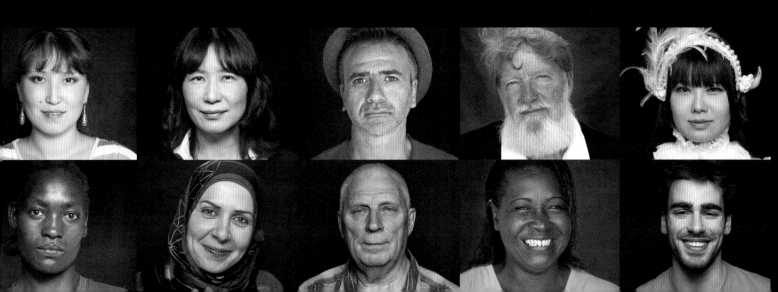

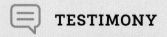
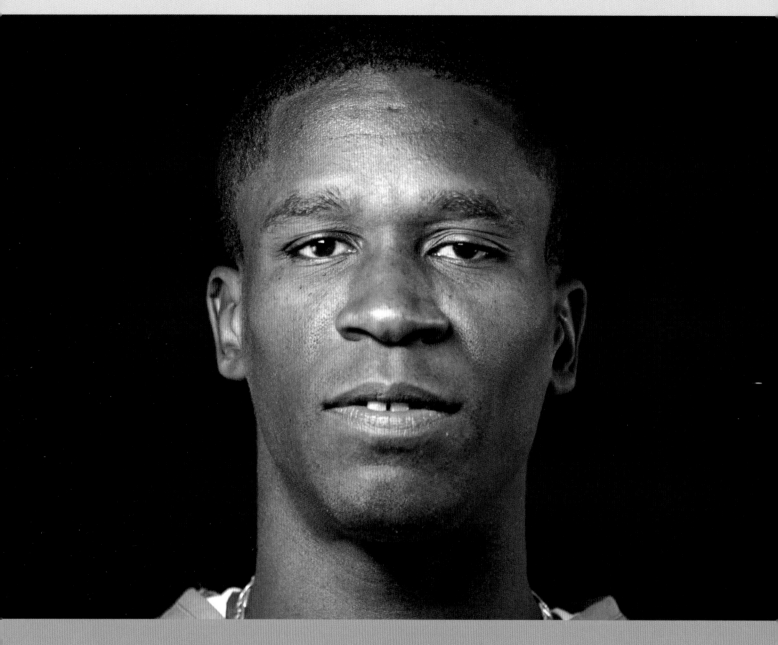

BECOMING HUMAN AGAIN

AFTER KILLING A WOMAN AND HER CHILD, LEONARD WAS SENTENCED TO LIFE IN PRISON. THERE HE BECAME AN ACTIVIST FOR A DIFFERENT KIND OF JUSTICE—ONE THAT REPAIRS AND HEALS.

I remember that my stepfather beat me. He beat me with electric cables, belts, sticks, and all sorts of things. And after each thrashing, he told me: "You know, this hurts me more than you," and "I did it because I love you." He taught me a false understanding of love. For many years, I tended to think that love meant hurting people. I have hurt all of those I have loved, and I measured my love according to the amount of pain I inflicted. That is, until I arrived in prison, in an environment devoid of love. Since then, I have begun to understand what love is and what it is not, because I met someone. She gave me my first insight into what love is, because she was able to look past my situation and the fact that I was in prison for the worst crime a man could commit: the murder of a woman and a child. It was Agnes, the mother and grandmother of Patricia and Chris, the woman and child I killed, who gave me the most beautiful lesson on love, because she had every reason to detest me but didn't give in to hatred. And as time went on, along the path we undertook together, which was rather incredible, she gave me love and taught me what it was. Or, what it is. It is in prison that I learned what love is.

Agnes contacted me in 2005. At that particular moment, I was in solitary confinement. I had learned, the previous week, that my brother had been killed. I was in mourning then, and at that particular moment I really did understand what it is to lose someone you love. When I received her first letter, I didn't know who she was because I had never seen her name; it wasn't

until she wrote me again that she told me who she was and that I knew what I had inflicted on her. Because I understood her loss, I didn't seek to obtain her forgiveness, and I don't think she was too interested in the idea of offering it to me. But we were interested in the idea of finding a way to heal, and while undertaking this process, we learned about forgiveness.

As a prisoner serving a life sentence, for having killed Patricia and Christopher, Agnes's daughter and grandson, I have a message for you, Agnes. This message is that I love you more than I could ever express and I thank you for the opportunity to become human anew.

For a long time I lived in anger. It is this anger that allowed me to commit this crime, which allowed me to murder Pat and Chris. Then, in this correctional system, I lost all of my fury; spending several years in isolation made me suffer, along with my family and several others close to me.

But this anger, against myself, above all, had its roots. I ended up understanding that it came from a profound sense of having been hurt. During all these years in prison, I have become aware that the great majority of men in my situation have been hurt, and they express their pain through anger. And if the wounds aren't healed, then they are condemned to repeat the pattern of abuse and addiction, again and again and again.

Therefore, for me, the problem isn't anger; the problem is the hurt. My goal is to try to help the numerous men in my situation to heal while, perhaps, healing

> IN PRISON,
> I HAVE BEGUN
> TO UNDERSTAND
> WHAT LOVE IS
> AND WHAT IT
> IS NOT

● ● ●

● ● ● my own wounds. You don't have to let yourself be dominated by anger; you don't have to destroy your life and the lives of others.

As a prisoner serving a life sentence for murder, the meaning of my life from now on is to serve. To me, that means cultivating love, which seems so illusory to us, in our society. In trying to clean up my life, I have come to see clearly why we are here: It is, as far as I'm concerned, to love. And one of the things I teach in the meetings I'm involved in is that you have a choice, that you don't have to resort to violence, that you don't have to allow emotions to dominate you, whatever they are. And if I accept responsibility for what I have done, instead of saying, "I was consumed by rage," it forces me to face my mistakes and makes me capable of moving on.

I am constantly confronted by men who want to prove they are men, to me and to themselves. In this correctional environment, in this culture, the most powerful way to do so is to use violence. It's easy to give in to it; it doesn't require much to hit someone or to make blood flow. The challenge comes when someone wants to draw your own blood, and rather than respond with violence, you respond with peace. It's difficult, because when someone confronts you and wants to

hit you, your adrenaline rises, your reflexes prepare you for fight or flight, and the easiest thing to do is to give in to that. To stop the process of violence requires an extraordinary amount of will—all the more so in this environment, where it's considered a weakness.

But I have come to understand that, because seeking peace demands more strength than resorting to violence, the true warrior is he who actively looks for peace. And that understanding reinforces my will and my resolve when faced with a situation that seems to call for violence. Moreover, I have spent so many years living violently that to continue doing so would be a weakness. It would confirm to those who believe I am bad, that I am a killer incapable of atonement.

It is important to me that the world understands that men and women commit crimes because they are hurt. As long as we don't take care of these injuries, we will be condemned to repeat endlessly the cycles of delinquency and imprisonment. This is why I believe that rehabilitative justice is an important practice, and a philosophy: It is centered on healing, on recovering the equilibrium that is broken in a community when crimes are committed. Punishment without recovery is incomplete.

> TO STOP THE PROCESS OF VIOLENCE REQUIRES AN EXTRAORDINARY AMOUNT OF WILL— ALL THE MORE SO IN THIS ENVIRONMENT, WHERE IT'S CONSIDERED A WEAKNESS

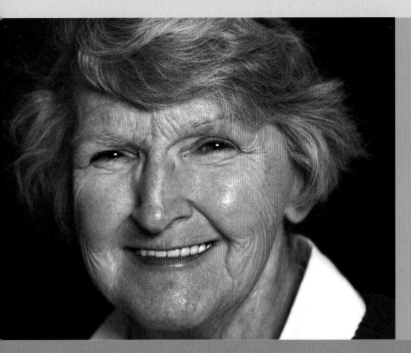

LEARNING TO FORGIVE

AFTER LEONARD MURDERED HER FAMILY, AGNES BECAME AN ACTIVIST FOR NONVIOLENCE.

My daughter and grandson were murdered. A few years back, I decided to contact the young man who committed these crimes. The correctional system at that time did not allow me to visit him. Therefore, I wrote to him. We maintained a correspondence for several years, and this exchange was healing.

Can I forgive this man? By and by, as I came to understand him, I saw that I could. But I think forgiveness is a gift you give yourself, so as to no longer carry any resentment and to free yourself of a weight that can become too heavy. This doesn't exonerate the other. It doesn't exempt him from his responsibility, because he lives with the consequences of his acts.

The man who has committed murder can understand and admit the suffering his crime has caused. During his imprisonment, he can learn to overcome and resolve his difficulties in a nonviolent manner; he can acquire social skills and begin to make good choices by adopting different behaviors and honoring the persons he has killed.

This is important, because most of the people we send to prison end up going home. If they have been locked up for thirty or forty years, they will probably leave prison less capable of living in the world than they were when they were first imprisoned. But some will have grown through their experiences and, probably, will not make the same mistakes.

One of the questions the man who murdered my daughter and grandson asked me was, "What can I do?" I answered, "Well! There is nothing you could do that would make things better. But what you can do is make a difference where you are, because we are all members of the same community."

My daughter and my grandson were murdered; this fact is a daily trial. One of the messages I would love to share with people who might be confronted by this experience is to continue living life no matter what. I would encourage them to honor life and those who have departed.

And the message I would relay to those who have committed murder would be to understand the wrong they have done and to do everything possible to make a positive contribution to their community, wherever they may be.

> ## FORGIVENESS IS A GIFT YOU GIVE YOURSELF

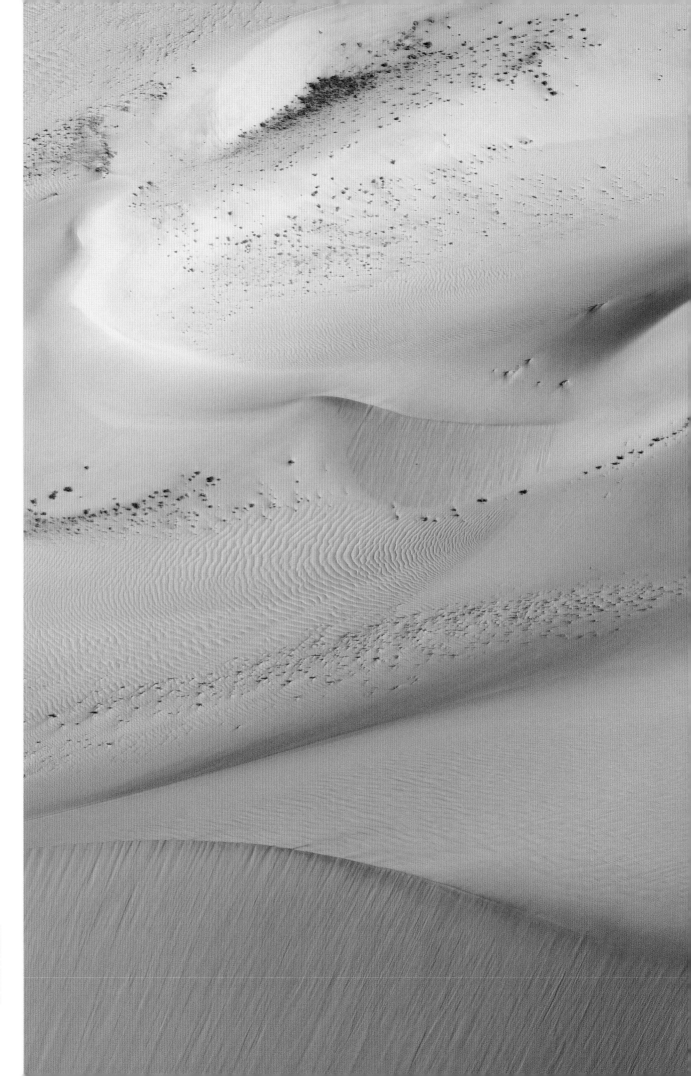

YAK CARAVAN IN THE DUNES NEAR SKARDU, INDUS VALLEY, GILGIT-BALTISTAN, PAKISTAN 35°19' N – 75° 43' E

Yaks live at an altitude of between 6,500 and 16,500 feet (2,000 and 5,000 m). Adapted to the Himalayan environment, these impressive mammals can transport loads of more than 250 pounds (113 kg), and females produce milk. Long yak caravans make possible the trade of numerous commodities in the most remote regions of the Himalaya. The number of domesticated yaks is estimated at twelve million.

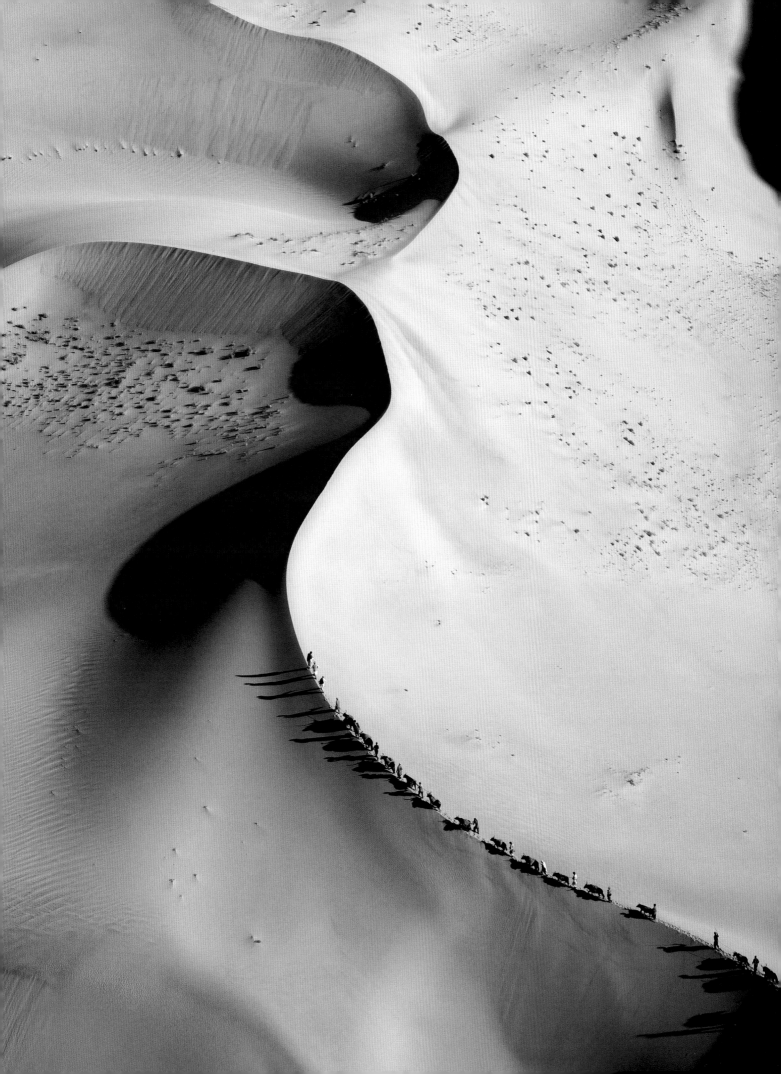

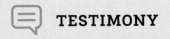
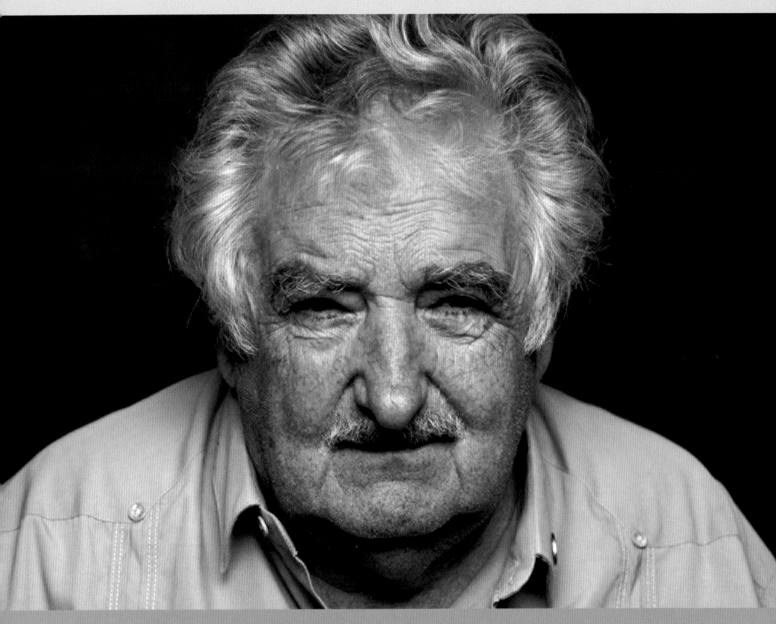

A VERY DIFFERENT KIND OF PRESIDENT

JOSÉ MUJICA CORDANO WAS PRESIDENT OF URUGUAY, BUT IN SPITE OF THIS, HE LEADS A SIMPLE AND MODEST LIFE.

My name is José Mujica Cordano. I am a descendant of immigrants. This means that my origin is that of boats and that by chance I set foot on land at the mouth of the river La Plata in the Atlantic. I am a peasant of sorts who loves nature...and I have devoted an important part of my life to trying to ameliorate the social circumstances of the world where I was born.

At this moment, I am president: I do a few things, I support others, and I give thanks to life. I have had certain disappointments, numerous injuries, and spent some years in prison—in effect, the path for someone who wants to change the world. It's a miracle that I'm still alive. And overall, I love life. I want to embark on the last journey as someone who steps up to the counter and asks the barkeeper for another round.

I spent more than ten years in solitary confinement in a dark cell, seven of those years without reading a single work. I had time to think, and here is what I discovered: Either you manage to be happy with very little, no baggage, because happiness is within you, or you accomplish nothing.

This is not an argument for poverty but for temperance. Nevertheless, just as we have invented a consumerist society, the economy will grow accordingly. We have invented a mountain of superficial needs; we live by buying and throwing out. But what we really spend is our time. When I buy something, or when you buy something, you don't buy it with money; you buy it with the time you have spent to earn that money. The difference is that the only thing that can't be bought is life. Life does nothing but flow, and what a misfortune it is to use it to lose our freedom!

Because when is it that I am free? I am free when I have time to do whatever pleases me, and I am not free when I need to spend a large part of my time in pursuit of the sole goal of acquiring material goods that supposedly allow me to live. In fact, fighting for freedom means fighting to make use of free time.

I know I belong to a civilization at the heart of which many folks would say, "How right he is, this gentleman." But they won't follow me, because we are trapped, like prisoners, in a spider's web. We need at least to begin thinking about this.

> # EITHER YOU MANAGE TO BE HAPPY WITH VERY LITTLE...OR YOU ACCOMPLISH NOTHING

To be temperate and to cultivate moderation is a better way to distribute resources. Here is an anecdote. In Uruguay, since we're a small country, we don't have a presidential airplane. And instead of buying one, we bought a helicopter because it's useful. We bought one in France that has a surgery station and provides several other urgent-care services, and those are for saving lives. Henceforth, there is a system at people's disposal that can rescue them quickly. This question is simple. Basically, "Do I buy a presidential airplane or do I buy a helicopter to save lives?"

It seems to me that moderation has to do with making this kind of choice. I'm not saying that we have to return to living in caves or under thatched roofs. No! What I propose is that we turn our backs to the world of waste, unnecessary expenses, and ostentatious houses that make you need two, three, or four servants! What is the point in all of that?

Then, we would have crowns, kings, and jesters who stop on the ramparts to play the trumpet when the sire leaves the castle, returning us to the Middle Ages. We must remember why we have had revolutions: in the ● ● ●

●●● name of equality. That is the republican meaning of life and it has been lost in politics.

During my years in prison, I learned to look for life where it is barely visible. Ants, they cry out; they have a language. Rats take on habits; they adjust to a schedule. Frogs are grateful for a glass of water in which they can bathe themselves. I learned the value of living. I also learned to converse with the one who exists within me, the one who accompanies you when you have no books or anyone to speak with. The only thing you have, in such a case, is the one who is within you. This person you often forget in face of the frivolity of life. And I recommend looking within you. Watch less television, which is oriented toward the external, and speak with the one within you, engage with his questions, his failures, his reproaches, his injuries.... I think people speak very little with themselves. From the moment I needed to preserve my psychic equilibrium by speaking to that person I have within myself, I developed other perspectives. I wouldn't be who I am if I hadn't lived those years of extraordinary solitude!

Such is our nature that we learn much more from adversity than from abundance. That doesn't mean I recommend the path of suffering, or anything of the sort. It means that I want to let people know that it is possible to fall and stand up again.

And it is always worth the effort of standing up again. One time or a thousand times—as long as you are alive. This is life's greatest message: "They are destroyed, those who stop fighting, and to stop fighting is to stop dreaming." Fighting, dreaming, and failing in the face of reality: This is what gives meaning to existence, to life.

> IN REALITY,
> I AM A
> DON QUIXOTE,
> ALWAYS BEATEN

For the younger generations, this is kind of a universal formula for dealing with existence. Failures are plentiful. The girl who told you she loved you when you were fifteen doesn't love you anymore! It's not as if you won't ever fall in love again. Defeats come when you contract an illness that you have a hard time beating, when you lose your job and have economic difficulties. But you can always begin again. And that, basically, is a love song to life. One must be grateful, because to be alive is a miracle.

In reality, I am a Don Quixote, always beaten. Our successes are far removed from our dreams...and from the ideas we concoct. Forty years ago, it was quite simple: We believed that it was possible to come to power and to construct a better society by changing the system of production, blah, blah, blah, and on and on. That cost us a lot, and then we came to understand that it was easier to change an economic reality than a cultural reality. The whole problem is that if you don't change, nothing changes.

The most transcendental reality for us on Earth is the one we think about the least! It is to be alive! Being alive is a miracle! For a human being, there are a million obstacles to this miraculous fact of life. How to underestimate this truth? How not to pay it attention? How not to fight to give meaning to this miracle?

Well...so long. I am José Mujica, a peasant for the first part of my life. After that, I engaged myself in the fight to change and improve the society in which I grow. At this moment, I am at a phase of being president, and tomorrow, like anybody else, I'll be a heap of worms, as I leave.

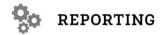
REACHING MY AUTISTIC SON THROUGH DISNEY

By Ron Suskind
First published in the *New York Times*, March 7, 2014

To reconnect with his autistic son, a father steps into the shoes of the animated heroes from the movies his child loves, using their dialogue to communicate. The Pulitzer Prize–winning journalist tells his story.

n our first year in Washington, our son disappeared. Just shy of his third birthday, an engaged, chatty child, full of typical speech—"I love you," "Where are my Ninja Turtles?" "Let's get ice cream!"—fell silent. He cried, inconsolably. Didn't sleep. Wouldn't make eye contact. His only word was "juice."

I had just started a job as the *Wall Street Journal*'s national affairs reporter. My wife, Cornelia, a former journalist, was home with him—a new story every day, a new horror. He could barely use a sippy cup, though he'd long ago graduated to a big-boy cup. He wove about like someone walking with his eyes shut. "It doesn't make sense," I'd say at night. "You don't grow backward." Had he been injured somehow when he was out of our sight, banged his head, swallowed something poisonous? It was like searching for clues to a kidnapping.

After visits to several doctors, we first heard the word "autism." Later, it would be fine-tuned to "regressive autism," now affecting roughly a third of children with the disorder. Unlike the kids born with it, this group seems typical until somewhere between 18 and 36 months—then they vanish. Some never get their speech back. Families stop watching those early videos, their child waving to the camera. Too painful. That child's gone.

In the year since his diagnosis, Owen's only activity with his brother, Walt, is something they did before the autism struck: watching Disney movies. *The Little Mermaid*, *Beauty and the Beast*, *Aladdin*—it was a boom time for Disney—and also the old classics: *Dumbo*, *Fantasia*, *Pinocchio*, *Bambi*. They watch on a television bracketed to the wall in a high corner of our smallish bedroom in Georgetown. It is hard to know all the things going through the mind of our six-year-old, Walt, about how his little brother, now nearly four, is changing....

Then Walt slips out to play with friends, and Owen keeps watching. Movie after movie. Certain parts he rewinds and rewatches. Lots of rewinding. But he seems content, focused.

We ask our growing team of developmental specialists, doctors, and therapists about it. We were never big fans of plopping our kids in front of Disney videos, but now the question seemed more urgent: Is this good for him? They shrug. Is he relaxed? Yes. Does it seem joyful? Definitely. Keep it limited, they say. But if it does all that for him, there's no reason to stop it.

So we join him upstairs, all of us, on a cold and rainy Saturday afternoon in November 1994. Owen is already on the bed, oblivious to our arrival, murmuring gibberish.... "Juicervose, juicervose." It is something we've been hearing for the past few weeks. Cornelia thinks maybe he wants more juice; but no, he refuses the sippy cup. *The Little Mermaid* is playing as we settle in, propping up pillows. We've all seen it at least a dozen times, but it's at one of the best parts: where Ursula the sea witch, an acerbic diva, sings her song of villainy, "Poor Unfortunate Souls," to the selfish mermaid, Ariel, setting up the part in which Ursula will turn Ariel into a human, allowing her to seek out the handsome prince, in exchange for her voice.

When the song is over, Owen lifts the remote. Hits rewind.

"Come on, Owen, just let it play!" Walt moans. But Owen goes back just twenty seconds or so, to the song's next-to-last stanza, with Ursula shouting:

Go ahead—make your choice!

I'm a very busy woman, and I haven't got all day.

It won't cost much, just your voice!

He does it again. Stop. Rewind. Play. And one more time. On the fourth pass, Cornelia whispers, "It's not 'juice.' " I barely hear her. "What?" "It's not 'juice.' It's 'just'…'just your voice'!"

I grab Owen by the shoulders. "Just your voice! Is that what you're saying?!"

He looks right at me, our first real eye contact in a year. "Juicervose! Juicervose! Juicervose!"

Walt starts to shout, "Owen's talking again!" A mermaid lost her voice in a moment of transformation. So did this silent boy. "Juicervose! Juicervose! Juicervose!" Owen keeps saying it, watching us shout and cheer. And then we're up, all of us, bouncing on the bed. Owen, too, singing it over and over—"Juicervose!"—as Cornelia, tears beginning to fall, whispers softly, "Thank God, he's in there."

We told his various therapists about what happened.…Owen reached out, if only for a moment, from his shut-in world. We spoke to our child.

The speech therapist tamped down our enthusiasm. Dr. Alan Rosenblatt, our trusted developmental pediatrician, did, too. He explained that echolalia is a common feature in kids like Owen.…Just like what the term suggests, they echo, usually the last word or two of a sentence.…Do those kids know what the words mean, we pressed Rosenblatt. "Usually not," he said. "They may want to make a connection, which is hopeful," he added.

"They just repeat the last sound," I croaked. He nodded. Why, I persisted, in a last stab, would he be rewinding that one part for weeks, maybe longer, and choose that phrase from so many in an eighty-three-minute movie? Rosenblatt shrugged. No way of knowing.

AUTISM EARLY SIGNS IN INFANTS

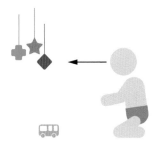

Unusual visual fixations
Unusually strong and persistent examination of objects

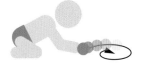

Abnormal repetitive behaviors
Spending unusually long periods of time repeating an action, such as flapping their hands or spinning a car wheel over and over again

Delayed intentional communication
Neutral facial expressions and decreased efforts to gesture and gain parental attention

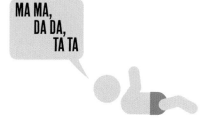

Lack of age-appropriate sound development
Delayed development of vowel sounds, such as "ma ma, da da, ta ta"

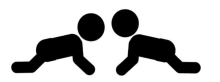

Decreased interest in interaction
Greater interest in objects than people and difficulty sustaining face-to-face interactions

Three weeks after the "juicervose" dance, we are at Walt Disney World. Walt grabs Owen's hand, and off they go down Main Street, U.S.A.... The boys sit in the flying galleon on Peter Pan's Flight.... They look like any other pair of brothers, and in the trick of this light, they are.

Each time Cornelia and I feel that, we catch ourselves. After the "juicervose" euphoria and then the cold water poured on us by doctors, we try to make sure we aren't just seeing what we want to see.

But by midafternoon, it's clear that Owen isn't self-talking in the streams of gibberish or flapping his hands as he usually does. He seems calm and focused—following the group, making eye contact—and oddly settled, with a slight smile, eyes alight, just as he is while watching the movies on our bed....

On the way out of Magic Kingdom, when Walt spots the Sword in the Stone near the carousel, we can't help indulging in fantasy. A Disney actor dressed as Merlin is there, reciting dialogue—"Let the boy try." As we approach the anvil, someone flips a hidden switch that loosens the sword. Walt pulls it out as Merlin cries, "You, my boy, are our king!"

Then both of them turn to Owen. "You can do it, Owie," Walt whispers. "I know you can." Owen looks evenly at his brother and Merlin, and then steps to the anvil and lifts the sword true. Did he understand what Walt was saying? Did he just imitate what he saw his brother do? What the hell difference did it make? Today, in the sunlight, he's the hero of his imagination.

It's Walt's ninth birthday, September 1997, in our new house near Chevy Chase Circle. Owen is six and a half. After roughhousing with buddies in the backyard at the end of his party, Walt gets a little weepy. He's already a tough, independent kid, often the case with siblings of disabled kids. But he can get a little sad on his birthdays. As Cornelia and I return to the kitchen, Owen walks in right behind us.

He looks intently at us, one, then the other. "Walter doesn't want to grow up," he says evenly, "like Mowgli or Peter Pan."

We nod, dumbly, looking down at him. He nods back and then vanishes into some private reverie.

It's as if a thunderbolt just passed through the kitchen. A full sentence, and not just an "I want this" or "Give me that." No, a complex sentence, the likes of which he'd not uttered in four years. Actually, ever.

IT'S AS IF OWEN HAD LET US IN, JUST FOR AN INSTANT

We don't say anything at first and then don't stop talking for the next four hours, peeling apart, layer by layer, what just happened. Beyond the language, it's interpretive thinking that he's not supposed to be able to do: that someone crying on his birthday may not want to grow up. Not only would such an insight be improbable for a typical six-year-old; it was an elegant connection that Cornelia and I overlooked.

It's as if Owen had let us in, just for an instant, to glimpse a mysterious grid growing inside him, a matrix on which he affixed items he saw each day that we might not even notice. And then he carefully aligned it to another one, standing parallel: the world of Disney.

After dinner is over and the boys retreat upstairs to their attic lair, Cornelia starts to think about what to do now. It's like he peeked out from some vast underground and then vanished. He's done this before, but never quite like this. "How on earth," she says almost to herself, "do you get back in there?"

I feel she's asking me. She has been the one lifting the burden each day, driving him to therapists and schools, rocking him to sleep as he thrashes at 3 a.m. I'm the one who tells stories, does voices, wears a propeller hat. Her look says, "Find a way."

Soon I'm tiptoeing up the carpeted stairs. Owen's sitting on his bed, flipping through a Disney book; he can't read, of course, but he likes to look at the pictures. The mission is to reach around the banister into his closet and grab his puppet of Iago, the parrot from *Aladdin* and one of his favorite characters. He has been doing lots of Iago echolalia, easy to identify because the character is voiced by Gilbert Gottfried, who talks like a busted Cuisinart. Once Iago's in hand, I gently pull the bedspread from the foot of Owen's bed onto the floor. He doesn't look up. It takes four minutes for Iago and me to make it safely under the bedspread.

Now crawl, snail-slow, along the side of the bed to its midpoint. Fine.

I freeze here for a minute, trying to figure out my opening line; four or five sentences dance about, auditioning.

Then, a thought: *Be* Iago. What would Iago say? I push the puppet up from the covers. "So, Owen, how ya doin'?" I say, doing my best Gilbert Gottfried. "I mean, how does it feel to be you?!" I can see him turn toward Iago. It's as if he is bumping into an old friend. "I'm not happy. I don't have friends. I can't understand what people say." I have not heard this voice, natural and easy, with the traditional rhythm of common speech, since he was two.

I'm talking to my son for the first time in five years. Or Iago is. *Stay in character.* "So, Owen, when did *yoooou* and I become such good friends?"

"When I started watching *Aladdin* all the time. You made me laugh so much. You're so funny."

My mind is racing—find a snatch of dialogue, anything. One scene I've seen him watch and rewind is when Iago tells the villainous vizier Jafar how he should become sultan.

Back as Iago: "Funny? OK, Owen, like when I say...um....So, so, you marry the princess and you become the chump husband." Owen makes a gravelly sound, like someone trying to clear his throat or find a lower tone: "I *loooove* the way your fowl little mind works." It's a Jafar line, in Jafar's voice....Then, I hear a laugh, a joyful little laugh that I have not heard in many years.

A week after the Iago breakthrough, we decide to try an experiment. Owen usually picks the animated movie whenever we gather in front of the 26-inch Magnavox in the basement. On this night, we pick it for him: *The Jungle Book*. It's a movie that the boys have long loved and one that Cornelia and I remember from our childhood: Disney's 1967 rendition of Rudyard Kipling's tales of Mowgli, a boy raised by wolves in the jungles of India,

schooled by Baloo, the obstreperous bear, and Bagheera, the protective black panther.

We watch the movie until, a few minutes along, we get to its signature song, "The Bare Necessities." We turn down the sound, and in my best attempt at the voice and inflection of Phil Harris, who voices the bear, I say: "'Look, now, it's like this, little britches. All you've got to do is...'"

Then we all sing, trying to get the words right:

Look for the bare necessities,
The simple bare necessities....
When you look under the rocks and plants
And take a glance at the fancy ants, and maybe try a few.

Just as Baloo looks at Mowgli, I look at Owen; he looks squarely back at me, and then it happens. Right on cue, he says, "'You eat ants?'" That's Mowgli's line; he speaks it as Mowgli, almost like a tape recording....

A few minutes later, when King Louie, the crazy orangutan, voiced by the jazz trumpeter and singer Louis Prima, sings to Mowgli about becoming a man, Walt's ready. "'Teach me the secret of man's red fire,'" he says, pulling on his ear, waiting for the whispered secret from the boy. Owen recoils, just as Mowgli does in the

movie, and says, "'I don't know how to make fire.'" Cornelia catches my eye; I shake my head. The inflection and ease of speech are things he can't otherwise muster. It's almost as though there's no autism. Mimicry is one thing. This isn't that. The movements, the tone, the emotions seem utterly authentic, like method acting....

So begin the basement sessions. During daylight, we go about our lives. Walt rides his bike to school each morning, back home each afternoon. Cornelia manages the house, the bills, the overloaded schedules of the kids. I am editing and writing for the *Journal*. No one knows we're all living double lives. At night, we become animated characters.

By the fall of 1999, the start of Owen's third year at the Lab School of Washington, a private school for kids with learning disabilities, we see his skills improving, his rudimentary reading, his new ability to do simple math. But the progress is uneven and unsteady, as is the building of social connections with potential friends. It's a struggle for him to keep up, the school warns us darkly, because his mind so often races through the parallel universe of movies.

We tell them what we've found: The key is to harness it. We discovered that

NO ONE KNOWS WE'RE ALL LIVING DOUBLE LIVES. AT NIGHT, WE BECOME ANIMATED CHARACTERS

UP TO $21,000

THE ADDITIONAL COST PER YEAR OF CARING FOR AN AUTISTIC CHILD IN THE UNITED STATES

he learned to read using the slowly scrolling credits at the end of movies. He'd hit pause and decode—animators, art directors, best boys, long-dead voice actors—desperate to know who was behind the flickering screen of light. The school rose to the challenge, up to a point, letting him cast and star in a play of "Br'er Rabbit and the Tar Baby"—with Owen reciting every line from our bootleg copy of "Song of the South."

But by his fifth year at Lab, we sense trouble has arrived. Owen is making progress, but the other kids, with lighter burdens, are moving faster. Sally Smith, the school's director, says it just isn't working out for Owen at Lab....I make my case: Owen is making progress in his own fashion, improving by the day. "He's turning these movies into tools that, more and more, he's using to make sense of the wider world," I tell her.

She looks at me sympathetically but doesn't budge. "Many of these kids are just too hard to teach," she says, then pauses. "Look, not picking up social cues is just too great a burden. They can't engage with teachers or peers with enough ease, enough capacity, to push themselves forward."

I rise from my chair. "You started this school so your son, who'd been

---

HE'S TURNING THESE MOVIES INTO TOOLS THAT, MORE AND MORE, HE'S USING TO MAKE SENSE OF THE WIDER WORLD

---

discarded, would have a place to go," I say, putting on my coat. Her son, Gary, now well into adulthood, has significant challenges, much like Owen. "Do you think he'd be accepted here today?"

Those are fighting words. I can't help it. I am thinking how difficult this is going to be for Owen. To her credit, Smith doesn't rise to battle.

"Look, I'm sorry," she says quietly. "Times change. We're serving a need and serving it well. Just not anymore for someone like Owen."

We call the school he was at six years before, Ivymount, which is for needier and more disabled kids, and tell the administrators that Owen will not be moving up with his class to the middle school at Lab. They're sympathetic and say they will gladly take him back. We're worried that he'll lose some of the gains he has made being in class with kids who have milder challenges, but we don't have much of a choice.

We tell Owen in early May 2002, a month before he will leave his school. We go out to dinner and say he'll be going back to Ivymount. He has made a few friends at Lab. They do things together, are starting to form little rituals. "It'll be great, Owie," Walt says, putting his arm around Owen's shoulder. "I'm sure some of your old friends at Ivymount will still be there."

Owen gets this look where he raises his eyebrows and presses his face into the widest of smiles. He calls it "happy face." He does it when he's worried he might cry.

Back at Ivymount in the fall, Owen, now eleven, is not being challenged academically or socially. Cornelia's response is to crank up his programming. She starts him in piano lessons with an Ivymount instructor who specializes in teaching special-needs kids. There are still the rounds of therapist visits and any after-school activity we can find. Not many playdates, though.

WHAT IS AUTISM?

Autism is a condition that is still not well understood. Its mechanism remains unknown, and no cause has been identified. While some treatments may attenuate symptoms, there is no cure.

Autism is characterized by emotional withdrawal, difficulties in communication and in the social domain, and repetitive behaviors. It arises most often in the first years of life. Other disorders, such as Asperger syndrome, are related and all of them are grouped under the term "autism spectrum disorder" (ASD). Combined, these disorders affect about 1 percent of the population and are more common in boys than in girls (in an approximate ratio of 4 to 1).

The reported number of autism cases has increased considerably in recent years; in certain regions, it has increased fivefold in the last twenty years. Specialists are actively researching the causes for this increase: On the one hand, it is possible that the revised, more inclusive definition of autism is at least partially responsible; on the other hand, the increase may be related to progress in research and medical practices that make autism spectrum disorders easier to identify.

DIFFICULT TREATMENT

Because there is no known cure for autism, helping children with the disorder means offering them the appropriate support. No one approach has proven to be universally effective. Families therefore try different approaches, going from one method or therapy to another. These efforts are expensive, and often one parent has to stop working. Public services are therefore crucial.

In this respect, France has more than once been accused of not fulfilling its obligations to people with autism. Autism-Europe launched the first collective complaint before the Council of Europe on behalf of people with disabilities in 2002. In 2004, the Council announced a landmark decision that France had failed its educational obligations to persons with autism. In 2014 the Council made a similar condemnation, reproaching France for not doing enough to educate children with autism, 80 percent of whom cannot secure enrollment in a school and have to stay in the hospital or at home. Close to forty thousand children affected by autism in France are believed to lack access to education.

The situation continues to be difficult because of the suspicion, even hostility, that has developed between families and part of the medical establishment: The former reproach the latter for favoring a psychoanalytic approach to the disorder over a neurodevelopmental one, which leads providers to recommend inappropriate treatments. This phenomenon is much less prevalent in English-speaking countries. "Here, we continue to send children to psychoanalysts who are going to explain that [autism] is a retaliation against the mother," laments the president of Vaincre l'Autisme, one of the most active autism-focused organizations in France.

Owen doesn't seem to mind. All he wants are sketch pads and pencils. Markers, too. He goes through a pad in a few days and wants another....

We've been observing him closely since the ouster from Lab. We know he was bruised, but he doesn't have enough expressive speech to explain his feelings. So we watch, collecting clues, like spies in our own home. He's distracted. He's watching lots of videos. The school reports that he's doing lots of "silly," the word we use for self-stimulatory behavior like flapping hands.

One Saturday afternoon, while Cornelia and Walt are running errands, I see Owen padding across the kitchen's Mexican tile floor on his way to the basement with pad, pencils, and one of his large animation books in hand. I wait a minute before I tiptoe behind him, stopping at the bottom of the stairs. He's on the rug, kneeling but hunched forward, flipping furiously through the book; as I edge closer, I see it contains artwork from *Learn to Draw Disney's The Little Mermaid*....

I can see he's stopping at pictures of Sebastian, the wise crab who watches over the heroine, Ariel.... He stops at a slide of Sebastian with a fearful look, mouth open and eyes wide.

The sketchbook flies open, the black pencil in hand. He looks from the picture to his pad, picture, pad, picture, pad. And then the tightly gripped pencil begins to move, a lead-lined crawl. Most kids, most anyone, would begin with the face—where we all tend to look first—but he starts on the edge, with the crab leg, then the claw, which take shape in a single line....

Every part of him starts moving except that rock-steady hand.... When he gets to the face, I look up and see a reflection of Owen's face, me behind him, in the darkened screen of the TV in front of us. The look on the crab's

WE WATCH, COLLECTING CLUES, LIKE SPIES IN OUR OWN HOME

face in the book is replicated in my son's reflection on the TV, where, of course, we've watched this scene—of Sebastian watching Ariel lose her voice—so many times....

He can't write his name legibly. But here is a rendering of a Disney character that might have easily appeared in any one of twenty animation books in his room....

I settle in cross-legged on the carpet to examine the pages. What do the drawings mean? Are the faces of these characters a reflection of hidden, repressed feelings? Does he race through the books looking for an expression that matches the way he feels and then literally draw that emotion to the surface?...

Time passes, pages turn. And then I see writing. On the next to last page of the sketchbook, there's something. It's his usual scrawl, the letters barely legible: "I Am the Protekter of Sidekicks."

I flip to the last page. In the chicken scratch of a kindergartner is a single sentence: "No Sidekick Gets Left Behind."

We need the right moment to respond. Every second we're with Owen in the coming days, Cornelia and I look for our opening—a moment when he's alone, or settled, or upbeat or a bit more talkative than usual.

Then the stars align. He's watching *Beauty and the Beast* and wants us all to join him. Soon we're together in the basement, watching the familiar opening, when the handsome prince spurns an old, ugly woman on a forbidding night, only to have her transform into a beautiful enchantress, who turns him into a hideous beast; a spell that can be broken only if he can "learn to love another and earn her love in return."

As the credits roll, we do a few voices—I say, "*Sacre bleu*, invaders!" as Lumiere. Cornelia throws in Mrs. Potts: "He's finally learned to love." Owen rises to each with a burst of follow-up lines. We respond in character. Nothing special. Just your average American family speaking in Disney dialogue.

Both characters are vividly drawn in his sketchbook. "They're a great pair of... sidekicks," Cornelia says. We've never used the word with him in conversation. Owen snaps to. "I love Mrs. Potts and Lumiere," he says.

"What is a sidekick?" Cornelia asks him.

"A sidekick helps the hero fulfill his destiny," he chirps. Rolls right off his tongue. A classical, elegant definition.

"Do you feel like a sidekick, Owie?" Cornelia asks him softly. Their eyes are aligned, just the two of them now, looking into each other, until he suddenly breaks into "happy face."

"I am one!" he says. His voice is high and cheery, no sign of a quaver. "I am a sidekick." The words come out flat, without affectation. But he compensates, giving them expression by nodding after every two syllables.

"And no...sidekick...gets left... behind."

There's no doubt, now, that he sees what we see: that kids of all kinds, including his classmates at Lab School, are moving on, while he's left behind. The sidekicks have emerged, sketch by sketch, in the difficult months since his ejection from Lab. His response has been to embrace it, the pain of it, and be a protector of the discarded. He starts giving sidekick identities to his classmates at Ivymount, so many of whom are heavily burdened—some with physical infirmities, and plenty of autistic kids with little speech. But they have qualities that he's identifying—this one was loyal, that one gentle, another one silly in some light-hearted way that makes him laugh.

It's often the supporting players in Disney fables who are more varied and vivid. Even in the earliest Disney movies, the first sidekicks—Goofy, Pluto, and then Donald Duck—often carried confusions, frailties, foolishness, pride, vanity, and hard-won, often reluctantly learned, insights. The spectrum of complex human emotions is housed with the sidekicks.

Owen and I walk gingerly down the icy steps of a side entrance to Dan Griffin's basement office in Takoma Park, Maryland. It's a particularly cold and stormy afternoon in December 2005, the week before Christmas....

WE RESPOND IN CHARACTER. NOTHING SPECIAL. JUST YOUR AVERAGE AMERICAN FAMILY SPEAKING IN DISNEY DIALOGUE

Owen started seeing the psychologist last year, when he was thirteen. More than any other therapist, Griffin took to the "Disney therapy," or more broadly, what might be called "affinity therapy," that Cornelia and I, with Walt's assistance, have been conducting for years in our home, and even more so recently. After Owen spent two years at Ivymount, Cornelia started home-schooling him last year, using Disney scripts as a bridge to teach him the basics of reading and math that he'll need to get into a high school for special-needs kids in Maryland. She regularly guides Griffin, who each week tries to use the scripts to teach Owen social and life skills as well....

Griffin had come up with an ingenious plan for Owen to protect and advise a sidekick. We had settled on Zazu, the proud but naïve hornbill charged with protecting a young Simba in *The Lion King*....

Hence:

Educating Zazu

I, Owen Harry Suskind, agree to undertake the challenging but critical task of providing stimulating educational experiences for my good friend Zazu. This project will take a good deal of work and

4 TIMES MORE

BOYS ARE FOUR TIMES MORE LIKELY THAN GIRLS TO BE DIAGNOSED WITH AUTISM OR RELATED DISORDERS

A MODERN DISORDER

Autism has only recently been identified. Leo Kanner was an Austrian physician who had emigrated to the United States, where he established the first pediatric psychiatry service in 1930. In 1943 he identified autism as a distinct neurological condition, naming the syndrome Early Infantile Autism. Previously, children who would now be diagnosed as autistic were often thought to have a form of schizophrenia.

In 1944 Hans Asperger, another physician, identified similar disorders in four young patients at his hospital in Austria. His work remained unknown until his death and was not translated until 1981. These translations enabled the rediscovery of his work. His work is at the source of what is called Asperger syndrome. Only then did specialists begin to discern a continuity between the two conditions.

In the 1950s an association with schizophrenia was still maintained—autism was frequently described as infantile schizophrenia. Furthermore, psychoanalytic hypotheses were prevalent; the disorders that appeared were frequently attributed to "refrigerator mothers," that is, women who were cold and distant. This was a term and a concept designed to foster feelings of guilt, but this theory is now rejected.

Today it is thought that these conditions are cerebral developmental disorders. In 2013 both autism and Asperger syndrome became categorized as "autism spectrum disorders" in the *Diagnostic and Statistical Manual of Mental Disorders*, Fifth Edition (DSM-5) by the American Psychiatric Association.

preparation, but should be a lot of fun and also immensely beneficial to Zazu. I agree to do this for the academic year of 2005-6.

Areas of Zazu's learning program shall include but will not be limited to:

1. Life in the world
2. How to concentrate
3. Following directions
4. Health
5. Asking questions
6. Making friends
7. Fun
8. Loving people
9. Science
10. Helping others

Signed,
Owen Suskind

We start today's therapy session in December with talk of Zazu and his progress. The focus is on contract item No. 6: Making friends.

Owen doesn't have friends, other than kids he encounters through carefully structured activities.... But when advising Zazu, Owen suddenly seems full of advice about how to make friends.

"To make a friend, you have to be a friend," he says, picking up a line that is used at Walt's summer camp; it's something Cornelia has said to him a few times but has never heard him repeat.

"And you need to be interested in what they're interested in," Owen adds. "And then they can be interested in what you're interested in."...

Owen mentions how Zazu has trouble with contract item No. 8—loving people—because he's "ashamed about how he failed Simba," who slipped away from the hornbill's watchful gaze and got into trouble—trouble that eventually led to his father's death.

Griffin takes the risk of asking Owen to elaborate about the fairly complex dynamic between Zazu and Simba; when you fail to meet your own expectations and disappoint someone you

AUTISTIC KIDS LIKE OWEN ARE NOT SUPPOSED TO DO THAT—THIS IS GETTING WEIRD IN A VERY GOOD WAY

care about, what does that feel like? As Owen is thinking, I mouth "P-h-i-l" to Griffin. He knows immediately which scene I'm thinking of and asks Owen if this is what happens to Phil in *Hercules*.

Owen starts to laugh. "Can I do it?"

Before we can nod, Owen's off and running, doing a scene in which Phil is trying to tell a crowd of doubters about Hercules's potential....He ends with a plea from Hercules: "How am I supposed to prove myself a hero if nobody will give me a chance?"

As the session ends, Griffin pulls me aside. "Autistic kids like Owen are not supposed to do that," he says. "This is getting weird in a very good way."...

April 2012. Owen is twenty, and we're visiting him at Riverview on Cape Cod. He's preparing for the Sunday-night meeting of Disney Club. Owen decided to start the group not long after he arrived at Riverview eight months ago....About a dozen students come to Owen's dorm each week, settle in to eat popcorn, chat a bit, and watch their favorites. A few times he described club meetings to us, and we tried to suggest activities over the phone. Then a few weeks ago, he asked if we could come out as Disney Club's parent advisers....

Tonight's selection is *Dumbo*, a fertile tale of self-recognition and emergence. After we watch a bit of the movie, we pause it and talk about how the thing that makes the little elephant a pariah, his huge ears, ultimately allows him to soar. I ask each of them about their "hidden ears," the thing "that makes them different—maybe even an outcast—that they've discovered is a great strength."

The room gets quiet. It's clear that many of these students have rarely, if ever, had their passion for Disney treated as something serious and meaningful.

One young woman talks about how her gentle nature, something that leaves her vulnerable, is a great strength in how she handles rescue dogs. Another mentions "my brain, because it can take me on adventures of imagination."…

It goes on this way for an hour. Like a broken dam. The students, many of whom have very modest expressive speech, summon subtle and deeply moving truths.

There's a reason—a good-enough reason—that each autistic person has embraced a particular interest. Find that reason, and you will find them, hiding in

there, and maybe get a glimpse of their underlying capacities. In our experience, we found that showing authentic interest will help them feel dignity and impel them to show you more, complete with maps and navigational tools that may help to guide their development, their growth. Revealed capability, in turn, may lead to a better understanding of what's possible in the lives of many people who are challenged.

As the Disney Club members now say, it's about "finding the hidden ears."

Owen and I are driving to Griffin's office in the summer of 2012 for a rare visit. Owen hasn't seen Griffin since Christmas break. As we drive, Owen says, let's do "that love business." Lately we've been doing this at least once a day.

"OK, you do Merlin," I say, which means I can do the young Arthur from Disney's 1962 *The Sword and the Stone*….

"You know, lad, this love business is a powerful thing," he says in Merlin's reedy, old man's voice.

"Greater than gravity?" I respond as Arthur.

THERE'S A REASON THAT EACH AUTISTIC PERSON HAS EMBRACED A PARTICULAR INTEREST. FIND THAT REASON, AND YOU WILL FIND THEM, HIDING IN THERE

"Well, yes, boy, in its way." Owen pauses, considering it all, just as the wizard does in this, one of his favorite passages. "Yes, I'd say it's the greatest force on earth."

Romantic love. It's running through him, first and fresh, which is what he tells Griffin as they sit in the office. "I've fallen in love with a wonderful, kind, beautiful, soft, and gentle girl, who likes the same things I like—animated movies, mostly hand-drawn, and mostly from Disney."

Griffin is giddy. He wants to know everything about Emily, Owen's girlfriend. He lays it all out: the tale of how they met at Riverview, how she's in Disney Club, their first kiss.…

Owen tells Griffin that Aladdin and Jasmine have been helpful. "I need to give her space," he says of Emily. "That's what Aladdin learns. Jasmine needs to make the choices for herself. She has to choose, and he needs to know what she wants."

Griffin presses forward on his chair, his face close to Owen's. "But how can you know what she wants?"

54

DISNEY HAS RELEASED FIFTY-FOUR FEATURE-LENGTH ANIMATED FILMS THAT ARE CONSIDERED CLASSICS, HAVING BEEN PRODUCED BY WALT DISNEY ANIMATION STUDIOS.

EXCEPTIONAL DESTINIES

Hans Asperger called his first patients "his little professors," because they possessed abilities that were at times surprising, along with a tendency to become passionately interested in subjects that were rather specialized (astronomy, prehistory, genealogy, etc.). They would memorize every detail of these subjects and discuss them at great length.

Some of Asperger's young patients have become brilliant celebrities, notably Elfriede Jelinek, who received the Nobel Prize in Literature in 2004, though it remains unclear whether she really suffered from the condition that bears Asperger's name.

Another of Asperger's patients became a professor of astrophysics who resolved an error defined by Isaac Newton. Many exceptional people are or have been suspected of suffering from Asperger's: the pianist Glenn Gould, the chess champion Bobby Fischer, the mathematician and theoretical physicist Paul Dirac, and others.

The list of personalities who could have been affected by Asperger's syndrome extends from Beethoven to Albert Einstein, although there is no solid argument to support this. Often the only indication is slightly asocial behavior. A document produced by the Pentagon in 2008 even considers the possibility that Vladimir Putin is affected by Asperger's. This is a hypothesis that is contested by the majority of specialists.

Yet one thing is certain: Asperger's syndrome is not incompatible with intellectual development, or even with exceptional talents.

Owen nods immediately. He's on it. "I have a song." He explains it is from a movie called *Quest for Camelot*. "The song is called 'Looking Through Your Eyes.'" He explains that he listens to the song every morning "to make sure I don't forget to see the world through her eyes."

For nearly a decade, Owen has been coming to see Griffin in this basement office, trying to decipher the subtle patterns of how people grow close to one another. That desire to connect has always been there as, the latest research indicates, it may be in all autistic people; their neurological barriers don't kill the desire, even if it's deeply submerged. And this is the way he still is—autism isn't a spell that has been broken; it's a way of being. That means the world will continue to be inhospitable to him, walking about, as he does, uncertain, missing cues, his heart exposed. But he has desperately wanted to connect, to feel his life, fully, and—using his movies and the improvised tool kit we helped him build—he's finding his footing. For so many years, it was about us finding him, a search joined by Griffin and others. Now it was about him finding himself.

"Owen, my good friend," Griffin says, his eyes glistening, "it's fair to say, you're on your way."

Owen stands up, "Thank you..." Owen says to Griffin. "For everything."

"Is friendship forever?" Owen asks me.

"Yes, Owen, it often is."

"But not always."

"No, not always."

It's later that night, and we're driving down Connecticut Avenue after seeing the latest from Disney (and Pixar), *Brave*. I think I understand now, from a deeper place, how Owen, and some of his Disney Club friends, use

"BUT IT CAN GET SO LONELY, TALKING TO YOURSELF," MY SON OWEN FINALLY SAYS. "YOU HAVE TO LIVE IN THE WORLD"

the movies and why it feels so improbable. Most of us grow from a different direction, starting as utterly experiential, sorting through the blooming and buzzing confusion to learn this feels good, that not so much, this works, that doesn't, as we gradually form a set of rules that we live by, with moral judgments at the peak.

Owen, with his reliance from an early age on myth and fable, each carrying the clarity of black and white, good and evil, inverts this pyramid. He starts with the moral—beauty lies within, be true to yourself, love conquers all—and tests them in a world colored by shades of gray. It's the sidekicks who help him navigate that eternal debate, as they often do for the heroes in their movies.

"I know love lasts forever!" Owen says after a few minutes.

We're approaching Chevy Chase Circle, five minutes from where we live. I know I need to touch, gently, upon the notion that making friends or finding love entails risk. There's no guarantee of forever. There may be heartbreak. But we do it anyway. I drop this bitter morsel into the mix, folding around it an affirmation that he took a risk when he went to an unfamiliar place on Cape Cod, far from his friends and home, and found love. The lesson, I begin, is "to never be afraid to reach out."

He cuts me off. "I know, I know," he says, and then summons a voice for support. It's Laverne, the gargoyle from *The Hunchback of Notre Dame*.

"Quasi," he says. "Take it from an old spectator. Life's not a spectator sport. If watchin's all you're gonna do, then you're gonna watch your life go by without you."

He giggles under his breath, then does a little shoulder roll, something he does when a jolt of emotion runs through him. "You know, they're not like the other sidekicks."

He has jumped ahead of me again. I scramble. "No? How?"

"All the other sidekicks live within their movies as characters, walk around, do things. The gargoyles only live when Quasimodo is alone with them."

"And why's that?"

"Because he breathes life into them. They only live in his imagination."

Everything goes still. "What's that mean, buddy?"

He purses his lips and smiles, chin out, as if he got caught in a game of chess. But maybe he wanted to. "It means the answers are inside of him," he says.

"Then why did he need the gargoyles?"

"He needed to breathe life into them so he could talk to himself. It's the only way he could find out who he was."

"You know anyone else like that?"

"Me." He laughs a sweet, little laugh, soft and deep. And then there's a long pause.

"But it can get so lonely, talking to yourself," my son Owen finally says. "You have to live in the world."

This article is adapted from Life, Animated *by Ron Suskind, published by Kingswell, an imprint of Disney Book Group. Disney exerted no influence over the content of the book. The author acknowledges the rights granted to him for the use of Disney materials.*

Ron Suskind is a Pulitzer Prize–winning journalist and the author of four books about presidential power. He is currently the senior fellow at Harvard's Edmond J. Safra Center for Ethics.

1 BILLION

DISNEY'S BIGGEST SUCCESS HAS BEEN *FROZEN*, WHICH GENERATED MORE THAN ONE BILLION DOLLARS OF REVENUE, MAKING IT THE TOP-GROSSING ANIMATED MOVIE OF ALL TIME.

THE SECRET TO HAPPINESS

Serious disorders, such as autism, are sometimes rich with lessons. This is true of approaching death, as well. As a nurse for palliative care services in Australia, Bronnie Ware is a witness to this truth. Drawing on her experience with people at the end of their lives, she wrote a book (*The Top Five Regrets of the Dying*) that explored the five regrets patients at the twilight of their existence most frequently expressed. These five regrets relate to unsatisfied wishes that were simple but not always easy to fulfill.

First, people wished they had lived a life true to themselves rather than the life others expected of them. Ware declares: "Most people had not honored even a half of their dreams and had to die knowing that it was due to choices they had made, or not made.... Health brings a freedom very few realize, until they no longer have it."

Second, and this regret was expressed more often by men, they wished they had valued those closest to them over work and career.

Third, they wished they had had the courage to express their feelings.

Fourth, they wished they had maintained their connections with their friends.

Fifth, they wished they had decided to be happy. Bonnie Ware writes of this final regret, "This is a surprisingly common one. Many did not realize until the end that happiness is a choice. They had stayed stuck in old patterns and habits." You have been warned.

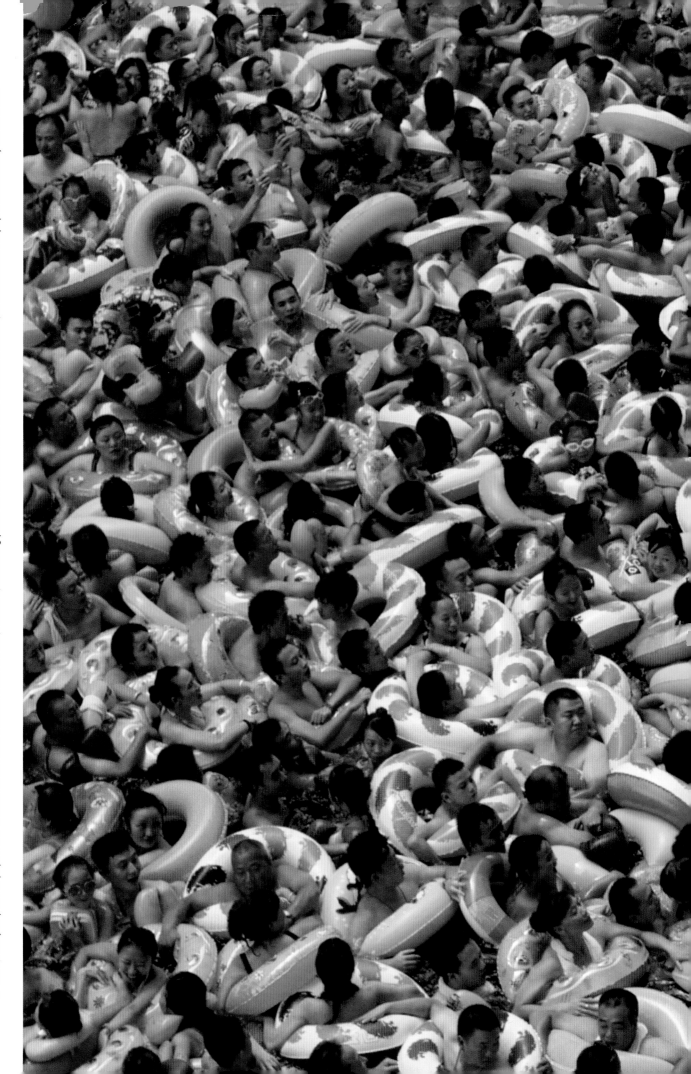

SWIMMING POOL IN CHENGDU, SICHUAN, CHINA 30° 39' N – 104° 04' E

In China, a majority of the population does not know how to swim. When it's hot, however, swimming pools are mobbed. With 1.357 billion inhabitants, China is the most populated country in the world.

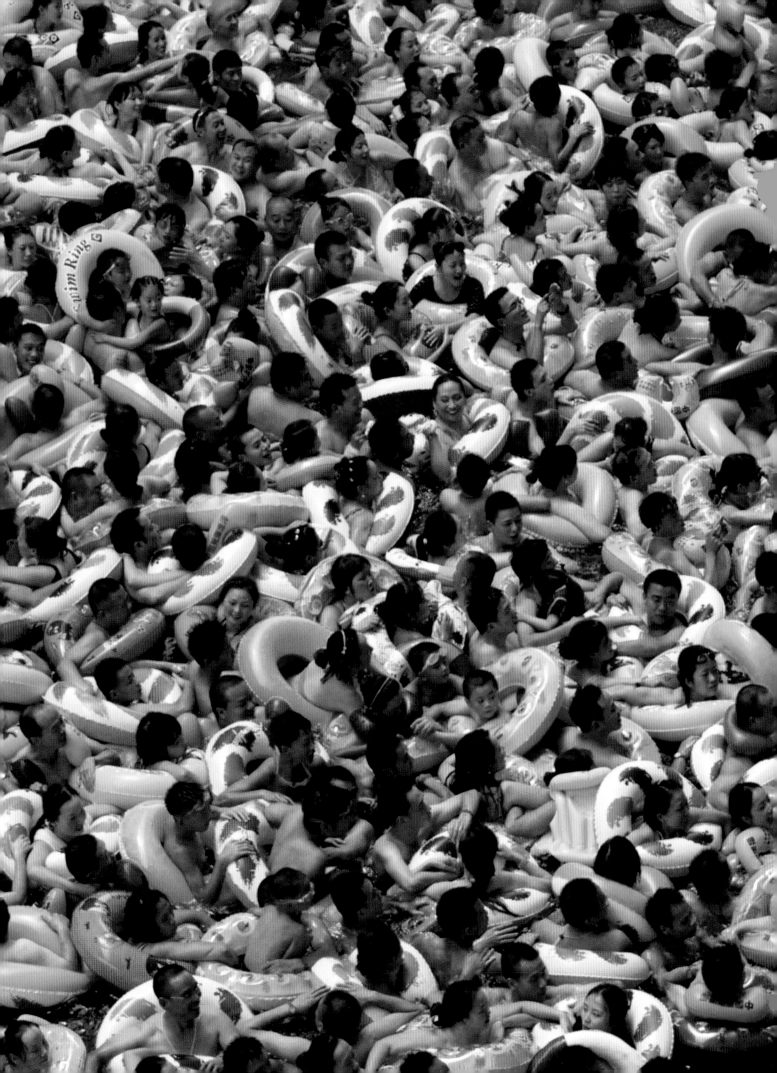

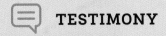
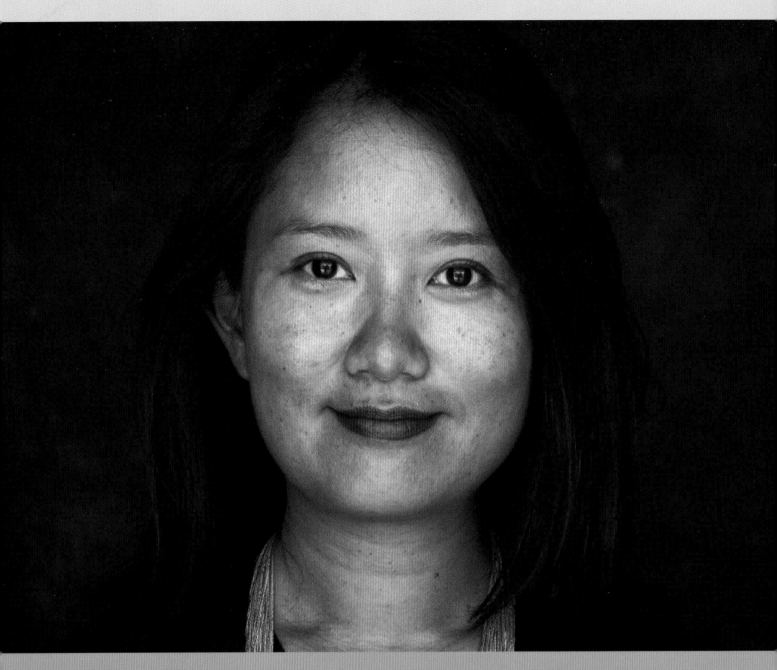

"STOLEN KISSES"

THE FILM SHOOT THAT TOOK PLACE IN MYANMAR WAS AMONG THE HARDEST. IT WASN'T BECAUSE WE HAD TO EXPOSE PRISONS, THE COUNTRY'S RELATIVE LACK OF FREEDOMS, OR EVEN CORRUPTION. NO. THE DIFFICULTY WAS THAT WE HAD TO TALK ABOUT LOVE.

As soon as we broached the subject, most of my interviewees stopped talking, as if we had touched upon the sacred, upon something that was far too vast to be broached in regular conversation, especially with a stranger. Other interviewees would turn to my translator with a serious look and answer totally obliquely. When I asked the translator whether they had really understood the question, he explained that this was their polite way of letting me know that we needed to move on to another topic. Because in Burma, one never says "no." That, of course, took me some time to understand. At first, I hung in there. For example, I ask a joyful-looking woman who was selling bananas at a market if she had experienced happiness in her married life. She answered that the only time she had known happiness was when she won a lottery. And after listening very attentively to my question, she asked me one in turn: "Love: is it that feeling that is like kindness but stronger, is it that?" I also tried to approach the subject with a much younger man, who seemed to be more modern, at least in appearance. Love, he answered, yes, he had seen it when he visited Japan. He noticed couples kissing in the street and holding hands without hiding. That openness really struck him, and he still talks about it with his friends.

I documented no intimate stories, no emotions, nobody who would talk about their feelings. At the end of four days of filming, I tried to take things in hand by conveying my unease to my translator. I asked him how to bring up the subject with the Burmese. Two hours later, he still had no answer for me. "Here," he told me, "we never speak about what we feel. It is considered bad, even bizarre. And since we don't talk about it, most of us don't know how to put certain concepts into words, such as love or even happiness." We were decidedly far from our Western world where we spend our time at the shrink trying to analyze our feelings!

> ## LOVE, HE ANSWERED, YES, HE HAD SEEN IT WHEN HE VISITED JAPAN

Then, on the fifth day, Yin Myo Su arrived, a forty-two-year-old Burmese woman and the owner of a beautiful hotel. She expressed herself very well in French. She had traveled, she told me in passing, and that day she had come to talk about everything, no matter the taboo. I knew that she was married and that she had children. So I was thrilled and hopeful for a beautiful love story! When we reached the middle of our conversation, I finally decided to go for it and ask her about the most beautiful proof of love she had received in her life. Suddenly, Yin Myo Su tensed up. She tried to answer, blushed, stammered, stopped, held her breath. Then she asked the translator to leave. She didn't want to tell anyone but us, away from the presence of Burmese men. My cameraman began to suspect that she would share something indecent. He whispers in my ear, "We should perhaps explain to her that we don't need to know her most inadmissible fantasies." I said nothing; I waited. The translator left the room. There was an unsettling silence. Then Yin Myo Su began to speak in Burmese. She stopped suddenly. Since I didn't understand, I asked her to summarize in French what she had just said. She turned redder than the wood of the chair she was sitting in, and sighed: "I just explained that the most beautiful gift that I've received in my life...was when...when...when he...my husband...for the first time...kissed me...on the mouth." Then, without waiting another second, Yin Myo Su yanked off her microphone and ran from the room. She couldn't stay with us once she had revealed her most intimate secret. At that instant, the conversation ended. Also at that instant I understood that the most universal subjects aren't always the simplest. And sometimes they are not simple at all.

— Anastasia Mikova

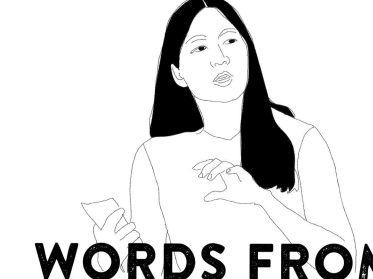

WORDS FROM CHINESE WORKERS

LESLIE CHANG

From her June 2012 TED Talk

Journalist Leslie Chang, former correspondent for the *Wall Street Journal* in China, visited one of the many Chinese villages where the young (70 percent of them women) must leave to find work. She tells their stories in a manner free from clichés and victimizing accusations.

I'd like to talk a little bit about the people who make the things we use every day: our shoes, our handbags, our computers and cell phones. Now, this is a conversation that often calls up a lot of guilt. Imagine the teenage farm girl who makes less than a dollar an hour stitching your running shoes, or the young Chinese man who jumps off a rooftop after working overtime assembling your iPad. We, the beneficiaries of globalization, seem to exploit these victims with every purchase we make, and the injustice feels embedded in the products themselves. After all, what's wrong with a world in which a worker on an iPhone assembly line can't even afford to buy one? It's taken for granted that Chinese factories are oppressive and that it's our desire for cheap goods that makes them so.

So, this simple narrative equating Western demand and Chinese suffering is appealing, especially at a time when many of us already feel guilty about our impact on the world, but it's also inaccurate and disrespectful....

Chinese workers are not forced into factories because of our insatiable desire for iPods. They choose to leave their homes in order to earn money, to learn new skills, and to see the world. In the ongoing debate about globalization, what's been missing is the voices of the workers themselves. Here are a few.

Bao Yongxiu: "My mother tells me to come home and get married, but if I marry now, before I have fully developed myself, I can only marry an ordinary worker, so I'm not in a rush."

Chen Ying: "When I went home for the new year, everyone said I had changed. They asked me, what did you do that you have changed so much? I told them that I studied and worked hard. If you tell them more, they won't understand anyway."

Wu Chunming: "Even if I make a lot of money, it won't satisfy me. Just to make money is not enough meaning in life."...

All of these speakers, by the way, are young women, eighteen or nineteen years old.

So I spent two years getting to know assembly-line workers like these in the south China factory city called Dongguan. Certain subjects came up over and over: how much money they made, what kind of husband they hoped to marry, whether they should jump to another factory or stay where they were. Other subjects came up almost never, including living conditions that to me looked close to prison life: ten or fifteen workers in one room, fifty people sharing a single bathroom, days and nights ruled by the factory clock. Everyone they knew lived in similar circumstances, and it was still better than the dormitories and homes of rural China.

The workers rarely spoke about the products they made, and they often had great difficulty explaining what exactly they did. When I asked Lu Qingmin, the young woman I got to know best, what exactly she did on the factory floor, she said something to me in Chinese that sounded like "qiu xi." Only much later did I realize that she had been saying "QC," or "quality control." She couldn't even tell me what she did on the factory floor....

Journalistic coverage of Chinese factories, on the other hand, plays up this relationship between the workers and the products they make. Many articles calculate: How long would it take for this worker to work in order to earn enough money to buy what he's making? For example, an entry-level assembly-line worker in China in an iPhone plant would have to shell out two and a half months' wages for an iPhone....

The workers I got to know had a curiously abstract relationship with the product of their labor. About a year after I met Lu Qingmin, or Min, she invited me home to her family village for the Chinese New Year. On the train home, she gave me a present: a Coach brand change purse with brown leather trim. I thanked her, assuming it was fake, like almost everything else for sale in Dongguan. After we got home, Min gave her mother another present: a pink Dooney & Bourke handbag, and a few nights later, her sister was showing off a maroon LeSportsac shoulder bag. Slowly it was dawning on me that these handbags were made by their factory, and every single one of them was authentic.

Min's sister said to her parents, "In America, this bag sells for $320." Her parents, who are both farmers, looked on, speechless. "And that's not all—Coach is coming out with a new line, 2191," she said. "One

bag will sell for $6,000." She paused and said, "I don't know if that's 6,000 yuan or 6,000 American dollars, but anyway, it's $6,000."

Min's sister's boyfriend, who had traveled home with her for the new year, said, "It doesn't look like it's worth that much." Min's sister turned to him and said, "Some people actually understand these things. You don't understand shit."…

The first time I met Min, she had just turned eighteen and quit her first job on the assembly line of an electronics factory. Over the next two years, I watched as she switched jobs five times, eventually landing a lucrative post in the purchasing department of a hardware factory. Later, she married a fellow migrant worker, moved with him to his village, gave birth to two daughters, and saved enough money to buy a secondhand Buick for herself and an apartment for her parents. She recently returned to Dongguan on her own to take a job in a factory that makes construction cranes, temporarily leaving her husband and children back in the village.

In a recent e-mail to me, she explained, "A person should have some ambition while she is young so that in old age she can look back on her life and feel that it was not lived to no purpose."

Across China, there are 150 million workers like her, one-third of them women, who have left their villages to work in the factories, the hotels, the restaurants, and the construction sites of the big cities. Together, they make up the largest migration in history, and it is globalization, this chain that begins in a Chinese farming village and ends with iPhones in our pockets and Nikes on our feet and Coach handbags on our arms, that has changed the way these millions of people work and marry and live and think. Very few of them would want to go back to the way things used to be.

When I first went to Dongguan, I worried that it would be depressing to spend so much time with workers. I also worried that nothing would ever happen to them, or that they would have nothing to say to me. Instead, I found young women who were smart and funny and brave and generous. By opening up their lives to me, they taught me so much about factories and about China and about how to live in the world.

> I FOUND YOUNG WOMEN WHO WERE SMART AND FUNNY AND BRAVE AND GENEROUS

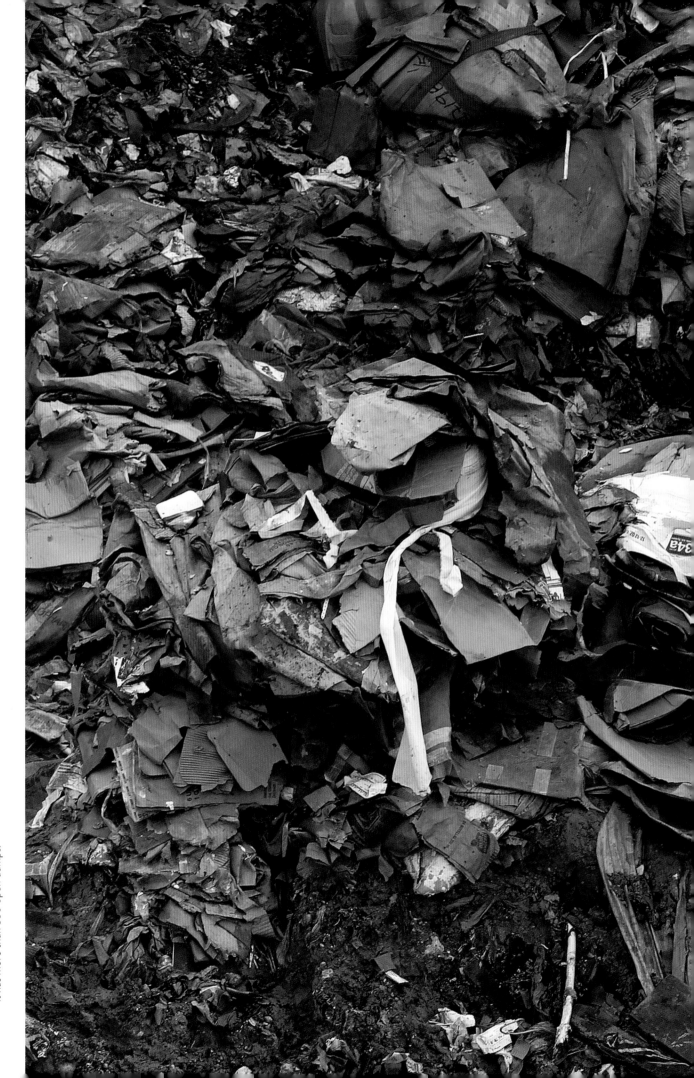

OPEN-AIR DUMP, SANTO DOMINGO, DOMINICAN REPUBLIC 18° 28′ N – 69° 53′ W

With the influx of tourists, the Dominican Republic has experienced an average GDP annual growth rate of 5.5 percent. Nevertheless, around 40 percent of the population still lives at or below the poverty line. What's more, although the millions of tourists bring in revenue, they also produce an enormous mass of garbage. Yet the country is completely lacking in infrastructure for treating waste; it has more than 350 open dumps.

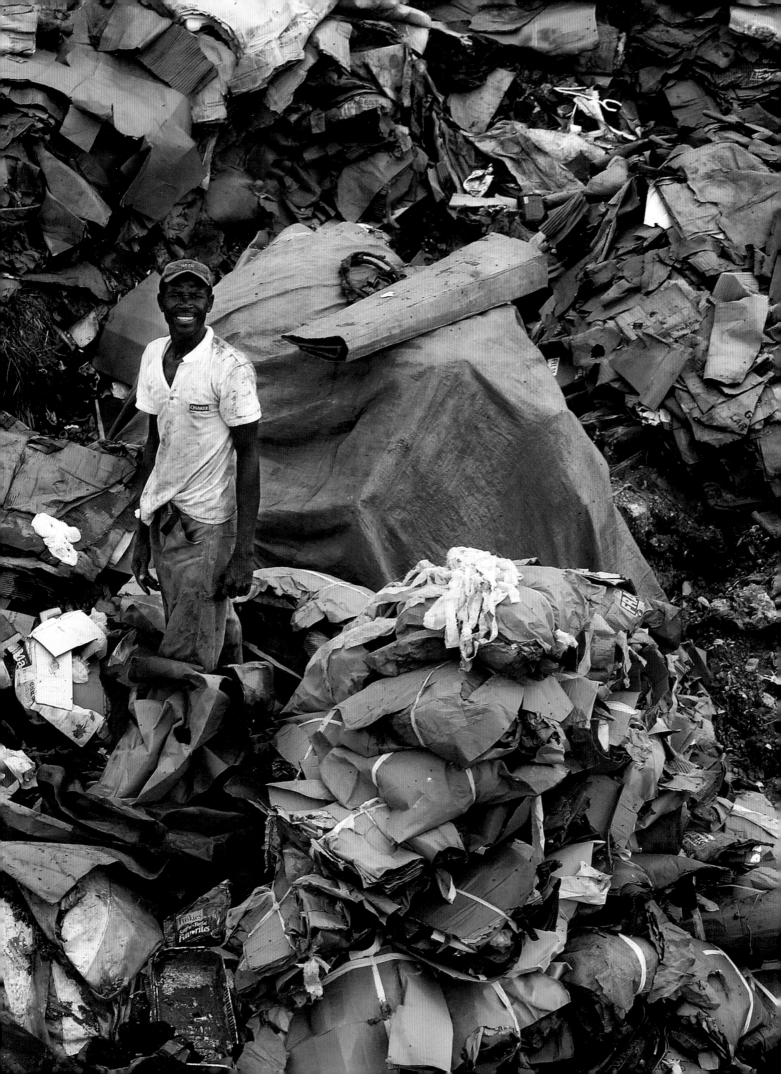

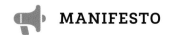

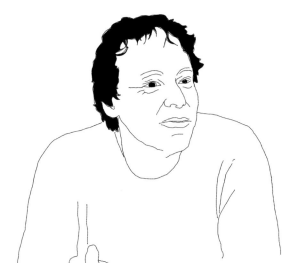

ON THE PHENOMENON OF BULLSHIT JOBS

DAVID GRAEBER

First published in *Strike!* magazine, August 17, 2013

Ever had the feeling that your job might be made up? That the world would keep on turning if you weren't doing that thing you do nine to five? Anthropology professor and bestselling author David Graeber explored the phenomenon of bullshit jobs for our recent summer issue—everyone who's employed should read carefully...

In the year 1930, John Maynard Keynes predicted that technology would have advanced sufficiently by century's end that countries like Great Britain or the United States would achieve a fifteen-hour work week. There's every reason to believe he was right. In technological terms, we are quite capable of this. And yet it didn't happen. Instead, technology has been marshaled, if anything, to figure out ways to make us all work more. In order to achieve this, jobs have had to be created that are, effectively, pointless. Huge swathes of people, in Europe and North America in particular, spend their entire working lives performing tasks they secretly believe do not really need to be performed. The moral and spiritual damage that comes from this situation is profound. It is a scar across our collective soul. Yet virtually no one talks about it.

Why did Keynes's promised utopia—still being eagerly awaited in the '60s—never materialize? The standard line today is that he didn't figure in the massive increase in consumerism. Given the choice between less hours and more toys and pleasures, we've collectively chosen the latter. This presents a nice morality tale, but even a moment's reflection shows it can't really be true. Yes, we have witnessed the creation of an endless variety of new jobs and industries since the '20s, but very few have anything to do with the production and distribution of sushi, iPhones, or fancy sneakers.

So what are these new jobs, precisely? A recent report comparing employment in the U.S. between 1910 and 2000 gives us a clear picture (and I note, one pretty much exactly echoed in the U.K.). Over the course of the last century, the number of workers employed as domestic servants, in industry, and in the farm sector has collapsed dramatically. At the same time, "professional, managerial, clerical, sales, and service workers" tripled, growing "from one-quarter to three-quarters of total employment." In other words, productive jobs have, just as predicted, been largely automated away (even if you count industrial workers globally, including the toiling masses in India and China, such workers are still not nearly so large a percentage of the world population as they used to be).

But rather than allowing a massive reduction of working hours to free the world's population to pursue their own projects, pleasures, visions, and ideas, we have seen the ballooning not even so much of the "service" sector as of the administrative sector, up to and including the creation of whole new industries like financial services or telemarketing, or the unprecedented expansion of sectors like corporate law, academic and health administration, human resources, and public relations. And these numbers do not even reflect on all those people whose job is to provide administrative, technical, or security support for these industries, or for that matter the whole host of ancillary industries (dog-washers, all-night pizza deliverymen) that only exist because everyone else is spending so much of their time working in all the other ones.

These are what I propose to call "bullshit jobs."

It's as if someone were out there making up pointless jobs just for the sake of keeping us all working. And here, precisely, lies the mystery. In capitalism, this is exactly what is *not* supposed to happen. Sure, in the old inefficient socialist states like the Soviet Union, where employment was considered both a right and a sacred duty, the system made up as many jobs as they had to (this is why in Soviet department stores it took three clerks to sell a piece of meat). But, of course, this is the very sort of problem market competition is supposed to fix. According to economic theory, at least, the last thing a profit-seeking firm is going to do is shell out money to workers they don't really need to employ. Still, somehow, it happens.

While corporations may engage in ruthless downsizing, the layoffs and speed-ups invariably fall on that class of people who are actually making, moving, fixing, and maintaining things; through some strange alchemy no one can quite explain, the number of salaried paper-pushers ultimately seems to expand, and more and more employees find themselves, not unlike Soviet workers actually, working forty or even fifty hour weeks on paper, but effectively working fifteen hours just as Keynes predicted, since the rest of their time is spent organizing or attending motivational seminars, updating their Facebook profiles or downloading TV box-sets.

The answer clearly isn't economic: It's moral and political. The ruling class has figured out that a happy and productive population with free time on their hands is a mortal danger (think of what started to happen when this even began to be approximated in the '60s). And, on the other hand, the feeling that work is a moral value in itself, and that anyone not willing to submit themselves to some kind of intense work discipline for most of their waking hours deserves nothing, is extraordinarily convenient for them.

Once, when contemplating the apparently endless growth of administrative responsibilities in British academic departments, I came up with one possible vision of hell. Hell is a collection of individuals who are spending the bulk of their time working on a task they don't like and are not especially good at. Say they were hired because they were excellent cabinet-makers, and then discover they are expected to spend a great deal of their time frying fish. Neither does the task really need to be done—at least, there's only a very limited number of fish that need to be fried. Yet somehow, they all become so obsessed with resentment at the thought that some of their co-workers might be spending more time making cabinets, and not doing their fair share of the fish-frying responsibilities, that before long there's endless piles of useless badly cooked fish piling up all over the workshop and it's all that anyone really does.

I think this is actually a pretty accurate description of the moral dynamics of our own economy.

Now, I realize any such argument is going to run into immediate objections: "Who are you to say what jobs are really 'necessary'? What's necessary anyway? You're an anthropology professor, what's the 'need' for that?" (And indeed a lot of tabloid readers would take the existence of my job as the very definition of wasteful social expenditure.) And on one level, this is obviously true. There can be no objective measure of social value.

I would not presume to tell someone who is convinced they are making a meaningful contribution to the world that, really, they are not. But what about those people who are themselves convinced their jobs

> IT'S AS IF SOMEONE WERE OUT THERE MAKING UP POINTLESS JOBS JUST FOR THE SAKE OF KEEPING US ALL WORKING

are meaningless? Not long ago I got back in touch with a school friend who I hadn't seen since I was twelve. I was amazed to discover that in the interim, he had become first a poet, then the front man in an indie rock band. I'd heard some of his songs on the radio having no idea the singer was someone I actually knew. He was obviously brilliant, innovative, and his work had unquestionably brightened and improved the lives of people all over the world. Yet, after a couple of unsuccessful albums, he'd lost his contract, and plagued with debts and a newborn daughter, ended up, as he put it, "taking the default choice of so many directionless folk: law school." Now he's a corporate lawyer working in a prominent New York firm. He was the first to admit that his job was utterly meaningless, contributed nothing to the world, and, in his own estimation, should not really exist.

There's a lot of questions one could ask here, starting with, What does it say about our society that it seems to generate an extremely limited demand for talented poet-musicians, but an apparently infinite demand for specialists in corporate law? (Answer: If 1 percent of the population controls most of the disposable wealth, what we call "the market" reflects what *they* think is useful or important, not anybody else.) But even more, it shows that most people in these jobs are ultimately aware of it. In fact, I'm not sure I've ever met a corporate lawyer who didn't think their job was bullshit. The same goes for almost all the new industries outlined above. There is a whole class of salaried professionals that, should you meet them at parties and admit that you do something that might be considered interesting (an anthropologist, for example), will want to avoid even discussing their line of work entirely. Give them a few drinks, and they will launch into tirades about how pointless and stupid their job really is.

This is a profound psychological violence here. How can one even begin to speak of dignity in labor when one secretly feels one's job should not exist? How can it not create a sense of deep rage and resentment? Yet it is the peculiar genius of our society that its rulers have figured out a way, as in the case of the fish-fryers, to ensure that rage is directed precisely against those who actually do get to do meaningful work. For instance: In our society, there seems a general rule that, the more obviously one's work benefits other people, the less one is likely to be paid for it. Again, an objective measure is hard to find, but one easy way to get

a sense is to ask: What would happen were this entire class of people to simply disappear? Say what you like about nurses, garbage collectors, or mechanics, it's obvious that were they to vanish in a puff of smoke, the results would be immediate and catastrophic. A world without teachers or dock-workers would soon be in trouble, and even one without science fiction writers or ska musicians would clearly be a lesser place. It's not entirely clear how humanity would suffer were all private equity CEOs, lobbyists, PR researchers, actuaries, telemarketers, bailiffs, or legal consultants to similarly vanish. (Many suspect it might markedly improve.) Yet apart from a handful of well-touted exceptions (doctors), the rule holds surprisingly well.

Even more perverse, there seems to be a broad sense that this is the way things should be. This is one of the secret strengths of right-wing populism. You can see it when tabloids whip up resentment against tube workers for paralyzing London during contract disputes: The very fact that tube workers can paralyze London shows that their work is actually necessary, but this seems to be precisely what annoys people. It's even clearer in the U.S., where Republicans have had remarkable success mobilizing resentment against school teachers, or auto workers (and not, significantly, against the school administrators or auto industry managers who actually cause the problems) for their supposedly bloated wages and benefits. It's as if they are being told, "but you get to teach children! Or make cars! You get to have real jobs! And on top of that you have the nerve to also expect middle-class pensions and health care?"

If someone had designed a work regime perfectly suited to maintaining the power of finance capital, it's hard to see how they could have done a better job. Real, productive workers are relentlessly squeezed and exploited. The remainder are divided between a terrorized stratum of the—universally reviled—unemployed and a larger stratum who are basically paid to do nothing, in positions designed to make them identify with the perspectives and sensibilities of the ruling class (managers, administrators, etc.)—and particularly its financial avatars—but, at the same time, foster a simmering resentment against anyone whose work has clear and undeniable social value. Clearly, the system was never consciously designed. It emerged from almost a century of trial and error. But it is the only explanation for why, despite our technological capacities, we are not all working three- to four-hour days.

TAKING ACTION LEADS TO HAPPINESS

YANN ARTHUS-BERTRAND

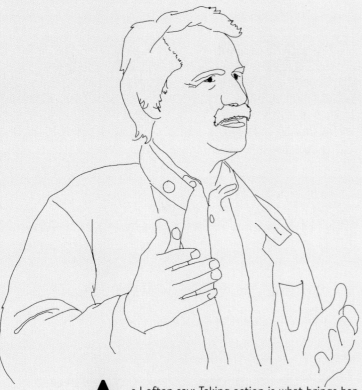

As I often say: Taking action is what brings happiness. It's a truth I'm personally convinced about and that I see confirmed every day: People who commit to good causes give off a vibrant, positive, and contagious energy—because taking action, taking your destiny into your own hands, is also a way to uncover your vitality, to feel fulfilled, to open yourself to the rest of the world.

In times of crisis and with pessimism all about, people turn inward. Yet when problems are evident, it's really the time to see bigger, to reconsider our society and our life. Gandhi taught: "Be the change that you want to see in the world." Start by changing yourself. Each person's effort can then build to transform the world. You'll see if you try. It's easier than you think, and you'll feel good as soon as you begin to do good for yourself or for others. This doesn't mean becoming perfect or stopping everything that makes you happy now. Rather, it means being vigilant, reconsidering what has become automatic through routine; it means becoming aware of the importance of the present moment in order to better take advantage of it. It's about finding a new way to live together so that we can reconcile ourselves with ourselves, with our society, and with our planet.

How do we do that? We each have to find our own answer. But in the chapters that follow, I wanted to include examples of NGOs (non-governmental organizations) that work on the themes evoked. I hope that reading these pages will make you want to get involved, and that the sample of ways we're suggesting will help you find your way down this path.

"It's not the thorns that protect me, says the rose. It's my scent," wrote Paul Claudel. In a similar way, it's not the terrible predictions of all the Cassandras that will save the world. It's our capacity to be moved. It's our capacity to see the beauty that resides in each and every one of us—and to make it blossom by opening ourselves to others and by letting our heart speak of love. Love, meant in the widest sense, that is, as a form of empathy and kindness; it is the cement of all social life, the bedrock of a "living together." Love is revolutionary. Love is the force that will change our world.

This is what I am trying to say in *Human*. This is what I've always tried to say.

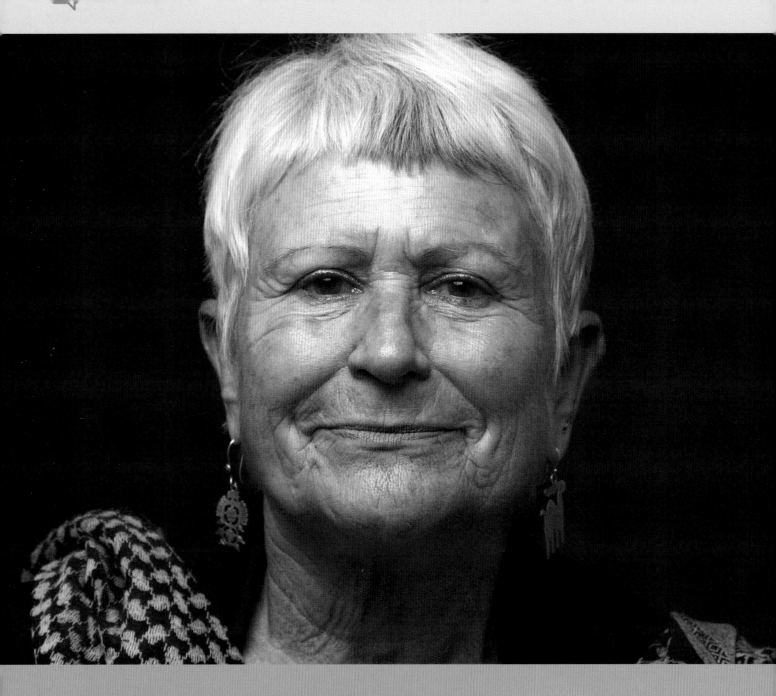

MEETING MIMI BONHEUR

YOU CAN FIND HAPPINESS EVERYWHERE—EVEN IN A SYRIAN REFUGEE CAMP. BUT WHAT IS HAPPINESS AND HOW CAN WE DEFINE IT?

What is *bonheur*; what is happiness? I posed the question to farmers in Dordogne and to Syrian refugees. I posed it to workers in Shenzhen and also to the beautiful Indian women in Kushinagar, to traders, actors, dancers, astronauts, Salafis, transgender people, mothers, and many more. Just the thought of these people who agreed to share their thoughts with me is a bit of happiness in itself. But I still don't have the answer.

Of all the stories I remember, of all the people who answered my question, Marie-Madeleine stands out the most. She's known as Mimi. We had just set up in Zaatari, a refugee camp located in northern Jordan, where Syrians fleeing the civil war arrive on a daily basis. Our tent was next to the Médecins du Monde clinic, and the movement in and out was constant. In the murmur of moans and crying children, I was suddenly stopped by a "Salam alaikum [Peace to you]" that had a whiff of French, a voice higher than all the others, colored with sun and cheer. The jovial dissonance was emanating from a small woman in a white blouse, her hair blonde and short. She had a dazzling smile. So there was a joyful soul in the camp!

Mimi worked as an emergency nurse with vivacious freshness. Her patent joie de vivre took away none of the difficulty of her battles. Confronted with tortured people who had lost everything—their private lives and their social lives, their professional and religious lives—she had to gently help them release their pain. "Often it ends with a smile or when possible, with a hand to the shoulder or a gesture to the heart to say, 'you're with me, you're close to me, you understand.' When I can do that, it's the sunshine of my day," she exclaims. This miracle unfolded before my eyes. I was amazed at her skill in dealing with Syrians, who could not, for the most part, speak her language. In observing the refugees—with the help of my Lebanese perspective—I saw they were reassured by the demonstration of warmth and the efforts Mimi made. In reality, it was as if she were speaking their language. Through her dedication, she seemed to dapple the camp with light. With her light.

Secretly, I had already given her the nickname Mimi Bonheur…Mimi Happiness…

SO THERE WAS A JOYFUL SOUL IN THE CAMP!

The notion of happiness was so difficult to articulate through all the interviews. Sometimes it was associated with a birth, a marriage or a happy moment, other times with a search, an absolute, an abstraction….About this mysterious grail, Mimi had a completely personal view, quite different from those of the others. "For me," she says, "happiness is made up of so many pieces that, theoretically, there's always one missing. But I think that happiness is above all an aptitude for happiness. An aptitude that isn't given to everyone: You have people, young to boot, who at age twenty are sad to death." This was someone who had crossed the globe, from Ethiopia to Darfur, Haiti, Kashmir, and Peru, to treat the afflictions of this world, so what was her secret? From where did her aptitude for happiness come?

Mimi told me, "My family was very happy, you could even say bawdy and a bit inappropriate, but I have mourned a lot. My three brothers all died violent deaths, in accidents, rather young." This was a dark period that could have thrown her off balance, but she decided to look to what was ahead, because "someone who sets out for a star never changes," she explains, interrupting her answer with mischievous bursts of laughter. Mimi considered herself lucky to be in such strong health, to never be tired. She saw her happy character as a gift from life. The only negative idea she came up against was that maybe she took everything from her brothers. In other words, maybe she had an excess of luck. I was mesmerized by her strength and resilience, which she says she transmitted to her two children. "My life consists of dedramatizing everything. Everything! So I think that's a secret of longevity. Maybe I'll do as well as Jeanne Calment!" she says, bursting out in laughter.

After the interview, I let my fixer accompany her back. At his side, she entered into a long silence. Why? Before leaving, she let me know that the questions I had asked had forced her to reflect deeply about herself. So why the silence? I picture her, eyes looking into the distance, and to this day, that silence torments me. Might there be a dark side to this sunny happiness? The mystery will never be solved. And neither will the mystery of happiness in general, which we all have to elucidate for ourselves.
                                                    —Mia Sfeir

HAPPINESS MAP

NATIONAL HAPPINESS RANKING

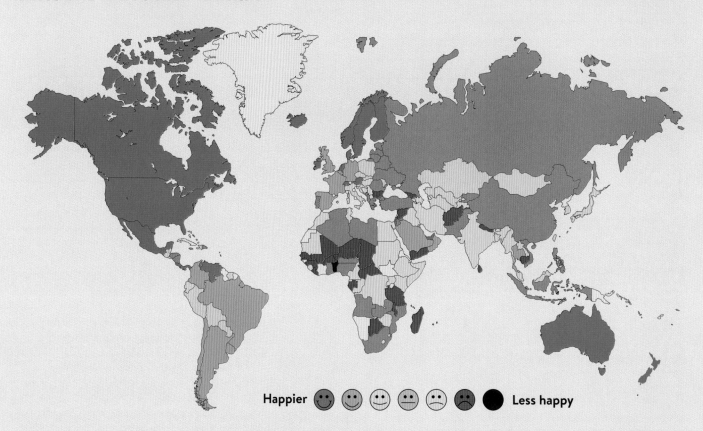

Happier 😄 🙂 🙂 😐 😕 ☹️ ⚫ Less happy

COMPARING WORLD AND REGIONAL HAPPINESS

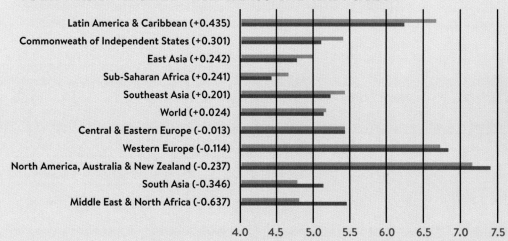

Latin America & Caribbean (+0.435)
Commonweath of Independent States (+0.301)
East Asia (+0.242)
Sub-Saharan Africa (+0.241)
Southeast Asia (+0.201)
World (+0.024)
Central & Eastern Europe (-0.013)
Western Europe (-0.114)
North America, Australia & New Zealand (-0.237)
South Asia (-0.346)
Middle East & North Africa (-0.637)

4.0 4.5 5.0 5.5 6.0 6.5 7.0 7.5

This report used data collected by the Gallup World Poll on three measures of happiness: life satisfaction on a scale of 1 to 10, positive emotional state the prior day (Did you smile a lot yesterday? Did you experience enjoyment?), and negative emotional state the prior day (Did you experience anger or sadness?).

— 2010–2012
— 2005–2007

LOVE IN TEXT MESSAGES

WHO IN COUPLES SENDS THE MOST TEXT MESSAGES?

Depending upon gender and stage of relationship

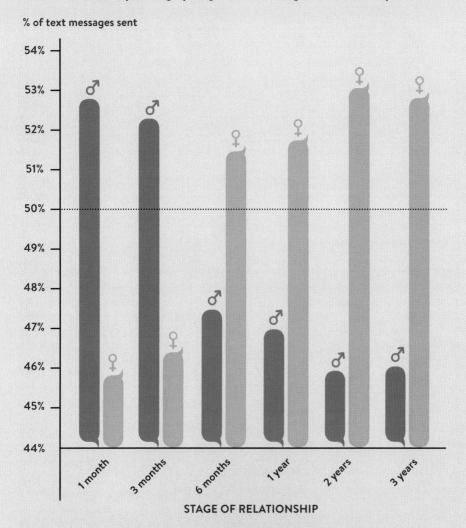

% of text messages sent

STAGE OF RELATIONSHIP

RESPONSE TIME IN A TEXT CONVERSATION

Depending upon gender

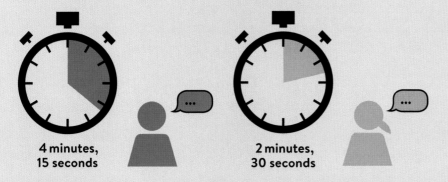

4 minutes, 15 seconds

2 minutes, 30 seconds

KEY FIGURES

According to the World Happiness Report, there has been an increase of 7% in happiness in South America and the Caribbean and an increase of 5.1% in Asia between 2005 and 2012.

According to a different ranking, the Happy Planet Index, which measures global well-being and the environment, Costa Rica, Vietnam, and Colombia are at the top of the list. Of course, everything depends upon the method of calculation.

The global average age for first sexual intercourse is 17.3 years.

The global average number of sexual partners is nine.

54% of the global population lives in cities.

More than 1.1 billion tourists traveled abroad in 2014.

Global advertising expenditures exceed $540 billion. This is about 4 times as much as public development assistance.

There are more than 7.5 billion mobile phone subscriptions in the world. This is more than the number of people who live on Earth.

95 of 100 residents have Internet access in Norway, which is the most connected country on Earth. Conversely, North Korea restricts Internet access to a minority of its elite. It is probably the country most isolated from the World Wide Web.

TIMELINE

c. 2000 B.C.
First identified love poem, on a Sumerian clay tablet. It is thought to have been recited to a wife of the Sumerian king Shu-Sin.

1631
Start of construction on the Taj Mahal, by the Mughal emperor Shah Jahan, in memory of his wife.

1776
The United States Declaration of Independence stipulates that "all men are created equal, that they are endowed by their creator with certain unalienable Rights, that among these are Life, Liberty, and the pursuit of Happiness."

1817
Robert Owen invents the concept of the eight-hour day; eight hours rest, eight hours work, and eight hours leisure time.

1908
The Ford Model T is created. This car symbolizes the triumph of the industrial revolution as a result of mass production and accompanies the development of the consumer society. More than fifteen million Ford Ts are factory produced.

1960s–1980s
These decades are considered a time of sexual revolution due to the availability of oral contraceptives and changing sexual norms.

BOOKS

Romeo and Juliet
William Shakespeare, 1597
Undoubtedly the best-known love story, this play takes place in Verona. The Capulets and the Montagues are at war, yet their children fall in love, hiding it from their families.

De l'Amour [On Love]
Stendhal, 1822
One of the key books on love, in which the author expounds on the theory of crystallization, a key phenomenon of love, in which one projects illusions of perfection onto the beloved.

Bartleby, the Scrivener
Herman Melville, 1853
As a conscientious scrivener, Bartleby copies texts for his boss. One day, he changes and responds to his employer's requests with the one phrase, "I would prefer not to." A text about the absurdity of bureaucratic work.

Lady Chatterley's Lover
D. H. Lawrence, 1928
Lady Chatterley is married to a man who has become paralyzed. She meets a gamekeeper with whom she enters into a passionate affair, thus defying social conventions.

Brave New World
Aldous Huxley, 1932
In the future, a new human society based on eugenics and extremely developed planning emerges. Guaranteeing peace and social order, it promises the best world possible for all. A critique of the "leisure society."

L'Amour et l'Occident [Love in the Western World]
Denis de Rougemont, 1939
An historic study based on the story of Tristan and Isolde and addressing courtly love and passionate love. The latter is thought to have emerged in the twelfth century in southwest France in connection with heretic Catharism.

The Catcher in the Rye
J. D. Salinger, 1951
Holden Caulfield has three days of freedom after being kicked out of private school. It's an experience that will change the course of his life.

Lolita
Vladimir Nabokov, 1955
Humbert Humbert feels mad passion for a twelve-and-half-year-old teenager. A novel about transgression, this book made its mark on the twentieth century. Ever since, the name Lolita suggests erotic ambiguity.

La Société du spectacle [The Society of the Spectacle]
Guy Debord, 1967
One of the most celebrated modern critiques of our consumer society.

The World Inside
Robert Silverberg, 1971
The highest possible good is to procreate and multiply endlessly. Enclosed in giant towers called monads, humans live in comfort and enjoy the greatest sexual liberty. But is this enough to guarantee happiness?

Fragments d'un discours amoureux [A Lover's Discourse: Fragments]
Roland Barthes, 1977
A collection of fragments, easy and pleasant to read, which untangle feelings and their manifestations.

No Logo: Taking Aim at the Brand Bullies
Naomi Klein, 1999
In this book, the Canadian journalist denounces the effects of the consumer society. She investigates the manner in which companies exploit workers to produce at low cost commercialized products that are much more expensive than they cost to make, a consequence of advertising. And she also warns of the effect of advertising on our societies: It infiltrates our mind and introduces an image of happiness based on consumerism.

Premier matin [Early Morning]
Jean-Claude Kaufmann, 2002
Sociological analysis of shared intimate moments like waking up, breakfast, and getting ready reveal numerous things about day-to-day love and the possible compatibility between two beings.

FILMS

The Meaning of Life
Monty Python, 1983
This comedy doesn't answer the question of what governs our existence. But through several skits, it proposes that we laugh about the absurdity of certain moments in life: from birth to death, education, restaurants, and war.

The Full Monty
Peter Cattaneo, 1997
The city of Sheffield in England is facing hard economic times. Unemployed, with no job prospects, several workers decide to form a male striptease act to make ends meet.

American Beauty
Sam Mendes, 1999
This acerbic film paints a disenchanted portrait of the American middle class, unable to find happiness in suburban life or in work. What's left when every illusion upon which you've built your life has crumbled?

In the Mood for Love
Wong Kar-Wai, 2000
The story takes place in Hong Kong in the 1960s. Two couples move into apartments on the same day and become next-door neighbors. Mr. Chow and Mrs. Chan find their respective spouses going out regularly. Little by little, they cross paths, slip away, seek each other out, discover adultery and shared feelings.

Devdas
Sanjay Leela Bhansali, 2002
Devdas has completed his studies in England, and returns to India where his childhood friend Parvati is waiting for him. They seem meant for one another—but social conventions oppose their union. A typically Bollywood movie, very colorful, with music and dance playing a preponderant role.

Eternal Sunshine of the Spotless Mind
Michel Gondry, 2004
The firm Lacuna offers its clients the opportunity to erase their memory. Feeling unhappy, Clementine erases Joel from her memory after a three-year relationship. He decides to do the same…

Into the Wild
Sean Penn, 2007
In the true story of Christopher McCandless, a recent graduate drops everything to live a life of adventures on the road. To escape society and its limitations, he takes refuge in Alaska where he spends the winter in an abandoned bus. The conclusion he comes to: "Happiness is only real when shared."

WEBSITES

World Autism Awareness Day, the United Nations
www.un.org/en/events/autismday

Better Life Index, OECD
www.oecdbetterlifeindex.org

The Happy Planet Index
www.happyplanetindex.org

Gross National Happiness
www.grossnationalhappiness.com

Ecological footprint
www.footprintnetwork.org

46,000 free digital books
www.gutenberg.org

Films, books, music, and software in the public domain
archive.org

ANTHROPOGENIC LANDSCAPE IN THE MARSHES NEAR OYO, CUVETTE, REPUBLIC OF THE CONGO [CONGO-BRAZZAVILLE] 1° 08' S – 15° 58' E

The small spots visible on the ground are evidence of ancestral agricultural practices. Archeological remains dating to the thirteenth century were discovered here.

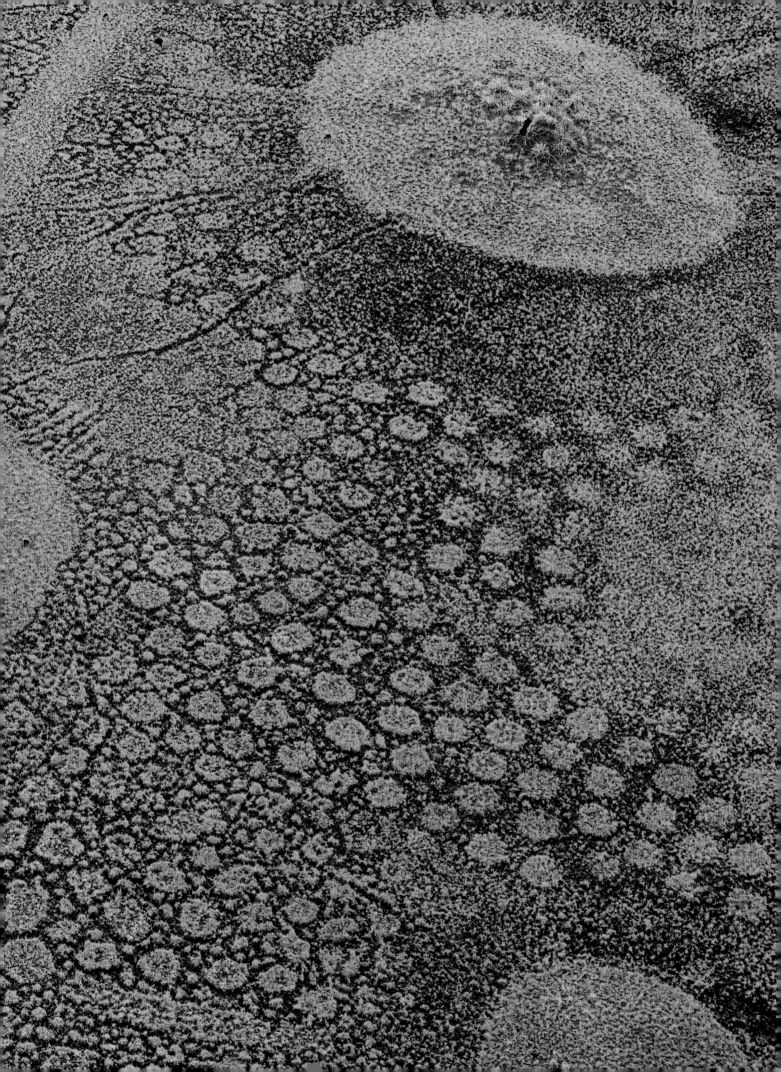

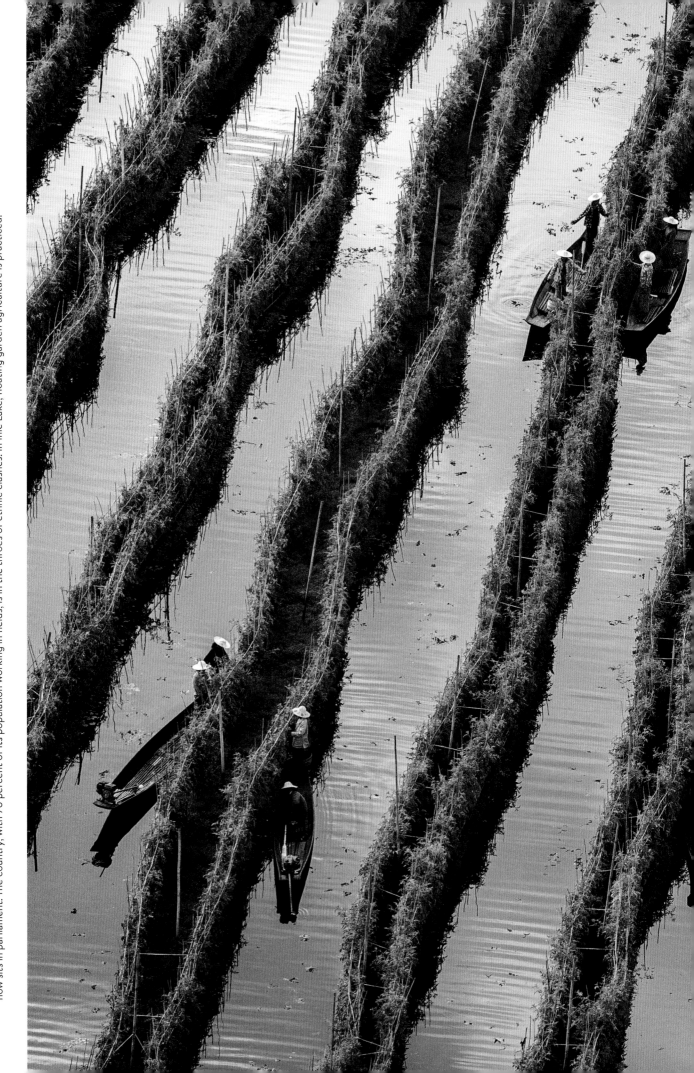

INLE LAKE, SHAN, MYANMAR [BURMA] 20°33' N – 96°55' E

For many years controlled by a junta, Myanmar today is a country in transition. The emblematic figure of this transformation is the opposition leader and Nobel Peace Prize winner Aung San Suu Kyi, who now sits in parliament. The country, with 70 percent of its population working in fields, is in the throes of ethnic clashes. In Inle Lake, floating garden agriculture is practiced.

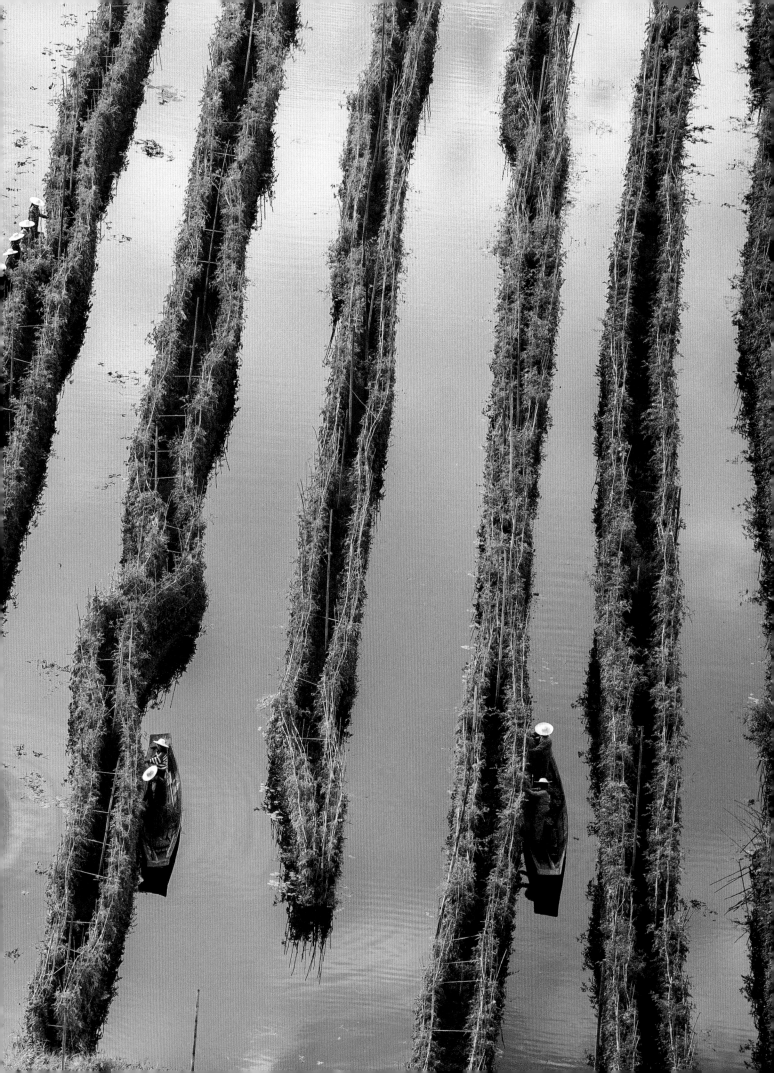

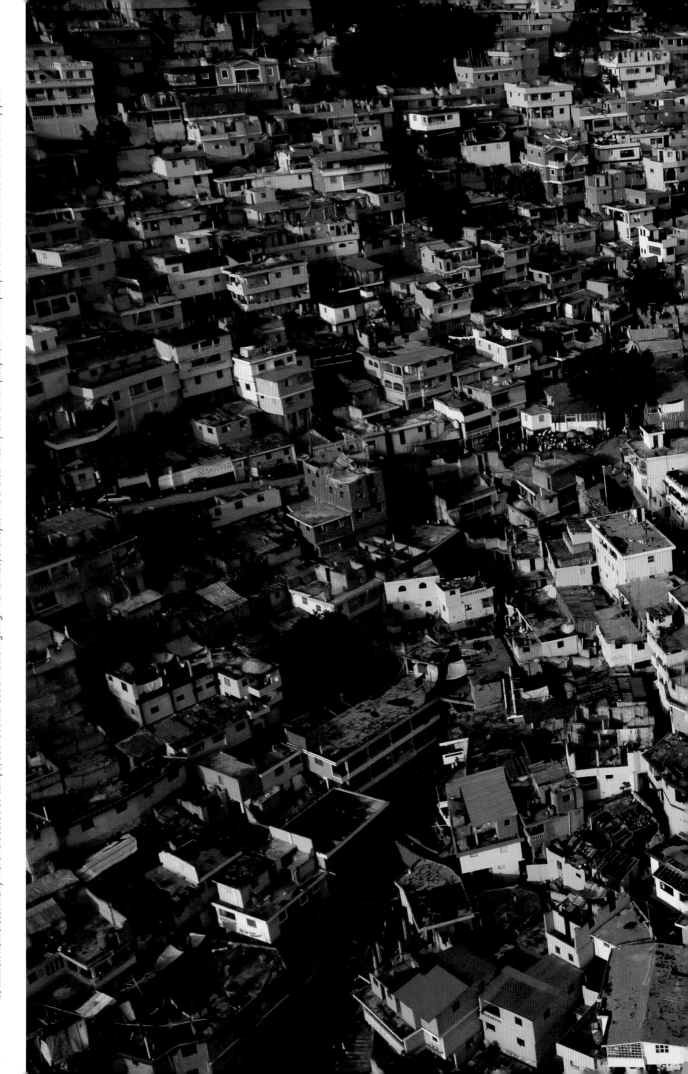

JALOUSIE, A SHANTYTOWN ON THE EDGE OF PÉTIONVILLE, A SUBURB OF PORT-AU-PRINCE, HAITI 18° 30' 41.57" N – 72° 17' 38.80" W

Parts of Jalousie were repainted in bright colors in 2013, as part of the Haitian government's Beauty versus Poverty initiative. Most houses still do not have water and electricity. The earthquake in 2010 left 1.3 million homeless. Many were relocated to camps, but reconstruction is slow going. Worldwide, shantytowns shelter nearly one billion people; 27 million people are added to these numbers every year.

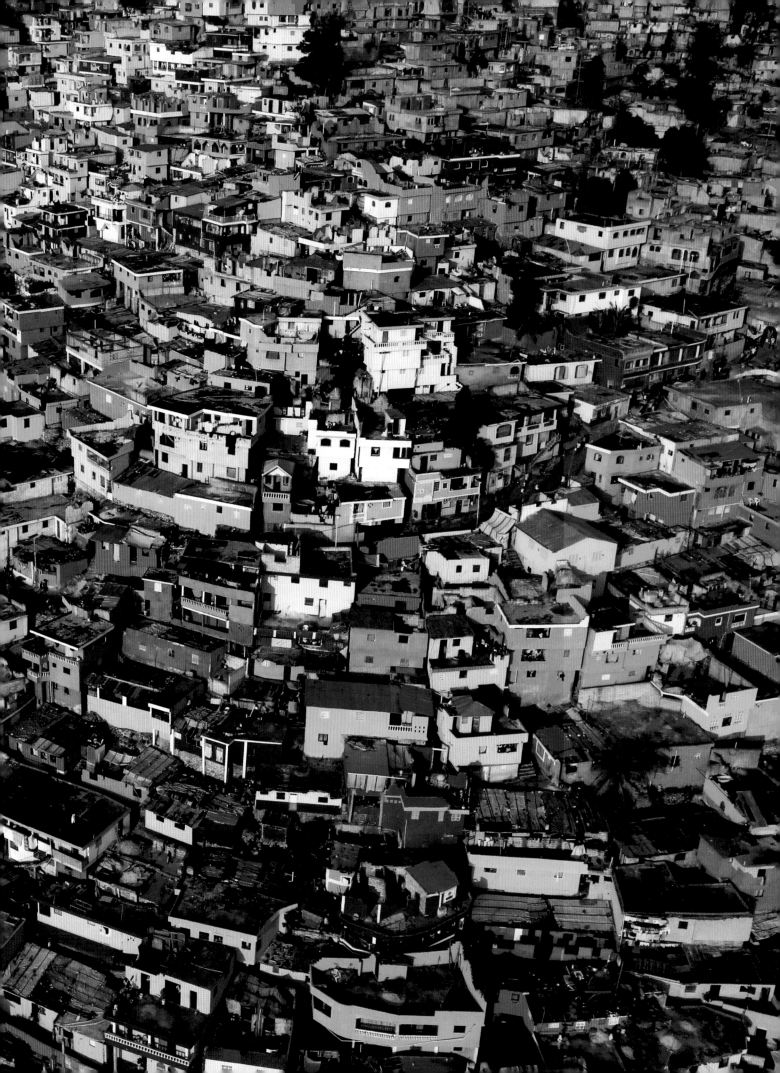

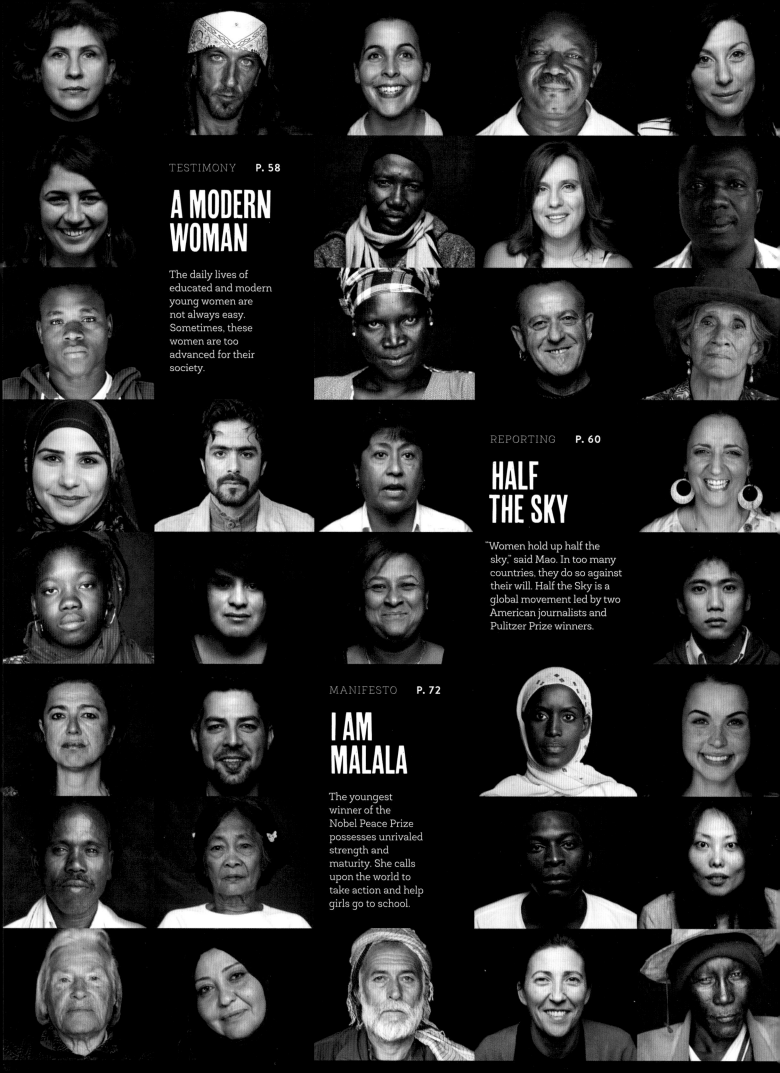

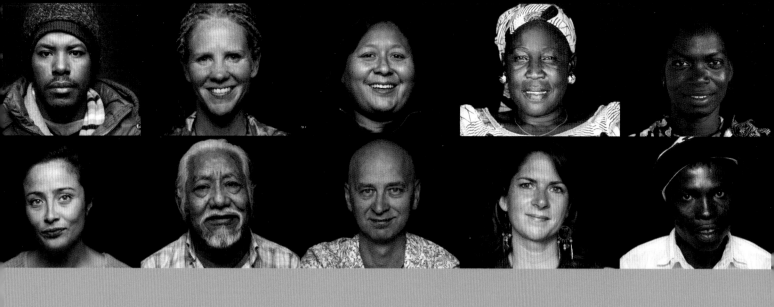

WOMEN'S RIGHTS

For many young girls, receiving an education means risking their lives. Malala in Pakistan and the young Nigerian girls kidnapped by Boko Haram—which in the Hausa language roughly translates to "Western education is a sin"—are poignant examples of women who have faced violence at the hands of fundamentalists. Ensuring that girls around the globe have the opportunity to go to school and attain a better life is one of the most urgent causes of the twenty-first century.

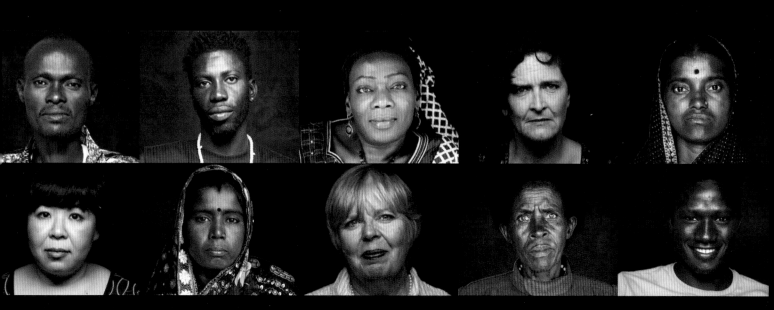

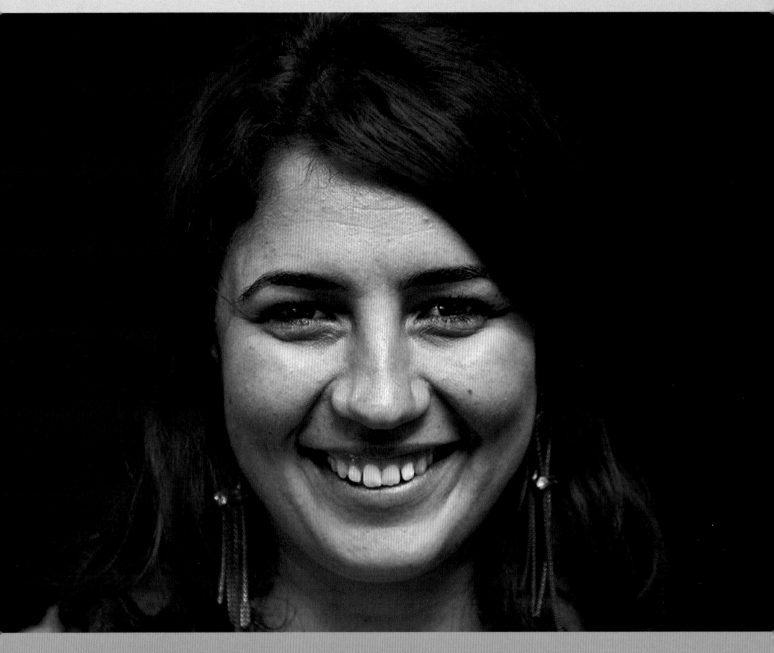

A MODERN WOMAN

NESRINE LIVES IN TUNISIA. SHE IS TWENTY-SEVEN YEARS OLD, HAS FOUNDED HER OWN ARCHITECTURE FIRM, AND DRIVES A CAR. BUT EVEN HER FAMILY HAS A HARD TIME ACCEPTING HER.

Being a woman here, in Tunisia, especially in the South, is more difficult than being a man because, here, men have all the rights and we have all the obligations.

For example, everyone finds it strange that at my age, I haven't yet married, that I don't have children, and that these aren't my top concerns. Here, a woman's fulfillment is linked to having a family and children. They couldn't care less whether she works or not, whether she has an education or not, even whether she's happy or not, so long as she has children and is married.

What bothers me the most about my immediate environment is that they call me a spinster. Yes, at twenty-seven! And the worst is that people think it's my fault. I completed my studies through a high-level baccalaureate, I have a car, I've opened my own architecture firm, and people think I'm too demanding because I want someone intelligent who accepts that I'm a free woman! It cannot be, they say, a woman doesn't have the right to ask a man to be intelligent. A woman has to obey her husband. And what pains me as well is that I have many European friends who find it completely normal that I'm waiting for someone with whom I can live in peace. But not here. Here, what's important in a marriage is knowing how to cook. The same is true with sex; it's taboo. We're supposed to be virgins, never touched. It really bothers me because, come on, I'm not fourteen anymore. And men, they act as if they're going to retrain you to fit their character. Honestly…What do you think I've been doing these past twenty years? Striving to be neutral so that I can adapt to your personality? And do I not have the right to have my own personality? I'm your doll? In any case, I don't know how to cook.

I find it strange that there are women who know their husbands are cheating on them and yet don't care, as long as he comes back at night, as long as he brings home enough to eat, as long as he brings home the money to buy jewelry so that they can look good out in the world.

And what pains me even more is that women aren't asking for the right to live as they want to live. They accept being reduced to an object that makes children, an object that makes dinner, an object that does the dishes. It pains me because I'm not like that. I want to have my own life; I want to live like other human beings.

Women have to wage their own revolution. They have to say, "Enough, I don't want to live like this." Because while I'm speaking out now, I think I'm going to end up giving in—because I'm alone. And I want children and a family life too, but only if I find the man to go with it. Then it would be better. And the problem is that for women, if it doesn't work, you can't divorce, because being divorced is even worse than being a spinster.

I just want to have a life. I went through school and I always worked hard, but that's not enough to make my parents happy and proud of me. And that hurts, because I think the effect is almost the opposite…I almost feel that I'm dishonoring them, that in their eyes I'm not fulfilling my role as their first daughter. But how can you change that? I'm trying, I'm trying, but honestly, I'm not sure I'll make it alone.

> WOMEN HAVE TO WAGE THEIR OWN REVOLUTION. THEY HAVE TO SAY, "ENOUGH, I DON'T WANT TO LIVE LIKE THIS"

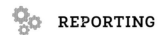

HALF THE SKY

By Nicholas D. Kristof and Sheryl WuDunn

From *Half the Sky: Turning Oppression into Opportunity for Women Worldwide*, 2009, Knopf

In the nineteenth century, the central moral challenge was slavery. In the twentieth century, it was the battle against totalitarianism. Nicholas D. Kristof and Sheryl WuDunn, both reporters at the *New York Times* and Pulitzer Prize awardees, believe that in the twenty-first century the paramount moral challenge will be the struggle for gender equality in the developing world.

Srey Rath is a self-confident Cambodian teenager whose black hair tumbles over a round, light brown face. She is in a crowded street market, standing beside a pushcart and telling her story calmly, with detachment. The only hint of anxiety or trauma is the way she often pushes her hair from in front of her black eyes, perhaps a nervous tic....

Rath is short and small-boned, pretty, vibrant, and bubbly, a wisp of a girl whose negligible stature contrasts with an outsized and outgoing personality....But Rath's attractiveness and winning personality are perilous bounties for a rural Cambodian girl, and her trusting nature and optimistic self-assuredness compound the hazard.

When Rath was fifteen, her family ran out of money, so she decided to go work as a dishwasher in Thailand for two months to help pay the bills. Her parents fretted about her safety, but they were reassured when Rath arranged to travel with four friends who had been promised jobs in the same Thai restaurant. The job agent took the girls deep into Thailand and then handed them to gangsters who took them to Kuala Lumpur, the capital of Malaysia. Rath was dazzled by her first glimpses of the city's clean avenues and gleaming high-rises, including at the time the world's tallest twin buildings; it seemed safe and welcoming. But then thugs sequestered Rath and two other girls inside a karaoke lounge that operated as a brothel. One gangster in his late thirties, a man known as "the boss," took charge of the girls and explained that he had paid money for them and that they would now be obliged to repay him. "You must find money to pay off the debt, and then I will send you back home," he said, repeatedly reassuring them that if they cooperated they would eventually be released.

Rath was shattered when what was happening dawned on her. The boss locked her up with a customer, who tried to force her to have sex with him. She fought back, enraging the customer. "So the boss got angry and hit me in the face, first with one hand and then with the other," she remembers, telling her story with simple resignation. "The mark stayed on my face for two weeks." Then the boss and the other gangsters raped her and beat her with their fists.

"You have to serve the customers," the boss told her as he punched her. "If not, we will beat you to death. Do you want that?" Rath stopped protesting, but she sobbed and refused to cooperate actively. The boss forced her to take a pill; the gangsters called it "the happy drug" or "the shake drug." She doesn't know exactly what it was, but it made her head shake and induced lethargy, happiness, and compliance for about an hour. When she wasn't drugged, Rath was teary and insufficiently compliant—she was required to beam happily at all customers—so the boss said he would waste no more time on her: She would agree to do as he ordered or he would kill her. Rath then gave in. The girls were forced to work in the brothel seven days a week, fifteen hours a day. They were kept naked to make it more difficult for them to run away or to keep tips or other money, and they were forbidden to ask customers to use condoms. They were battered until they smiled constantly and simulated joy at the sight of customers, because men would not pay as much for sex with girls with reddened eyes and haggard faces. The girls were never allowed out on the street or paid a penny for their work.

"They just gave us food to eat, but they didn't give us much because the customers didn't like fat girls," Rath says. The girls were bused, under guard, back and forth between the brothel

> RATH'S SAGA OFFERS A GLIMPSE OF THE BRUTALITY INFLICTED ROUTINELY ON WOMEN AND GIRLS IN MUCH OF THE WORLD, A MALIGNANCY THAT IS SLOWLY GAINING RECOGNITION AS ONE OF THE PARAMOUNT HUMAN RIGHTS PROBLEMS OF THIS CENTURY

and a tenth-floor apartment where a dozen of them were housed. The door of the apartment was locked from the outside. However, one night, some of the girls went out onto their balcony and pried loose a long, five-inch-wide board from a rack used for drying clothes. They balanced it precariously between their balcony and one on the next building, twelve feet away. The board wobbled badly, but Rath was desperate, so she sat astride the board and gradually inched across.

"There were four of us who did that," she says. "The others were too scared, because it was very rickety. I was scared, too, and I couldn't look down, but I was even more scared to stay. We thought that even if we died, it would be better than staying behind. If we stayed, we would die as well."

Once on the far balcony, the girls pounded on the window and woke the surprised tenant. They could hardly communicate with him because none of them spoke Malay, but the tenant let them into his apartment and then out its front door. The girls took the elevator down and wandered the silent streets until they found a police station and stepped inside. The police first tried to shoo them away, then arrested the girls for illegal immigration. Rath served a year in prison under Malaysia's tough anti-immigrant laws, and then she was supposed to be repatriated. She thought a Malaysian policeman was escorting her home when he drove her to the Thai border—but then he sold her to a trafficker, who peddled her to a Thai brothel.

Rath's saga offers a glimpse of the brutality inflicted routinely on women and girls in much of the world, a malignancy that is slowly gaining recognition as one of the paramount human rights problems of this century....

A similar pattern emerged in other countries, particularly in South Asia and the Muslim world. In India, a "bride burning"—to punish a woman for an inadequate dowry or to eliminate her so a man can remarry—takes place approximately once every two hours, but these rarely constitute news. In the twin cities of Islamabad and Rawalpindi, Pakistan, five thousand women and girls have been doused in kerosene and set alight by family members or in-laws—or, perhaps worse, been seared with acid—for perceived disobedience just in the last nine years. Imagine the outcry if the Pakistani or Indian governments were burning women alive at those rates. Yet when the government is not directly involved, people shrug.

MAO ZEDONG, FEMINIST?

Mao Zedong is attributed with coining the Chinese proverb "Women hold up half the sky," hence the title of the book *Half the Sky* that journalists Nicholas D. Kristof and Sheryl WuDunn devoted to the oppression and courage of women throughout the world. After taking power in 1949, the Great Helmsman notably banned in China the binding of women's feet, which resulted in necrosis of the toes and sometimes death by septicemia. He is said to have publicly paid homage to women and to have invoked their importance in the face of the misogynist society. Mao also ended polygamy and the system of concubinage and promoted the education of women. In Communist China, women were to be "comrades" like everyone else.

These Maoist measures were undoubtedly inspired by the effort to mobilize the entire Chinese workforce, which was summoned to bring the country that Great Leap Forward. Ultimately, this leap caused the largest famine in the history of China and killed some thirty million people.

The saying is nevertheless beautiful, and above all, true.

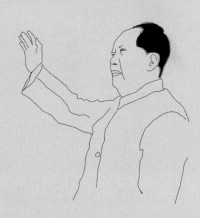

When a prominent dissident was arrested in China, we would write a front-page article; when 100,000 girls were routinely kidnapped and trafficked into brothels, we didn't even consider it news. Partly that is because we journalists tend to be good at covering events that happen on a particular day, but we slip at covering events that happen every day—such as the quotidian cruelties inflicted on women and girls. We journalists weren't the only ones who dropped the ball on this subject: Less than 1 percent of U.S. foreign aid is specifically targeted to women and girls....

The owners of the Thai brothel to which Rath was sold did not beat her and did not constantly guard her. So two months later, she was able to escape and make her way back to Cambodia. Upon her return, Rath met a social worker who put her in touch with an aid group that helps girls who have been trafficked start new lives. The group, American Assistance for Cambodia, used $400 in donated funds to buy a small cart and a starter selection of goods so that Rath could become a street peddler. She found a good spot in the open area between the Thai and Cambodian customs offices in the border town of Poipet. Travelers crossing between Thailand and Cambodia walk along this strip, the size of a football field, and it is lined with peddlers selling drinks, snacks, and souvenirs.

Rath outfitted her cart with shirts and hats, costume jewelry, notebooks, pens, and small toys. Now her good looks and outgoing personality began to work in her favor, turning her into an effective saleswoman. She saved and invested in new merchandise,

> WOMEN AREN'T THE PROBLEM BUT THE SOLUTION. THE PLIGHT OF GIRLS IS NO MORE A TRAGEDY THAN AN OPPORTUNITY

her business thrived, and she was able to support her parents and two younger sisters. She married and had a son, and she began saving for his education....

Rath's eventual triumph is a reminder that if girls get a chance, in

THE TRAP OF MODERN SLAVERY

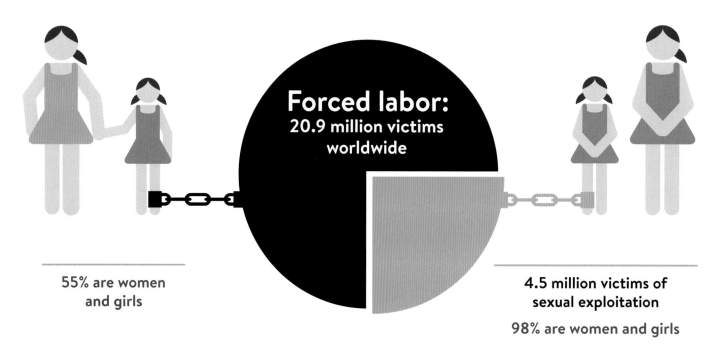

Forced labor:
20.9 million victims worldwide

55% are women and girls

4.5 million victims of sexual exploitation

98% are women and girls

the form of an education or a micro-loan, they can be more than baubles or slaves; many of them can run businesses. Talk to Rath today—after you've purchased that cap—and you find that she exudes confidence as she earns a solid income that will provide a better future for her sisters and for her young son.... *Women aren't the problem but the solution. The plight of girls is no more a tragedy than an opportunity.*

That was a lesson we absorbed in Sheryl's ancestral village, at the end of a dirt road amid the rice paddies of southern China. For many years we have regularly trod the mud paths of the Taishan region to Shunshui, the hamlet in which Sheryl's paternal grandfather grew up. China traditionally has been one of the more repressive and smothering places for girls, and we could see hints of this in Sheryl's own family history. Indeed, on our first visit, we accidentally uncovered a family secret: a long-lost step-grandmother. Sheryl's grandfather had traveled to America with his first wife, but she had given birth only to daughters. So Sheryl's grandfather gave up on her and returned her to Shunshui, where he married a younger woman as a second wife and took her to America. This was Sheryl's grandmother, who duly gave birth to a son—Sheryl's dad. The previous wife and daughters were then wiped out of the family memory.

Something bothered us each time we explored Shunshui and the surrounding villages: Where were the young women? Young men were toiling industriously in the paddies or fanning themselves indolently in the shade, but young women and girls were scarce. We finally discovered them when we stepped into the factories that were then spreading throughout Guangdong Province, the epicenter of China's economic eruption. These factories produced the shoes, toys, and shirts that filled America's shopping malls, generating economic growth rates almost unprecedented in the history of the world—and creating the most effective antipoverty program ever recorded. The factories turned out to be cacophonous hives of distaff bees. Eighty percent of the employees on the assembly lines in coastal China are female, and the proportion across the manufacturing belt of East Asia is at least 70 percent. The economic explosion in Asia was, in large part, an outgrowth of the economic empowerment of women. "They have smaller fingers, so they're better at stitching," the manager of a purse factory explained to us. "They're obedient and work harder than men," said the head of a toy factory. "And we can pay them less."

THE ECONOMIC EXPLOSION IN ASIA WAS, IN LARGE PART, AN OUTGROWTH OF THE ECONOMIC EMPOWERMENT OF WOMEN

Women are indeed a linchpin of the region's development strategy. Economists who scrutinized East Asia's success noted a common pattern. These countries took young women who previously had contributed negligibly to gross national product (GNP) and injected them into the formal economy, hugely increasing the labor force. The basic formula was to ease repression, educate girls as well as boys, give the girls the freedom to move to the

EDUCATING WOMEN

Educating women means fixing an injustice: gender inequality. But it also means fighting against two other problems in our world: overpopulation and poverty.

Today, 64 percent of the world's 781 million illiterate adults are women and more than 50 percent of the world's 121 million unschooled children are girls. The causes of this situation are many: cultural preferences and stereotypes that favor boys, the burden of household chores, poverty, and more.

In a world with a rapidly growing population, every study shows that the most important factor determining women's fertility rate is neither a matter of revenue nor of educating men, but of education for women themselves. Women who have gone to school tend to marry later, are more likely to use contraception, and prefer smaller families. Even religious customs can change: In Iran, mullahs began encouraging lower birth rates starting in 1989 and this yielded rapid results. Better access to education for women plays an important role in this. Today, three-quarters of married couples in Iran use contraception—that's the highest rate in the Muslim world.

Moreover, a drop in the birth rate (even if it started high) contributes to a nation's development. When parents have fewer children, they can better take care of themselves, and they can invest more in their children's education and health. This ensures that future generations will have better living conditions and economic opportunities. Educating women, therefore, fights poverty; according to UNESCO, every additional year of schooling raises the average annual GDP growth by 0.4 percent.

cities and take factory jobs, and then benefit from a demographic dividend as they delayed marriage and reduced childbearing. The women meanwhile financed the education of younger relatives, and saved enough of their pay to boost national savings rates. This pattern has been called "the girl effect." In a nod to the female chromosomes, it could also be called "the double X solution."

Evidence has mounted that helping women can be a successful poverty-fighting strategy anywhere in the world, not just in the booming economies of East Asia. The Self Employed Women's Association was founded in India in 1972 and ever since has supported the poorest women in starting businesses—raising living standards in ways that have dazzled scholars and foundations.

In Bangladesh, Muhammad Yunus developed microfinance at the Grameen Bank and targeted women borrowers—eventually winning a Nobel Peace Prize for the economic and social impact of his work. Another Bangladeshi group, BRAC, the largest antipoverty organization in the world, worked with the poorest women to save lives and raise incomes—and Grameen and BRAC made the aid world increasingly see women not just as potential beneficiaries of their work, but as agents of it.

In the early 1990s, the United Nations and the World Bank began to appreciate the potential resource that women and girls represent. "Investment in girls' education may well be the highest-return investment available in the developing world," Lawrence Summers wrote when he was chief economist of the World Bank. "The question is not whether countries can afford this investment, but whether countries can afford not to educate more girls."...The United Nations Development Programme (UNDP)

summed up the mounting research this way: "Women's empowerment helps raise economic productivity and reduce infant mortality. It contributes to improved health and nutrition. It increases the chances of education for the next generation."

More and more, the most influential scholars of development and public health—including Sen and Summers, Joseph Stiglitz, Jeffrey Sachs, and Dr. Paul Farmer—are calling for much greater attention to women in development. Private aid groups and foundations have shifted gears as well. "Women are the key to ending hunger in Africa," declared the Hunger Project. French foreign minister Bernard Kouchner, who founded Doctors Without Borders, bluntly declared of development: "Progress is achieved through women."—The Center for Global Development issued a major report explaining "why and how to put girls at the center of development." CARE is taking women and girls as the centerpiece of its antipoverty efforts. The Nike Foundation and the NoVo Foundation are both focusing on building opportunities for girls in the developing world. "Gender inequality hurts economic growth," Goldman Sachs concluded in a 2008 research report that emphasized how much developing countries could improve their economic performance by educating girls. Partly as a result of that research, Goldman Sachs

THE QUESTION IS NOT WHETHER COUNTRIES CAN AFFORD THIS INVESTMENT, BUT WHETHER COUNTRIES CAN AFFORD NOT TO EDUCATE MORE GIRLS

committed $100 million to a "10,000 Women" campaign meant to give that many women a business education.

Concerns about terrorism after the 9/11 attacks triggered interest in these issues in an unlikely constituency: the military and counterterrorism agencies. Some security experts noted that the countries that nurture terrorists are disproportionally those where women are marginalized. The reason there are so many Muslim terrorists, they argued, has little to do with the Koran but a great deal to do with the lack of robust female participation in the economy and society of many Islamic countries. As the Pentagon

31 MILLION

31 MILLION GIRLS DID NOT GO TO SCHOOL IN 2011.

gained a deeper understanding of counterterrorism, and as it found that dropping bombs often didn't do much to help, it became increasingly interested in grassroots projects such as girls' education. Empowering girls, some in the military argued, would disempower terrorists. When the Joint Chiefs of Staff hold discussions of girls' education in Pakistan and Afghanistan, as they did in 2008, you know that gender is a serious topic that fits squarely on the international affairs agenda. That's evident also in the Council on Foreign Relations. The wood-paneled halls that have been used for discussions of MIRV warheads and NATO policy are now employed as well to host well-attended sessions on maternal mortality....

It's true that there are many injustices in the world, many worthy causes competing for attention and support, and we all have divided allegiances. We focus on this topic because, to us, this kind of oppression feels transcendent—and so does the opportunity. We have seen that outsiders can truly make a significant difference.

Consider Rath once more. We had been so shaken by her story that we wanted to locate that brothel in Malaysia, interview its owners, and try to

IT'S TRUE THAT THERE ARE MANY INJUSTICES IN THE WORLD, MANY WORTHY CAUSES COMPETING FOR ATTENTION AND SUPPORT

free the girls still imprisoned there. Unfortunately, we couldn't determine the brothel's name or address. (Rath didn't know English or even the Roman alphabet, so she hadn't been able to read signs when she was there.) When we asked her if she would be willing to return to Kuala Lumpur and help us find the brothel, she turned ashen. "I don't know," she said. "I don't want to face that again." She wavered, talked it over with her family, and ultimately agreed to go back in the hope of rescuing her girlfriends.

Rath voyaged back to Kuala Lumpur with the protection of an interpreter and a local antitrafficking activist. Nonetheless, she trembled in the red-light districts upon seeing the cheerful neon signs that she associated with so much pain. But since her escape, Malaysia had been embarrassed by public criticism about trafficking, so the police had cracked down on the worst brothels that imprisoned girls against their will. One of those was Rath's. A modest amount of international scolding had led a government to take action, resulting in an observable improvement in the lives of girls at the bottom of the power pyramid. The outcome underscores that this is a hopeful cause, not a bleak one.

Honor killings, sexual slavery, and genital cutting may seem to Western readers to be tragic but inevitable in a world far, far away. In much the same way, slavery was once widely viewed by many decent Europeans and Americans as a regrettable but ineluctable feature of human life. It was just one more horror that had existed for thousands of years. But then in the 1780s a few indignant Britons, led by William Wilberforce, decided that slavery was so offensive that they had to abolish it. And they did. Today we see the seed of something similar: a global movement to emancipate women and girls.

BRING BACK OUR GIRLS

The kidnapping, during the night of April 14–15, 2014, of 276 secondary school girls by the Islamist sect Boko Haram in northeast Nigeria illustrates the sad reality of the violence and hostility perpetuated by certain groups of men when faced with the education of women. Unfortunately, this isn't the only example.

Despite the worldwide indignation that this kidnapping triggered, despite the #BringBackOurGirls campaign, supported by Michelle Obama and other public figures, despite the awarding of the Nobel Peace Prize to Malala Yousafzai, and despite the statements made by heads of state, no military or diplomatic action of consequence has been launched.

The Nigerian army seems incapable of confronting the situation and was itself accused of crimes against humanity. Boko Haram continues to kill; for example, in January 2015 the sect massacred more than two thousand people in Baga and surrounding villages.

Immediately following the kidnapping, which was perpetrated at the Chibok boarding school, 57 young girls escaped, but the 219 other girls remain prisoners of Boko Haram, which has bound them to sexual slavery and forced them to be married or sold as slaves. The families fear that their daughters' cause has been abandoned by those in power.

Even though international solidarity seems weak in the face of Boko Haram's bloodthirsty determination, we must not forget the young girls of Chibok.

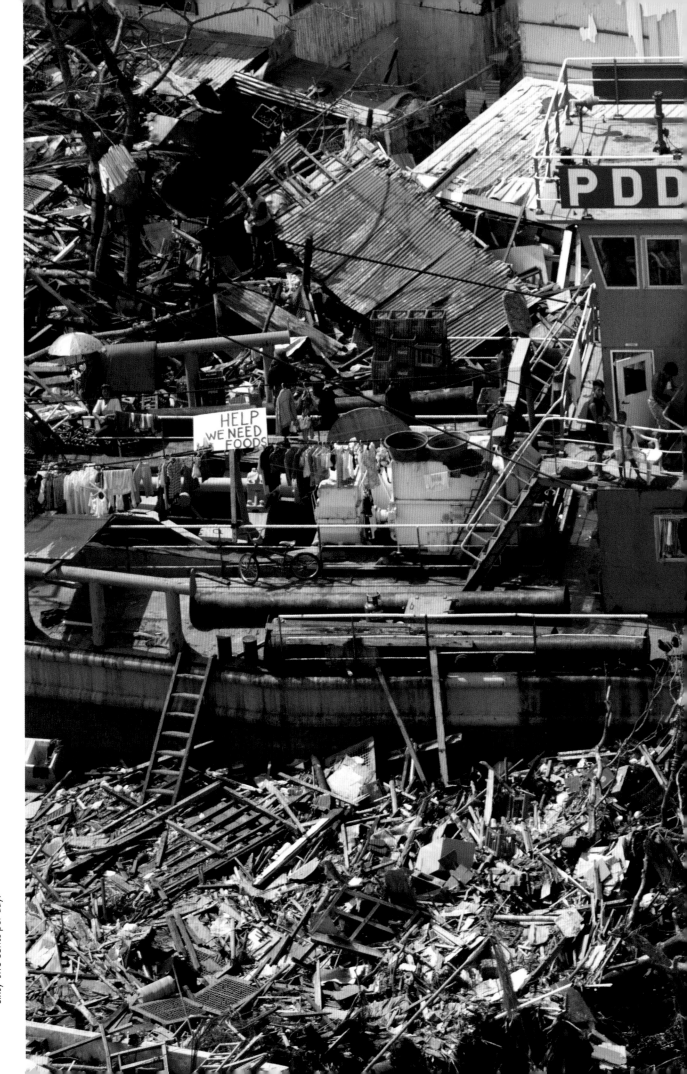

TACLOBAN, AFTER TYPHOON HAIYAN, EASTERN VISAYAS, PHILIPPINES 11° 14' 00" N – 125° 00' 14" E

In 2013, Typhoon Haiyan caused the death of some 6,200 people and widespread damage in the Philippines. The city of Tacloban was heavily affected. The country consists of 7,017 islands populated by more than 107 million people and is particularly vulnerable to typhoons. In spite of rapid economic growth in recent years, more than a quarter of the country's population still lives on the equivalent of sixty-two cents per day.

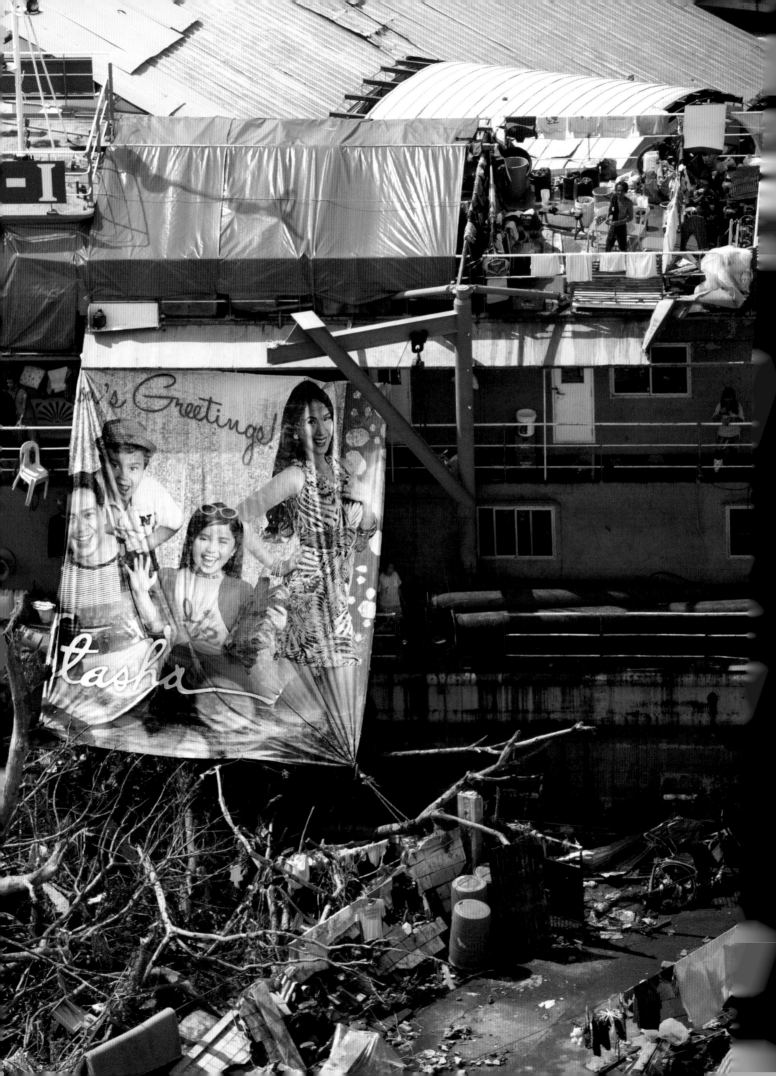

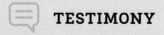

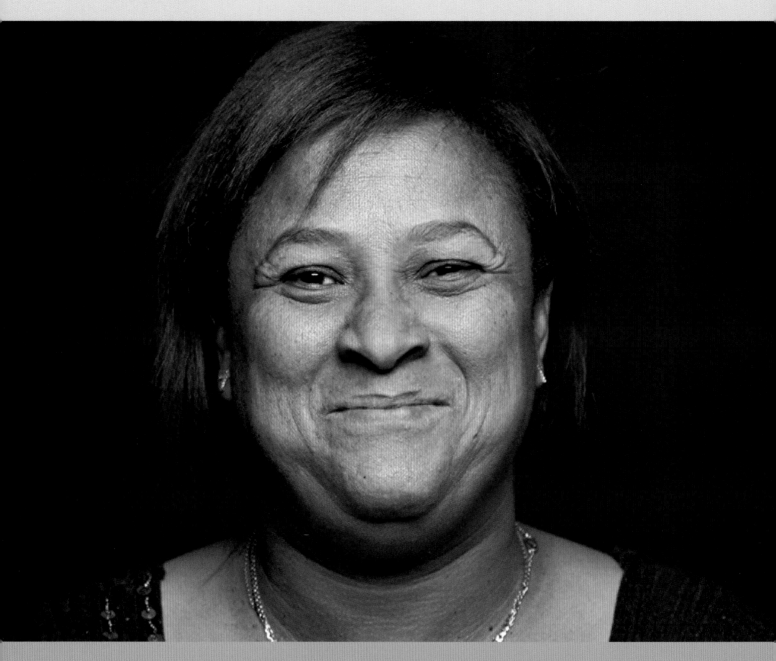

THE PRICE OF HAPPINESS

ESCAPING ABUSE IS POSSIBLE. LOVED ONES OR ACQUAINTANCES OFTEN PLAY THE ROLE OF CATALYST OR GUIDE TOWARD ANOTHER LIFE.

I immediately could see that Donesia's soul was magnificent but that something was standing in its way. We were in a small village in the depths of Australia, where initially we were to meet members of the Aboriginal community. Donesia was not Aboriginal; she wasn't even Australian. She was from South Africa and had moved to Australia almost nine years earlier. My assistant, who organized the interview, had told me that Donesia was a "super positive" woman, always in a good mood, always smiling.

"At this point, I don't think I need anything more in my life," Donesia explains to me. "I'm happy, just happy; you know the song *I'm happy*? I love it....When I feel annoyed, I prefer to stay in my room and not see anyone, but I have to smile. I'm just like that."

I don't know why, but that "I have to smile" tips me off. It is as if Donesia feels she has to prove her happiness, as if sometimes that smile hides something else. We continue to talk. Donesia speaks to me easily: Her children? The best! Her work? Extraordinary! Her husband? They've been in love since they were twenty, she met him at school, and it's still like the first day now. This perfect trajectory would make many jealous. Then suddenly, Donesia adds: "Even though, of course, I've had my ups and downs. I even divorced my husband only to remarry him a year later."

Then she continues telling her story as if nothing had been said.

But at that moment, I felt that something had just opened. So, I ask Donesia another question about her relationship. She begins to answer, joyfully as always. Then something happens. Tears replace the smile. She begins a whole other story. "You can get out of domestic violence," she says somberly. Then she tells me that for years, she was a battered woman, that her husband would come home drunk, that he would point a gun at her temple, force her to kneel and beg for her life. "And I would do it; I would do it in front of

I'VE HAD MY UPS AND DOWNS. I EVEN DIVORCED MY HUSBAND ONLY TO REMARRY HIM A YEAR LATER

my son." Donesia has a hard time finishing her sentence. She endured this ordeal for a long time. Like millions of other battered women, she thought that what was happening to her was her fault, that she had asked for it, and that she had to accept it. Then one day, another woman wanted to help her, a colleague at work who saw the suffering behind the façade of Donesia's smile. They spoke for hours: about her life, her children. From that moment on, Donesia realized that by staying with this man, she was running the risk of ending up, at best, crippled, and at worst, in the cemetery.

With the support of this colleague, Donesia leaves her husband, sees a therapist, enters a program for battered women. A year later, she begins to see the light at the end of the tunnel. It is at that very moment that her husband comes back to see her, tells her he loves her and can't live without her, that he'll do anything it takes: stop the alcohol, go to a therapist, leave South Africa and his bad influences. And that's what they do. This is the reason for moving to Australia—it's a way to turn over a new leaf. Through love, Donesia is able to forgive.

"Today, he is a better man," she tells me about her husband, "He hasn't raised a hand against me in nine years. But nine years ago, I was still a battered woman....It was hard finding happiness, that's why I'm always happy, because I try to stay happy so that my life can move on."

I'm a woman, too, and inside, I feel like crying out in protest: "How can you forgive someone who was capable of such cruelty?" Yet, when Donesia talks to me about her husband, the smile reappears on her lips, and it's no longer the façade of a smile. It's the smile of a woman who has just bared her soul, of a strong woman who has fought for her happiness and who knows its price. It's the smile of a Woman, with a capital W.

—Anastasia Mikova

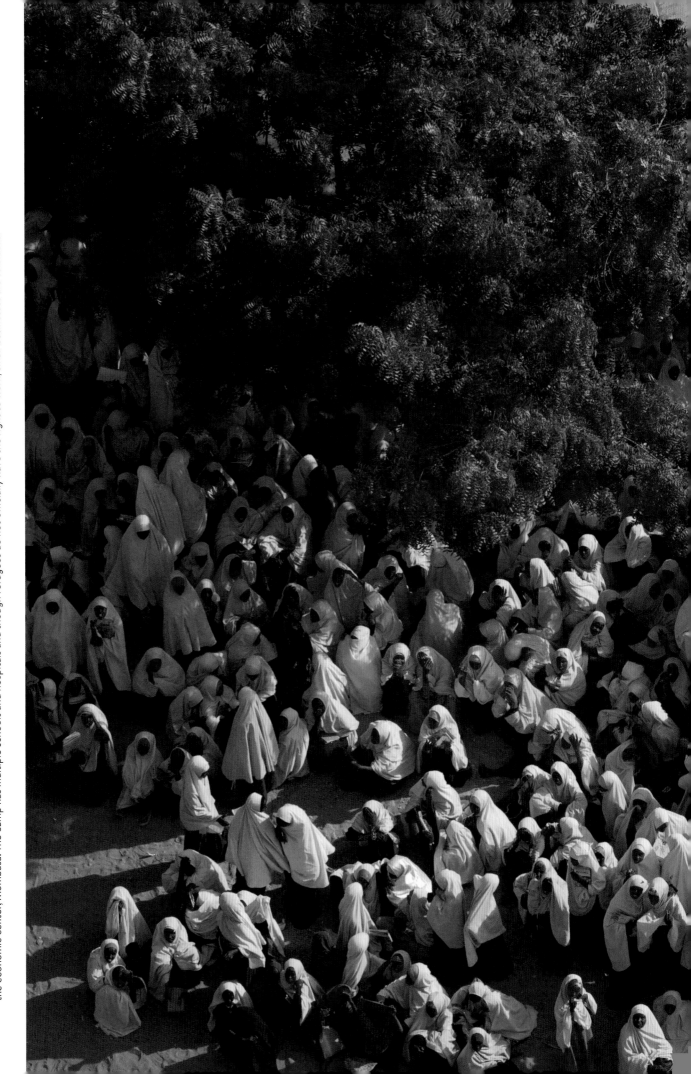

SCHOOL IN HAGADERA, A SOMALI REFUGEE CAMP IN DADAAB, KENYA 0° 0' S – 40° 22' E

Dadaab hosts one of the largest refugee camps in the world; 103,801 people live there, some for as long as twenty years. Dadaab is the third most populated city in Kenya, after the capital, Nairobi, and the economic center, Mombasa. The camp has multiple schools and hospitals and though refugees do not officially have the right to work, small businesses are tolerated.

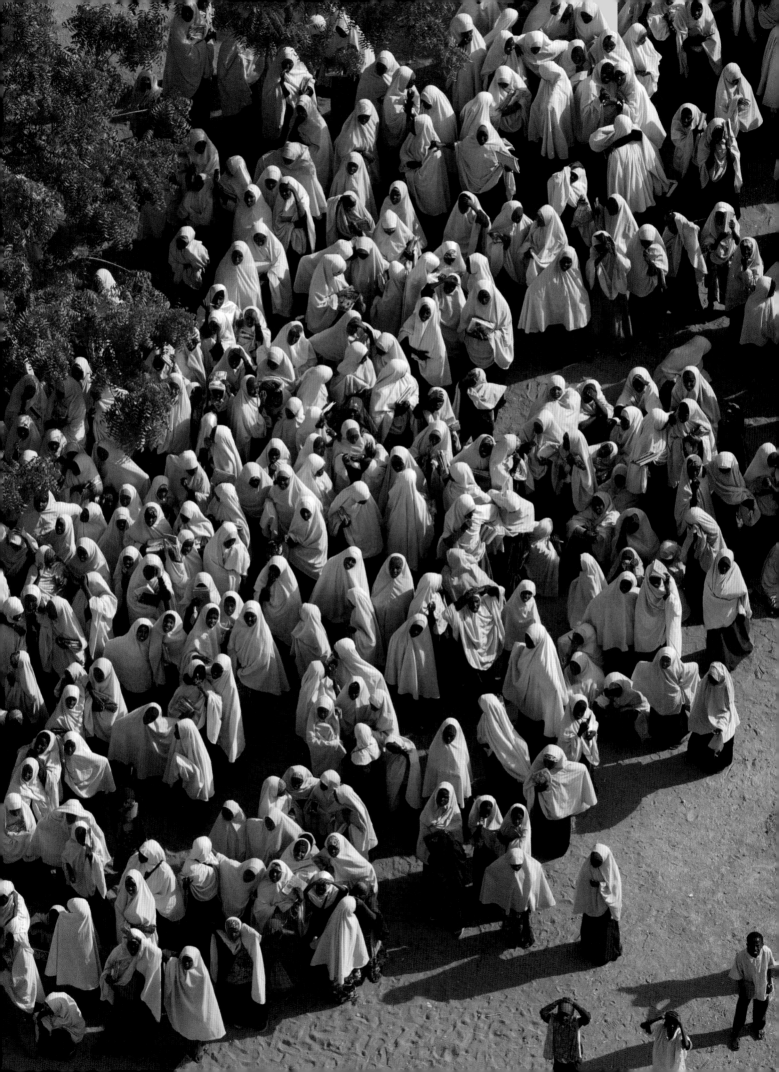

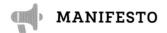
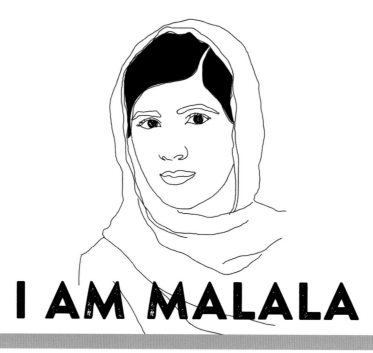

I AM MALALA

MALALA YOUSAFZAI

From her Nobel lecture, December 10, 2014

In December 2014, Malala Yousafzai, along with Indian children's rights advocate Kailash Satyarthi, received at age seventeen the Nobel Peace Prize, making her the youngest laureate in the history of the prize. The young Pakistani made a name for herself at age eleven, in 2009, with her blog _Diary of a Pakistani Schoolgirl_, in which she denounced the violence of the Taliban and their actions against the education of girls. In October 2012, a member of the Taliban attempted to assassinate her by shooting her on the bus that took her to school. She was critically wounded. Here are extensive excerpts from the lecture she delivered upon receiving her Nobel Prize.

...I am proud, well, in fact, I am very proud to be the first Pashtun, the first Pakistani, and the youngest person to receive this award. Along with that...I am pretty certain that I am also the first recipient of the Nobel Peace Prize who still fights with her younger brothers. I want there to be peace everywhere, but my brothers and I are still working on that.

I am also honored to receive this award together with Kailash Satyarthi, who has been a champion for children's rights for a long time. Twice as long, in fact, than I have been alive. I am proud that we can work together...and show the world that an Indian and a Pakistani, they can work together and achieve their goals of children's rights.

Dear brothers and sisters, I was named after the inspirational Malalai of Maiwand, who is the Pashtun Joan of Arc. The word "Malala" means "grief stricken," "sad," but in order to lend some happiness to it, my grandfather would always call me "Malala, the happiest girl in the world," and today I am very happy that we are together fighting for an important cause.

This award is not just for me. It is for those forgotten children who want education. It is for those frightened children who want peace. It is for those voiceless children who want change.

I am here to stand up for their rights, to raise their voice....It is not time to pity them. It is time to take action so it becomes the last time...that we see a child deprived of education.

I have found that people describe me in many different ways.

Some people call me the girl who was shot by the Taliban.

And some, the girl who fought for her rights.

Some people call me a "Nobel Laureate" now.

However, my brothers still call me that annoying bossy sister. As far as I know, I am just a committed and even stubborn person who wants to see every child getting quality education, who wants to see women having equal rights and who wants peace in every corner of the world.

Education is one of the blessings of life—and one of its necessities. That has been my experience during the seventeen years of my life. In my paradise home, Swat, I always loved learning and discovering new things. I remember when my friends and I would decorate our hands with henna on special occasions. And instead of drawing flowers and patterns, we would paint our hands with mathematical formulas and equations.

We had a thirst for education…because our future was right there in that classroom. We would sit and learn and read together. We loved to wear neat and tidy school uniforms and we would sit there with big dreams in our eyes. We wanted to make our parents proud and prove that we could also excel in our studies and achieve those goals, which some people think only boys can.

But things did not remain the same. When I was in Swat, which was a place of tourism and beauty, [it] suddenly changed into a place of terrorism. I was just ten [when] more than four hundred schools were destroyed. Women were flogged. People were killed. And our beautiful dreams turned into nightmares.

Education went from being a right to being a crime.

Girls were stopped from going to school.

When my world suddenly changed, my priorities changed, too.

I had two options. One was to remain silent and wait to be killed. And the second was to speak up and then be killed.

I chose the second one. I decided to speak up.

We could not just stand by and see those injustices of the terrorists denying our rights, ruthlessly killing people, and misusing the name of Islam. We decided to raise our voices and tell them: Have you not learnt, have you not learnt that in the Holy Quran Allah says: "If you kill one person it is as if you kill the whole [of] humanity"?

I AM NOT A LONE VOICE, I AM MANY

Do you not know that Mohammad, peace be upon him, the prophet of mercy, he says, "do not harm yourself or others"?

And do you not know that the very first word of the Holy Quran is the word "Iqra," which means "read"?

The terrorists tried to stop us and attacked me and my friends, who are here today, on our school bus in 2012, but neither their ideas nor their bullets could win.

We survived. And since that day, our voices have grown louder and louder.

I tell my story, not because it is unique but because it is not.

It is the story of many girls.

Today, I tell their stories, too. I have brought with me some of my sisters from Pakistan, from Nigeria, and from Syria, who share this story. My brave sisters Shazia and Kainat who were also shot that day on our school bus. But they have not stopped learning. And my brave sister Kainat Soomro, who went through severe abuse and extreme violence, even her brother was killed, but she did not succumb.

Also my sisters here, whom I have met during my Malala Fund campaign. My sixteen-year-old courageous sister, Mezon from Syria who now lives in Jordan as a refugee and goes from tent to tent encouraging girls and boys to learn; and my sister Amina, from the north of Nigeria, where Boko Haram threatens and stops girls, and even kidnaps girls, just for wanting to go to school.

Though I appear as one girl…one person, who is five feet two inches tall, if you include my high heels (it means I am five feet only), I am not a lone voice, I am not a lone voice, I am many.

I am Malala. But I am also Shazia.

I am Kainat.

I am Kainat Soomro.

I am Mezon.

I am Amina. I am those sixty-six million girls who are deprived of education. And today I am not raising my voice; it is the voice of those sixty-six million girls.

Sometimes people like to ask me why should girls go to school, why is it important for them. But I think the more important question is why shouldn't they, why shouldn't they have this right to go to school.

Dear sisters and brothers, today, in half of the world, we see rapid progress and development. However, there are many countries where millions still suffer from the very old problems of war, poverty, and injustice.

We still see conflicts in which innocent people lose their lives and children become orphans. We see many people becoming refugees in Syria, Gaza, and Iraq. In Afghanistan, we see families being killed in suicide attacks and bomb blasts.

Many children in Africa do not have access to education because of poverty. And as I said, we still see, we still see girls who have no freedom to go to school in the north of Nigeria.

Many children in countries like Pakistan and India, as Kailash Satyarthi mentioned, many children, especially in India and Pakistan, are deprived of their right to education because of social taboos, or they have been forced into child marriage or into child labor.

One of my very good school friends, the same age as me, who had always been a bold and confident girl, dreamed of becoming a doctor. But her dream remained a dream. At the age of twelve, she was forced to get married. And then soon she had a son, she had a child when she herself was still a child—only fourteen. I know that she could have been a very good doctor.

But she couldn't…because she was a girl.

Her story is why I dedicate the Nobel Peace Prize money to the Malala Fund, to help give girls quality education, everywhere, anywhere in the world and to raise their voices. The first place this funding will go to is where my heart is, to build schools in Pakistan—especially in my home of Swat and Shangla.

In my own village, there is still no secondary school for girls. And it is my wish and my commitment, and now my challenge, to build one so that my friends and my sisters can go there to school and get quality education and to get this opportunity to fulfill their dreams.

This is where I will begin, but it is not where I will stop. I will continue this fight until I see every child, every child in school.

Dear brothers and sisters, great people who brought change, like Martin Luther King and Nelson Mandela, Mother Teresa and Aung San Suu Kyi, once stood here on this stage. I hope the steps that Kailash Satyarthi and I have taken so far and will take on this journey will also bring change—lasting change.

My great hope is that this will be the last time, this will be the last time we must fight for education. Let's solve this once and for all.

We have already taken many steps. Now it is time to take a leap.

It is not time to tell the world leaders to realize how important education is—they already know it; their own children are in good schools. Now it is time to call them to take action for the rest of the world's children….

Some will say this is impractical, or too expensive, or too hard. Or maybe even impossible. But it is time the world thinks bigger.

Dear sisters and brothers, the so-called world of adults may understand it but we children don't. Why is it that countries which we call "strong" are so powerful in creating wars but are so weak in bringing peace? Why is it that giving guns is so easy but giving books is so hard? Why is it, why is it that making tanks is so easy but building schools is so hard?…

Let us become the first generation to decide to be the last, let us become the first generation that decides to be the last that sees empty classrooms, lost childhoods, and wasted potentials.

Let this be the last time that a girl or a boy spends their childhood in a factory.

Let this be the last time that a girl is forced into early child marriage.

Let this be the last time that a child loses life in war.

Let this be the last time that we see a child out of school.

Let this end with us.

> WHY IS IT THAT MAKING TANKS IS SO EASY BUT BUILDING SCHOOLS IS SO HARD?

ALL FOR EQUALITY

HE FOR SHE

Women aren't the only ones getting involved with equal rights for women. Gender equality concerns everyone on this planet: This is one of the messages of the United Nations campaign He for She. This campaign invites everyone, young men in particular, to come together and speak out against violence and discrimination against women. It also takes concrete action, offering asylum to refugees in Jordan, finding work for female untouchables in India, and helping women open small businesses in South Africa.
www.heforshe.org

HEALING VICTIMS

MÉDECINS DU MONDE [DOCTORS OF THE WORLD]

Most of the big international NGOs have established programs dedicated to women. Such is the case with Doctors of the World, which implements programs against violence toward women. Beyond medical initiatives, the organization coordinates the construction of networks that offer victims total care, including psychological and juridical support.
www.medecinsdumonde.org

OPPORTUNITIES FOR WOMEN

FÉDÉRATION NATIONALE SOLIDARITÉ FEMMES [WOMEN'S NATIONAL SOLIDARITY FOUNDATION]

According to the United Nations, up to 70 percent of women are victims of violence at least once in their lives; this average applies to all countries and all social classes. But this violence is not inevitable. In every country, in every region, there are organizations that support battered women, emergency shelters, and phone numbers. Get the information you need.
www.solidaritefemmes.org

HALF THE SKY

JOIN THE MOVEMENT

The authors of the book *Half the Sky*, excerpts of which are published in this chapter (see page 60), have launched a movement to help women and to offer anyone interested ways to get involved with these issues, from volunteering at health centers and promoting fair trade to fundraising for local NGOs.
www.halftheskymovement.org

WOMEN IN WAR ZONES

WOMEN FOR WOMEN

This NGO, founded by Zainab Salbi, helps women in war zones. In its twenty-plus years of operation, it has helped nearly 420,000 women, in Afghanistan, the Democratic Republic of the Congo, Iraq, Kosovo, Nigeria, Rwanda, and South Sudan.
www.womenforwomen.org

ENCOURAGING TALENT

MADRE

This American NGO works to identify and help remarkable women throughout the world to become leaders so that they might contribute to the transformation of the societies in which they live.
www.madre.org

WOMEN'S RIGHTS

POLITICS

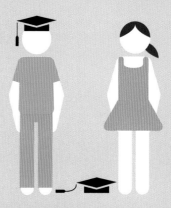

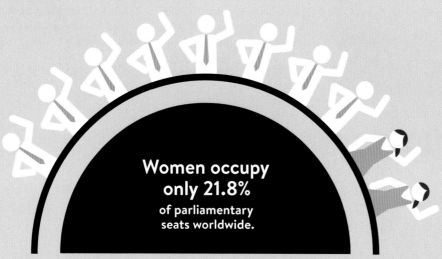

Women occupy only 21.8% of parliamentary seats worldwide.

IMPACT: Decisions on policies affecting societies are often made without women's substantive contributions or a gender perspective, and therefore may neglect their needs.

EDUCATION

781 million adults and 126 million youth worldwide lack basic literacy skills. More than 60% of them are women and girls.

IMPACT: Far and wide-ranging effects from reduced access to economic and productive resources to poorer health and well-being; and greater barriers to engagement in decision-making spheres.

INTIMATE PARTNER VIOLENCE

1 in 3 women worldwide has experienced physical or sexual violence—mostly by an intimate partner.

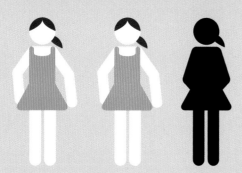

IMPACT: Detrimental impact on the lives and health of women; significant socioeconomic implications for individuals, families, communities, and society.

FEMALE GENITAL MUTILATION

133 million girls and women have experienced female genital mutilation in the 29 countries in Africa and the Middle East where the harmful practice is most common.

IMPACT: Severe emotional and physical trauma; potential health risks, including reproductive and sexual health complications, and possible death through loss of blood or sepsis.

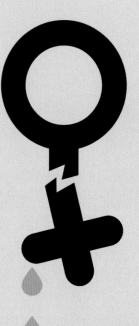

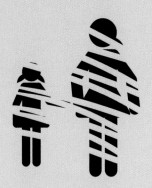

FAMILY

Husbands are the legally designated heads of households in 29 out of 143 countries.

IMPACT: Husbands control key decisions, such as choosing the family residence or obtaining official documents, and in some cases are allowed to restrict the wife's right to work or open a bank account.

NATIONALITY

In more than 60 countries, women are denied the right to acquire, change, or retain their nationality, including to confer nationality on non-national spouses.

IMPACT: Inability to exercise the same citizenship rights as men and to pass along rights afforded to citizens. This includes the right of abode; the right to vote, work, own land and property; and to access benefits, such as education and health care.

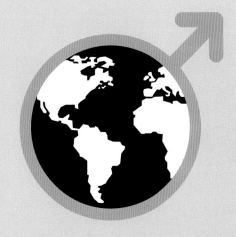

EMPLOYMENT

Women earn between 10% and 30% less than men in most countries out of 83 evaluated.

IMPACT: Higher incidence of poverty among women; lower propensity to save and invest, more vulnerable to external shocks, more likely to concentrate in lower paid, more insecure employment.

LAND AND OTHER RESOURCES

In 26 of 143 countries, statutory inheritance laws (i.e., written laws passed by legislature) differentiate between women and men.

IMPACT: Increased vulnerability to poverty and food insecurity; limited or no access to resources and credit; dependency on men to secure livelihood.

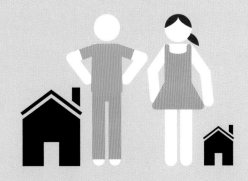

KEY FIGURES

It is estimated that nearly half of the women murdered in 2012 perished at the hand of their partner or a member of their family.

Most of the time, violence against women is subject to the unspoken law of silence. For example, of the 42,000 women, hailing from the 28 member states of the European Union, interviewed for a study, only 14% notify police about extreme violence committed by an intimate partner (man or woman).

Millions of women and girls find themselves trapped in modern slavery as victims of human trafficking. On the global scale, they represent 55% of the victims of forced labor, estimated at 20.9 million, and 98% of the victims of sexual exploitation, estimated at 4.5 million.

Rwanda has the most women in parliament in the world: Women occupy 63.8% of seats in the Lower Chamber.

A study of Fortune 500 companies showed that the total return offered to shareholders was 34% higher in companies with the largest percentage of women in senior management positions.

Analysis of data from 219 countries during the period 1970–2009 has shown that infant mortality decreased by 9.5% with each additional school year completed by women of child-bearing age. This means that between 1970 and 1990, 4.2 million children owe their survival to the improved education of women.

TIMELINE

30 B.C.
Death of Cleopatra VII, the most famous queen in history. The notoriety of her reign illustrates how much power certain women had during antiquity.

1215
The Fourth Council of the Lateran declares marriage a sacrament. Divorce is henceforth no longer permitted.

1791
Olympe de Gouges publishes Declaration of the Rights of Woman and of the [Female] Citizen. She would be executed by guillotine in 1793.

1893
New Zealand organizes the first national election in which women have the right to vote.

1903
Marie Curie becomes first woman to receive the Nobel Prize.

1960
The birth control pill is approved by the United States Food and Drug Administration (FDA) for contraceptive use.

BOOKS

A Room of One's Own
Virginia Woolf, 1929
This extended essay by the renowned writer explains why there are so few women writers in the history of literature. For Woolf, women must have "money and a room of her own" to be able to write.

The Golden Notebook
Doris Lessing, 1962
This is a powerful portrait of a woman writer. Lessing received the Nobel Prize in Literature in 2007.

Women as Lovers
Elfriede Jelinek, 1995
The overlapping destinies of two women seeking to get out of their status received through men. A vitriolic critique about relationships between the sexes by an iconoclastic Austrian Nobel Prize winner.

Persepolis
Marjane Satrapi, 2000
In this autobiographical graphic novel (also adapted into a movie), the author recounts her childhood memories in Iran. With the Islamic Revolution, the country changes and the plight of women evolves.

King Kong Théorie [King Kong Theory]
Virginie Despentes, 2006
Between rape, prostitution, and pornography, the writer offers "a manifesto for a new feminism."

Half the Sky
Nicholas D. Kristof and Sheryl WuDunn, 2009
This chapter's introduction is extracted from this astounding book, written by two New York Times journalists.

Les Assoiffées [The Thirsty Ones]
Bernard Quiriny, 2010
A humorous science fiction novel. Following the feminist revolution in 1970, women in Belgium impose their law on the land. A few years later, a group of French intellectuals are invited to visit the country. Female power as fantasized about by a man, a bit in the manner of Robert Merle's The Virility Factor.

Message from an Unknown Chinese Mother
Xue Xinran, 2010
Journalist Xinran has set out to meet Chinese women who had to give up their babies at birth. 120,000 Chinese children were adopted between 1992 and 2010. The majority are girls adopted by couples from Europe and North America. Xinran answers questions asked by these children about their origins by investigating adoption, orphanages, infanticides, one-child policy, and the trafficking of children in China.

I Am Malala: The Girl Who Stood Up for Education and Was Shot by the Taliban
Malala Yousafzai, 2013
This is the biography of the now-famous young woman.

FILMS AND TELEVISION

Salt of the Earth
Herbert Biberman, 1954
Made practically in secret by filmmakers who had to contend with McCarthyism and the witch hunt in Hollywood, this film is one of the first to be outspokenly feminist.

Raise the Red Lantern
Zhang Yimou, 1991
This film explores the condition of women in China at the start of the twentieth century.

Thelma and Louise
Ridley Scott, 1991
This crime drama movie follows two women on the difficult path to freedom.

The Piano
Jane Campion, 1993
This film is resolutely female, as is all of Jane Campion's work. In 1993, Campion was the first woman to be awarded the Palme d'Or at the Cannes Film Festival. She presided over its jury in 2014.

The Virgin Suicides
Sofia Coppola, 1999
The five Lisbon sisters live in suburban Michigan. Their parents subject them to a strict upbringing, giving them little freedom. Suffocated, the sisters commit suicide.

North Country
Niki Caro, 2005
This film was inspired by the true story of the first sexual harassment lawsuit in the United States in 1984.

Volver
Pedro Almodóvar, 2006
This is an homage to women by the celebrated Spanish director. The actresses shared the Best Actress award at Cannes.

Agora
Alejandro Amenábar, 2009
This strange film follows the life of Hypatia, a Greek woman from Alexandria, who is a mathematician and philosopher. She is assassinated by extremist Christians in 415.

678
Mohamed Diab, 2010
In Cairo, Egypt, women are perpetually the victims of sexual harassment. Even on the bus. Exasperated by this situation, three women from different backgrounds decide to defend themselves against daily, ordinary machismo, standing up to society.

Wadjda
Haifaa Al-Mansour, 2012
The first feature-length film made by a Saudi woman, *Wadjda* tells the story of a young girl's determination to buy a bicycle, even though it is forbidden for girls to ride one in Saudia Arabia.

Borgen
Television series, 2010–2013
This series gives a fictionalized account of the first female prime minister of Denmark.

ARTISTS

Female artists were rarely celebrated before the twentieth century. Let us cite Hildegard of Bingen, mystic, poet, and composer from the Middle Ages, and the sculptor Camille Claudel, relegated by her family to a psychiatric hospital in the twentieth century. More recently, major figures have emerged, including Louise Bourgeois, Nan Goldin, and Sophie Calle.

WEBSITES

An important reference on the subject is the website of UN Women, the United Nations organization dedicated to gender equality and the empowerment of women. The site is rich with facts and information (much of which is reproduced in this book), as well as portraits and analyses.
www.unwomen.org

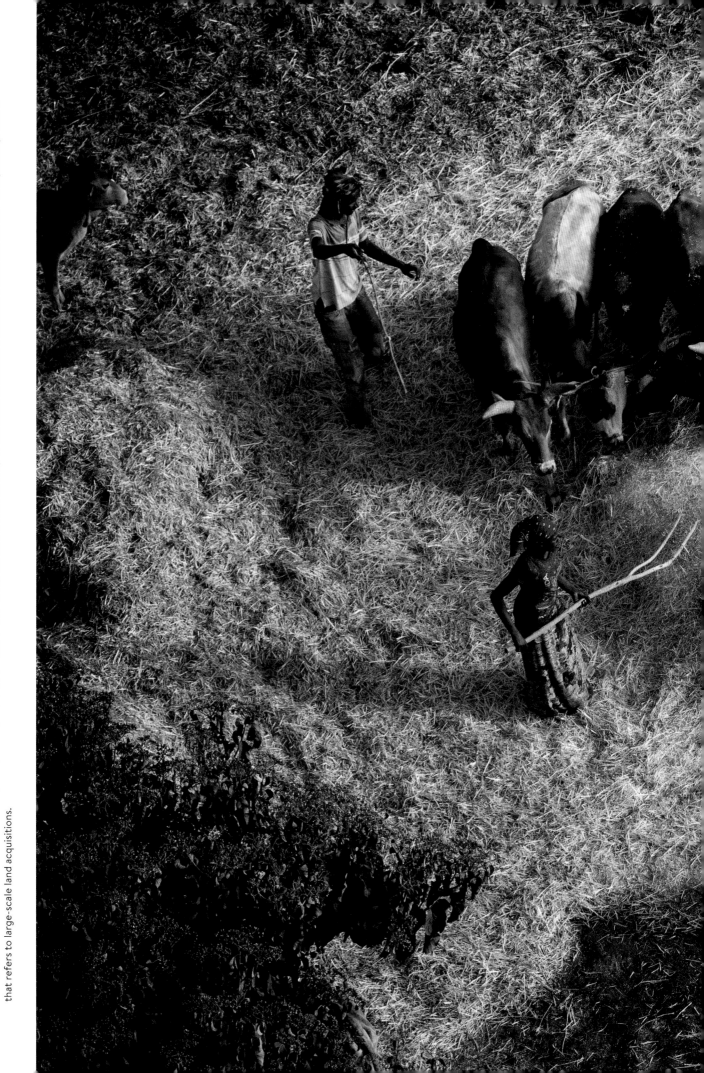

HARVEST, TIGRAY REGION, ETHIOPIA 13° 29' N – 32° 38' E

Ethiopia, the second most populated country in Africa, is essentially agricultural: The sector represents 85 percent of employment and 45 percent of the GDP. Under the constitution, land is owned by the state, which rents it to farmers. The state can therefore grant large concessions to foreign investors, sometimes up to one hundred thousand hectares. Detractors call this "land grabbing," a term that refers to large-scale land acquisitions.

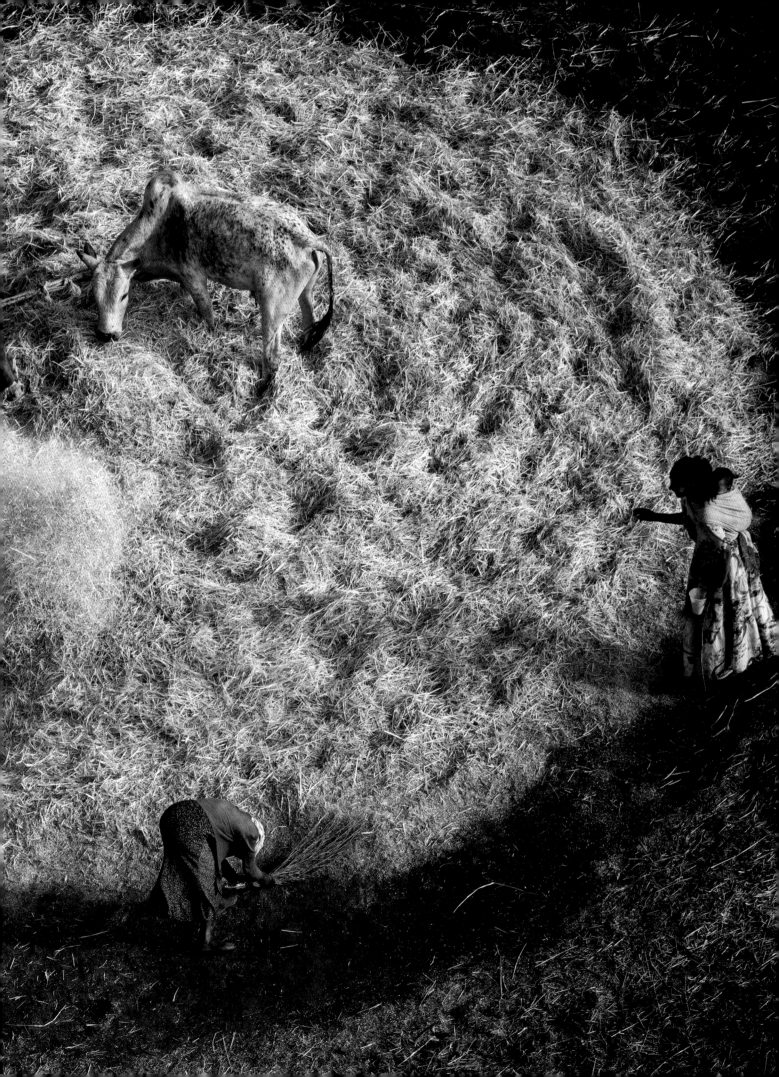

PADDY FIELD NEAR BETAFO, VAKINANKARATRA, MADAGASCAR 19° 48' 57" S – 46° 52' 12" E

Agriculture is the main economic activity of Madagascar. But the arable land, primarily located in the plains of the Central Highlands, is dependent on irrigation. Only a limited percentage of arable land is actually worked, mostly because of water shortages.

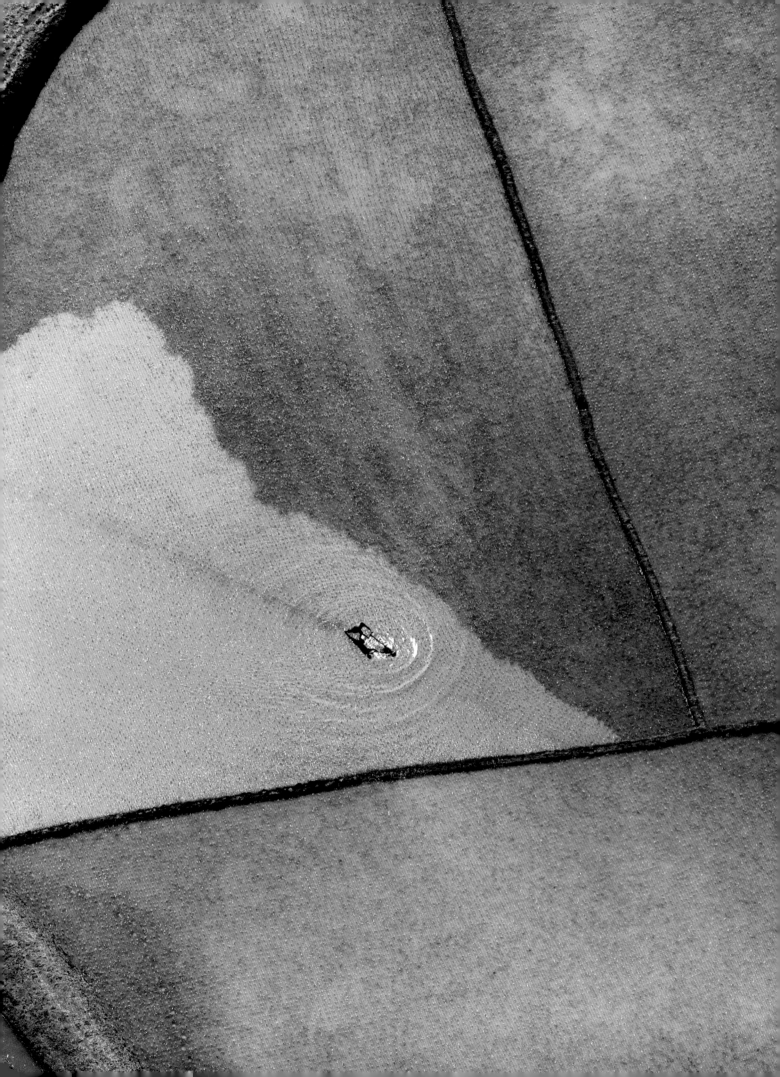

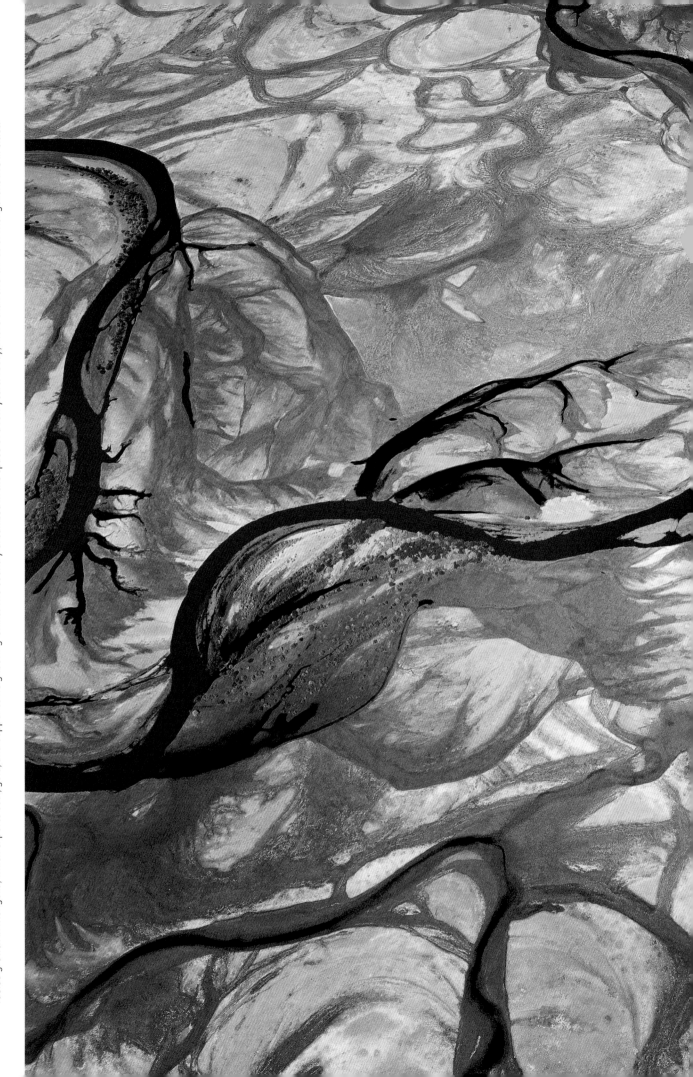

WATERCOURSES OF THE TUUL RIVER, TÖV PROVINCE, MONGOLIA 47° 16' N – 105° 27' E

The Tuul River runs through more than four hundred miles of central and northern Mongolia. Sacred to Mongolians, it flows to the south of Ulan-Bator, the country's capital. Underground resources have fueled growth in Mongolia, which exports coal, gold, and copper to neighboring China. The country urbanized in the space of a few years. Today, more than two-thirds of Mongolians live in cities.

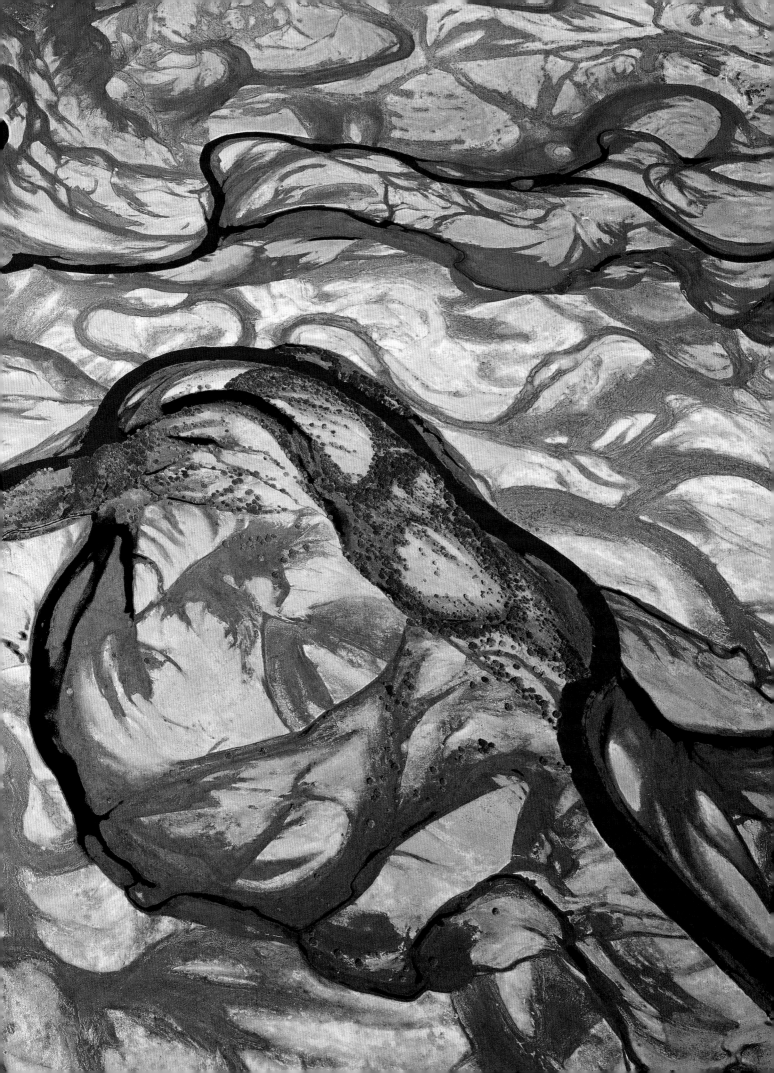

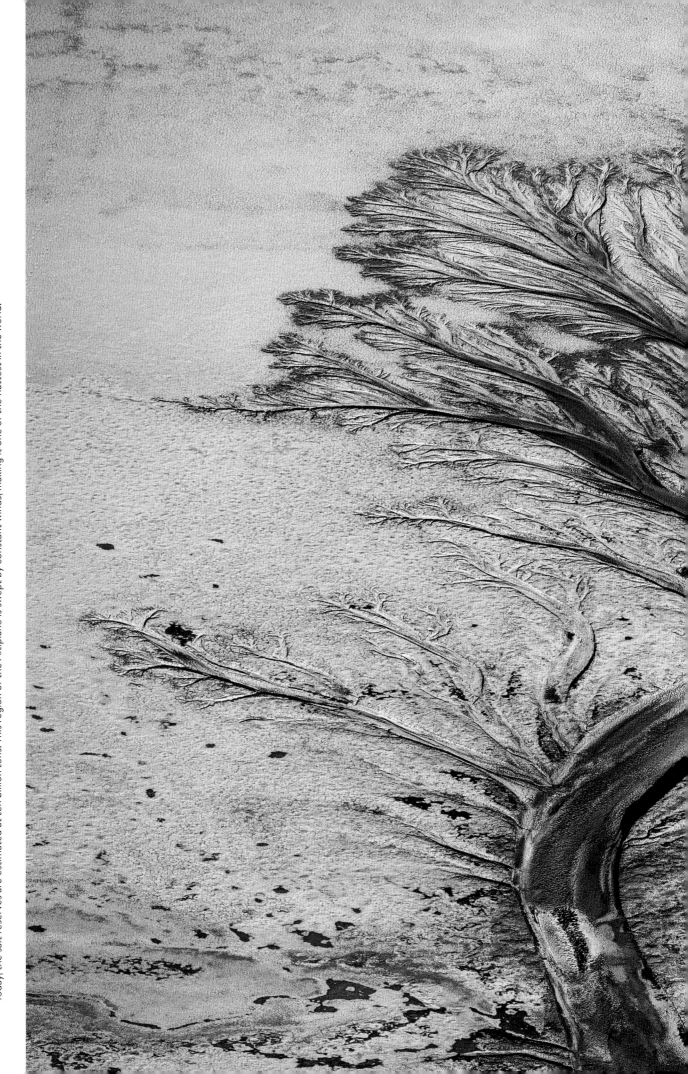

SALAR DE UYUNI, DANIEL CAMPOS, POTOSÍ, BOLIVIA 20° 12' S – 67° 36' W

The Salar de Uyuni is an exceptional geological formation, the result of the gradual evaporation of a prehistoric lake called Lake Minchin. Eleven thousand years ago, this lake was many hundred feet deep. Today, the salt reserves are estimated at ten billion tons. This region of the Altiplano is swept by constant winds, making it one of the flattest in the world.

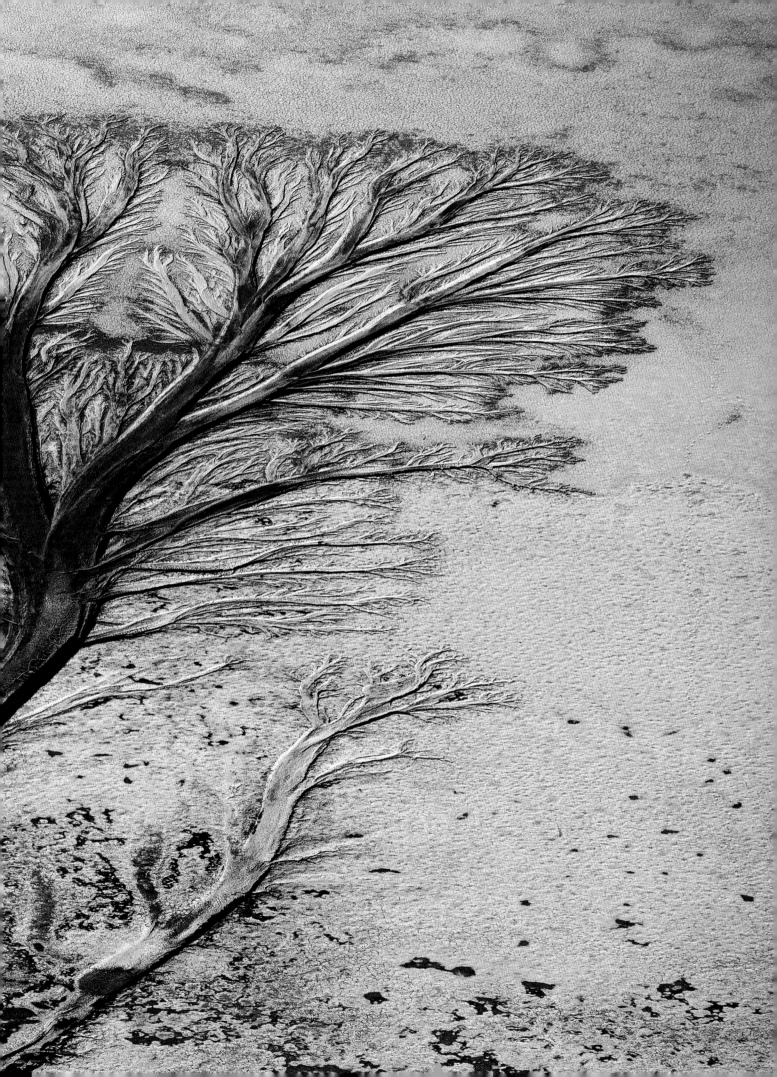

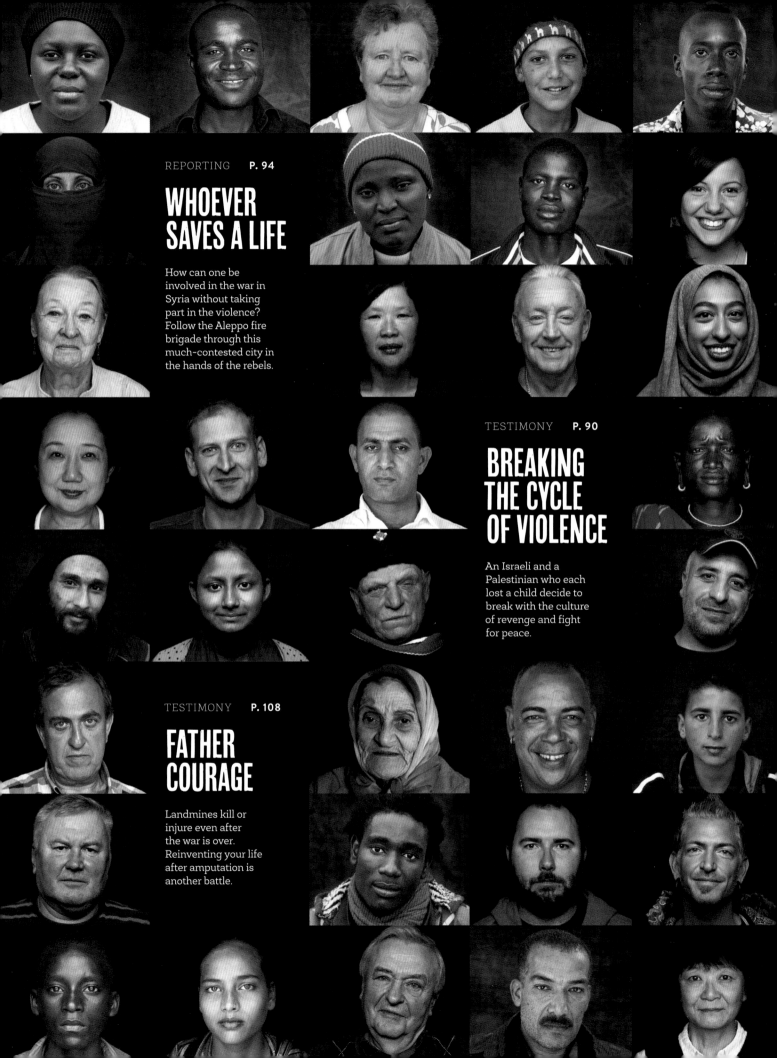

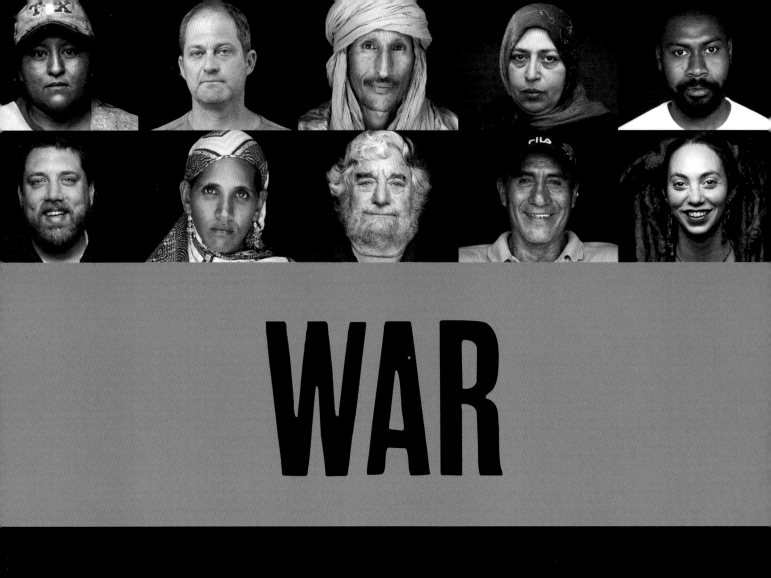

WAR

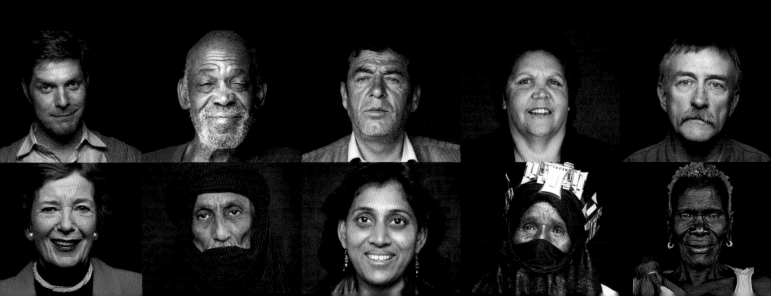

Twenty-first-century wars kill nearly fifty thousand people annually.
While this is fewer than during the previous century of world wars, atrocities
are still numerous, terrible, and diffuse, with machetes and AK-47s producing
more victims than do drones and intercontinental missiles.

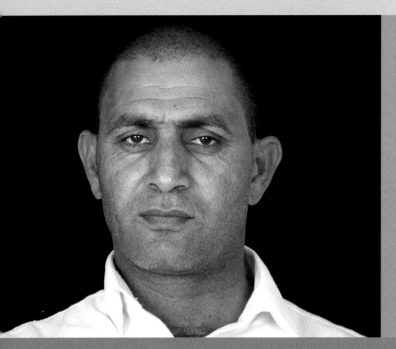

BREAKING THE CYCLE OF VIOLENCE

AN ISRAELI KILLED THE DAUGHTER OF BASSAM, A PALESTINIAN. DESPITE HIS PAIN, HE CAMPAIGNED FOR PEACE.

On January 5, 2007, an Israeli policeman killed my ten-year-old daughter, Abir, in front of her school. She was with her sister and two friends, and it was nine o'clock in the morning. She was shot by a plastic bullet in the head, from the back, at a distance of 50 to 65 feet (15 to 20 m).

Abir wasn't a combatant; she was just a child. She knew nothing of the conflict and did not take part in it. Unfortunately, she lost her life because she was a Palestinian.

Because I'm a human being, I asked myself: "If I kill the killer, or anyone else on the other side, one of the Israelis, or perhaps ten of them, would that give me back my daughter? No. I would cause more sorrow and another victim on the other side."

I chose to break the cycle of violence, of blood and vengeance, by stopping the killings and the revenge, and my support of vengeance.

It's very easy to create another enemy, but it's very difficult to make a friend. An Israeli soldier shot and killed my daughter. But more than a hundred Israeli ex-soldiers built her play yard, her garden and courtyard, her school....

Israeli and Palestinian children, our most innocent citizens, are the people who pay the highest price in this mortal conflict. They deserve our protection and to receive an education. They are all children; they are all our sons and daughters. This is what I said after Abir was killed. And on that day, I prayed that Abir would be the last victim in the conflict between Israelis and Palestinians.

When I speak to Abir, and I speak to her often, I ask her to be proud of me, because she pushes me every morning to get up and spread this message of humanity, against the murder of children, against the murder of civilians and the innocent, against violence, simply.

Many people have told me, "It's not your right to forgive in her name." And my reply is, "It's not my right to avenge myself in her name either."

I hope she is satisfied. I hope that she rests in peace. I promise her that justice will be done for her. It is the meaning of my life.

> ## IT'S NOT MY RIGHT TO AVENGE MYSELF IN HER NAME

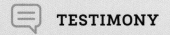
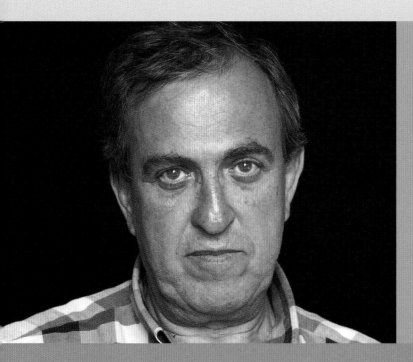

LEARNING TO MAKE PEACE

RAMI'S DAUGHTER WAS KILLED IN A SUICIDE BOMBING, BUT HE REFUSES TO GIVE IN TO HATRED.

I am an Israeli and I lost my daughter during a suicide attack on September 4, 1997. Since then, I have not been able to stop thinking about her. I feel her presence fifty-nine seconds per minute; the wound doesn't heal. It doesn't improve with time.

I am also the product of the educational system of two warring nations who train their young to be willing to sacrifice themselves come the time. This is as much the case for Palestinian society as it is for Israeli society. The educational system rests on a poisoning of the mind, on concealing the truth, on demonizing and dehumanizing the other. The walls it erects are worse than concrete ones: They are mental walls.

I was a victim of this educational system. I didn't hate anyone, because to hate isn't in my nature—in general, I don't hate people. But I can say quite frankly that I had never seen the other side. It didn't exist for me; I didn't pay it any attention. Even in my youth, when I was a soldier, I never looked at it up close: I was in a battalion of tanks. I fired sometimes from a distance of six miles (ten km).

> ## I CROSSED THAT BRIDGE OF HATRED AND FEAR AND WAS ABLE TO SEE THE OTHER SIDE OF HUMANITY

That's why when, for the first time in my life, I crossed that bridge of hatred and fear and was able to see the other side of humanity, the encounter was powerful. The journey I've been on since has led me down a profound road into the culture...of what I no longer consider "the other side." My definition of "side" has totally changed: Today I stand with those who want peace and who are ready to pay its price. The other side, for me, are all those who don't want peace and who are not ready to pay its price.

From now on, when I talk to Israeli and Palestinian students, I think not only about my daughter but also about them, about their families. I think about the heavy price they will have to pay if they continue hating each other. I do everything in my power to tell them that it's not worth it, that nothing is worth losing a child. I would go to the ends of the earth to see even just one student, who in the back of the classroom nods in approval at these words. Because for me, that would be a miracle: I'd have saved one drop of blood, and in Judaism the whole world exists in a drop of blood.

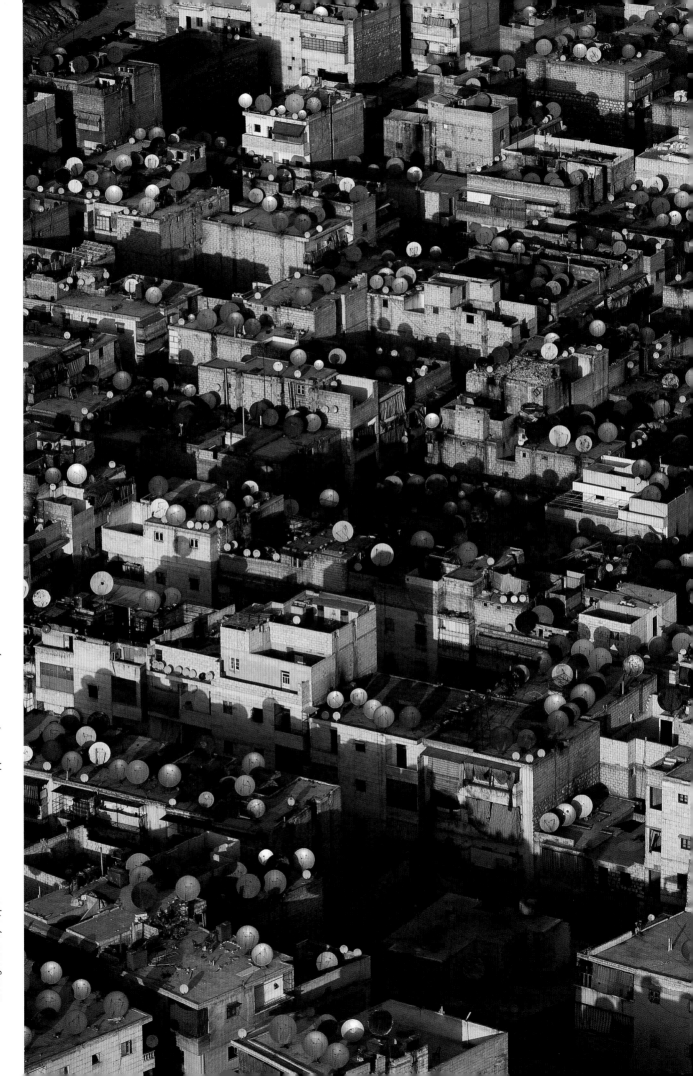

SATELLITE DISHES ON THE ROOFS OF ALEPPO, SYRIA 36°13' N – 37°10' E

This is what Aleppo looked like before the civil war, which has been ravaging Syria since 2011: a city covered with satellite dishes, all windows onto neighboring countries when the Arab Spring agitated the region. In Syria, peaceful demonstration was suppressed, and the country fell into chaos.

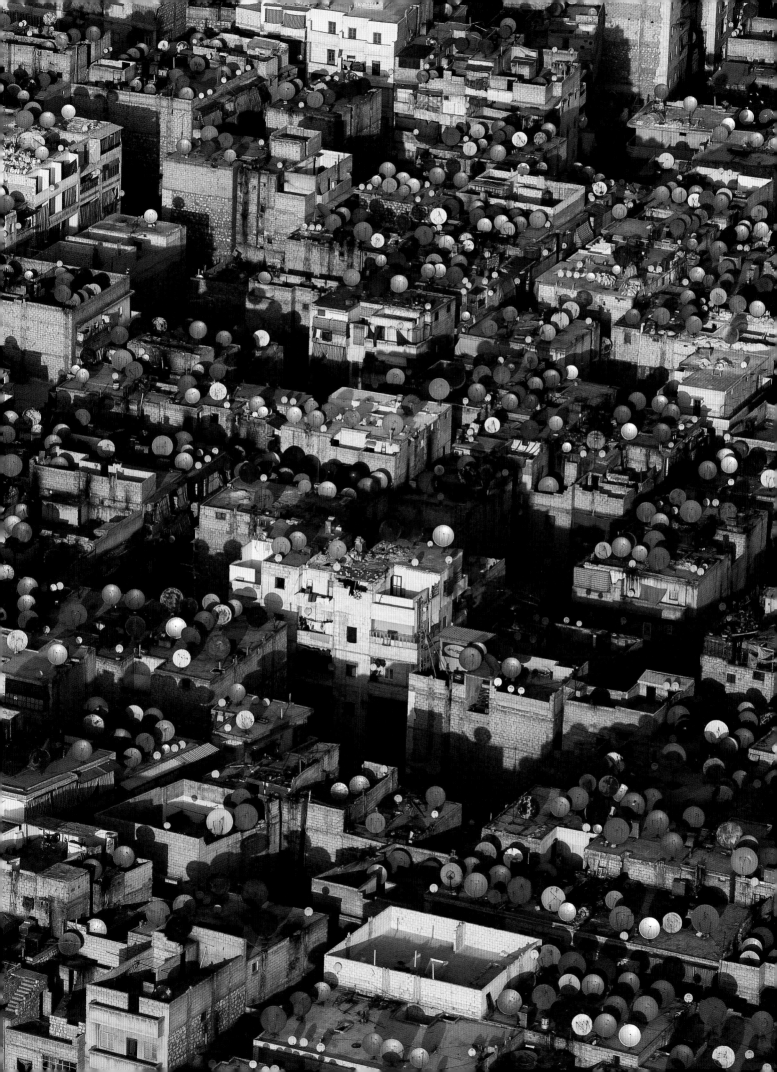

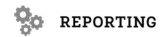

WHOEVER SAVES A LIFE

By Matthieu Aikins
First published in *Matter*, September 14, 2014

Under the bombs and mortar fire from troops of President Bashar al-Assad, a voluntary youth team, now famous in Syria and beyond, operates day and night to free survivors from the rubble. This amazing story offers a look inside the life-and-death world of Syria's first responders—the last hope for civilians caught in the chaos.

ALEPPO CITY, JUNE 18, 2014

The dawn found them sprawled like corpses around the cramped station room, atop a collection of soiled floor mats and a metal bunk that listed heavily to one side. They lay close together, some still wearing their uniforms from the night before. On a typical day in Aleppo, they would soon be woken by the sound of helicopters and jets roaring in to drop the first bombs on the rebel-held side of the city, which the regime has sought to pound to dust. But it was quiet this morning, and so they slept.

Standing outside his office next door, Khaled Hajjo, leader of the Hanano Civil Defense team, dragged on the first of many Gitanes and surveyed his small domain. The one-story, cinder-block station house was set in the corner of a large concrete lot the size of a soccer pitch, its perimeter hemmed by a twelve-foot stone wall. At the far

end of the lot was a mass of stacked old tires and a broken-down lifting crane. It had once been a car impound, but like so many buildings in Aleppo it had been repurposed for the war.

The station wasn't particularly sturdy. The neighborhood it was in, Hanano, was close to the front line and exposed not only to bombing but to artillery fire. Even a mortar round would probably cave in the roof, never mind the big howitzer shells that sometimes crashed into the lot. But the station had its advantages: It was set on a rise, with only a few low buildings surrounding it, and from here they could quickly spot the telltale smoke and dust pillars that mark the sites of bombs, and then rush to the rescue. They had been in this station since the very beginning, more than a year ago, when the team was first formed, and they had stayed in it through the long winter of massacres, through the worst times when the population had desperately fled the city, so that now the government's bombs fell as often as

not on abandoned buildings. This was their home.

Parked out front was a cherry-red truck with FREIW. FEUERWEHR, shorthand in German for "Volunteer Fire Department," along the side door in raised letters and, beneath it in Arabic, "Aleppo Civil Defense," spray painted in black. A well-built truck, donated by the West, it was starting to show its months of use in a war zone, with several bullet holes pocking the door and crazing the windshield. But it still got the job done, speeding them to blast sites.

The members of Civil Defense were attendants to the city's trauma, one of the few first responders left to care for the civilians caught on the front lines in a war between Syrian President Bashar al-Assad and rebel fighters. The team evacuated the injured, cleaned up the bodies, and fought fires. But what they were best known for—what they had become famous for in Syria and abroad—were the dramatic rescues, the lives they pulled from under the rubble.

When they spotted a blast, they'd cram into the cabin, ten or more on its two bench seats, and set off in search of the impact site. The truck had a loose, shaky suspension and the cab would smash up and down off the craters and potholes, jangling the men like change inside of a tin cup. The siren atop was an old-school wailer, deafening and sonorous. Sometimes they'd catch sight of an ambulance and give chase; often they'd be the first to the scene. As they rushed along, they'd lean out and ask pedestrians where the bomb had fallen. They could tell by the reaction if they were getting closer. At first it was just a pointed arm or a shrug, but as they neared, the onlookers would get increasingly agitated, until they saw in their eyes the wildness of a close brush with death or the panic for a trapped neighbor. The missions were all the more dangerous because of the regime's tactic of "double-tap" strikes, where they would return to bomb the same site and hit the rescuers and whatever crowd had gathered. In March, three members of the Hanano team had been killed that way, along with an Egyptian-Canadian photographer who had come to document their work.

> THE REGIME WOULD RETURN TO BOMB THE SAME SITE AND HIT THE RESCUERS AND WHATEVER CROWD HAD GATHERED

Khaled flicked the cigarette into the parking lot. Thirty years old, he looked more like a graduate student than someone who had spent the last year immersed in blood and rubble: shaggy hair, a straight, full-bridged nose, and a pointed jaw softened by full lips and cheeks. In a city dominated increasingly by anti-Western Islamist groups, he had until recently worn a ponytail. He was growing a slight paunch from all the nights spent sitting up snacking on fruit and nuts, listening to the sound of the city's bombardment and waiting for a call. When he smiled, a net of crow's feet crinkled into the corners of his eyes, but mostly his face maintained an unshakable placidity, even in the presence of death. It was this stillness, more than anything else, that accounted for his unruly team's respect and obedience. "It's the quiet ones you should fear," was how Surkhai, the group's joker, had put it....

Khaled could hear the rest of the team stirring. Present that day were some of his most reliable veterans—though of course they were really still boys. At twenty-eight, the twins, Surkhai and Shahoud, heavyset with thick hair covering everywhere but the top of their heads, were among the eldest. The rest were mostly twenty or twenty-one. Scrawny Ali, with his mullet, was only nineteen. Only Ahmed, a lanky, goateed kid who had been a firefighter like his father, had any experience as a first responder before the war. In all, there were thirty of them, but they worked in shifts, so that only a dozen or so were typically in the station at any one time. Except for the leader, Khaled. He had not taken a single day off. He loved the team—loved the physical closeness, the emotional bond. These guys had become his life. His old self, the former law student who taught at a trade school, seemed

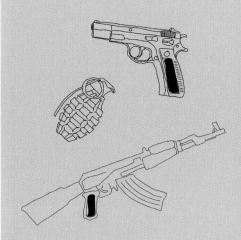

THE RAVAGES OF TWO DECADES OF WAR IN SOMALIA

Chaos reigns in Syria, where different regions, sometimes even different districts of the same town, are controlled by different armies. But before Syria, another country fell apart: Somalia. Islamist terrorism, famine, refugees, piracy: The country is considered a typical example, or rather, the worst example, of a failed state in which chaos reigns because the state is no longer assuming its role.

In 1991, civil war began the destruction of the state's infrastructure; the country soon fell into the hands of warlords. United Nations troops sustained heavy losses, and even the U.S. Army, sent in 1992 as part of a humanitarian intervention, had to retreat following a defeat in Mogadishu, the capital.

Profiting from violence, indigence, and the dissolution of the state, radical Islamist groups flourished, centered around a federation of courts called the Islamic Courts Union, which includes the military organization al-Shabaab, whose goal is to impose an Islamic state based on Sharia. These groups succeeded in taking over Mogadishu and a large part of the country when Somalia was struck by a new famine. In December 2006, Ethiopia intervened, and then, under the aegis of the African Union, other countries joined to obstruct the progress of the militias. Gradually, the large cities were retaken. But in 2009, al-Shabaab retook part of Mogadishu; Kenyan troops joined the conflict in 2011. At the end of 2014, al-Shabaab retreated from its last bastion and its leader, Ahmed Abdi Godane, was taken down by a U.S. drone. Today, the state exercises its power, but feebly and only over scattered regions, and the country remains in ruins.

as remote to him as his family's home, now behind regime lines.

The morning's quiet extended into the afternoon. Khaled couldn't believe how calm it was. Almost eerily so. It had been two days since the last big slaughter, when a bomb hit a vegetable market and killed several dozen people. Perhaps, the men speculated, the regime had been as stunned as everyone else by the fall of Mosul, in western Iraq, to the Al Qaeda splinter group known as ISIS. The summer heat was waxing in Aleppo, and Khaled decided not [to] push them to train or clean. So as the day unspooled, Ahmed played with Lulu, the mangy calico who hung around the station, while Surkhai and Ali took part in the listless card game in the bunk room.

Meanwhile Khaled pulled aside Annas, whom he was grooming for a leadership role, and they sat close on a love seat and talked about the team—who was doing well, who looked like they needed a rest. Annas was slender and had the long eyelashes and finely turned jaw of a teen idol; he looked much younger than his twenty-one years. He carried a pistol tucked into the back of his belt....

They should enjoy the lull, thought Khaled. Everyone in Syria was hungry for work, except them. But he knew the team would grow restless without action. The shared risk was what held them together. They even had a chant they sung as they rushed to the impact site:

Hey fucker, you're buried
We're coming to find you.
Hey fucker, you're burning
We're coming to put you out.

As the evening light began to lengthen shadows, the team heard a dull roar in the distance. The regime's helicopters were back. The group was highly attuned to the noises of the

city, like hunter-gatherers listening to the animal sounds of a forest. At night, Ahmed would describe them from his bunk. "That's an artillery shell. That's a jet. It's going to fire its Dushka," he'd say, and then would come the crash of the MiG hitting the front line with its cannon, like someone pulsing a blender. Sometimes a helicopter would be flying directly above them and they'd remain unmoved, noting that the thump of its rotor meant it was traveling somewhere, its blades digging in like an oarsman's. A helicopter getting ready to bomb you hovered, the noise it made more akin to the deep growl of a jet engine.

This one was way high up, a pale speck, and as they stood out in the parking lot watching it, a dot detached from it and tumbled slowly to earth, its impact announced by a mid-distance boom. It was a Russian-made Hind transport helicopter dropping a barrel bomb, the improvised but lethal explosives the regime had come to favor. Made out of empty fuel barrels or propane tanks, barrel bombs combine crude fuses with as much as two thousand pounds of TNT, along with pieces of junk steel and rebar that turn into red-hot shrapnel on detonation. They are as big as most conventional bombs, and a single hit is often enough to collapse the shoddily built concrete apartment complexes that comprise much of the city. The Syrian forces couldn't really aim them, but that didn't matter. The objective of the barrel-bomb campaign was to terrorize the population and render the city uninhabitable.

The team waited for the second bomb to fall away—the helos usually carried two—and then jumped in the truck and rattled out toward the bomb site. Their wheel man, Abu Sabet, a mournful-faced older taxi driver, had worked big rigs before the war. He had an artful command of the little truck, whipping it nimbly through the rubble-filled streets. The bomb had fallen in a sparsely built neighborhood; several local men standing nearby said that no one had been hit. Khaled decided to get down and make sure; toddling over strewn cinder blocks, the team moved forward among the shattered little houses. The air was still thick with pulverized concrete dust, golden in the dusk. "Al defa al madani, hada houn?" they yelled, into the rubble. "Civil Defense, anyone there?" There was no answer. "Guys, let's go," said Khaled, waving with his radio. The helicopter might come back.

Back at the station, they stood outside, joking. The brief call had stirred them out of their daylong torpor. Suddenly, Abu Sabet pointed directly above them. "A plane!" he said. They all jumped and looked skyward—but it was just a star in the lavender sky.

"Planes don't fly with their lights," scoffed Annas.

"Maybe the pilot left his handbrake on," joked Surkhai.

Looking sheepish, Abu Sabet got into his little taxi and drove home. He had a wife and kids who still lived in the city. The rest of the team settled into their nightly routine of laying about the bunk room, which held, in addition to the bed and sleeping mats, a fan, a propane burner, and a small television on which they would get the rebel and regime news broadcasts. One of the guys had brought a plate of cool, purple plums from the market. The rebel-held half of the city was still not yet fully besieged—the regime and ISIS were closing in from both sides—and there was still food in the few markets that remained open. They sucked the sour pits and cracked open a bowl of peanuts. An hour passed. And then there was a tremendous flash and boom.

To be hit by an explosion at close range is to experience light and sound as darkness and silence; silence as your ears ring louder than any sound, darkness as dust and smoke envelop you. The air filled with flying chunks of cinder block, and the men were pitched forward onto their hands, the floor suddenly gritty with debris. Khaled leaped to his feet and rushed with the rest of the team out into the pitch-black lot. The station had half-collapsed, and the power had gone out. One of the guys, Omar, had been hurt and a group led by Khaled threw

TO BE HIT BY AN EXPLOSION AT CLOSE RANGE IS TO EXPERIENCE LIGHT AND SOUND AS DARKNESS AND SILENCE; SILENCE AS YOUR EARS RING LOUDER THAN ANY SOUND, DARKNESS AS DUST AND SMOKE ENVELOP YOU

him into the cab of the truck and peeled out. The rest of the team ran across the road and crouched in a narrow space between two houses—they could hear the planes coming back in, and could see red antiaircraft tracers arc up from the rebel positions to meet them. Another blast sounded close by; the door to one of the houses opened and a young couple, the man cradling an infant in his arms, came out and hurried off into the night.

After about twenty minutes, the bombing subsided, and they dared to smoke again. Annas and Surkhai came out and stood by the road. The moon had risen in a yellow half-circle above the station; no one wanted to go back in, for fear the planes would return. An ambulance screeched up, and the driver got out, gaping at them in astonishment. "When I saw the bomb drop here, I came as fast as I could," he said.

300,000

TODAY, 300,000 CIVILIANS STILL LIVE IN ALEPPO. BEFORE THE CIVIL WAR, THE CITY WAS HOME TO NEARLY 2 MILLION PEOPLE.

You could see the whites of his eyes. "God has saved you because he wants you to save others."

The firetruck returned, and Khaled got out. "Omar's okay," he told the group. "He just cut his foot." He stood for a moment and surveyed the grim-faced half circle. The guys were badly rattled. But the Hanano team had never run from the site of a blast. He quickly made a decision. "We're going to stay here tonight and guard the station," he announced. "And in the morning, we'll go somewhere new."…

By daylight, they saw how close the bomb had fallen. The large house next door had vanished; in its place was an enormous crater filled with crushed debris. At the center of the crater were a few twisted sheets of heavy steel, the kind used in underground propane tanks—all that remained of a very large barrel bomb. It had obliterated the house and blown down a twenty-yard section of the heavy stone boundary wall, before smashing in part of the station. If the bomb had

dropped ten yards closer, they would all have been killed.

The loss of the station was a psychological blow. They had mourned their teammates there. But the building was on the verge of collapsing, and they had no choice but to move. There was no shortage of empty buildings in Aleppo to choose from, and early that morning Khaled had surveyed a school in a neighboring area. It was a sturdy, three-story building with a basement they could shelter in and a big parking lot for the trucks. It would do.

MAP OF THE CONFLICT IN SYRIA, LATE 2014

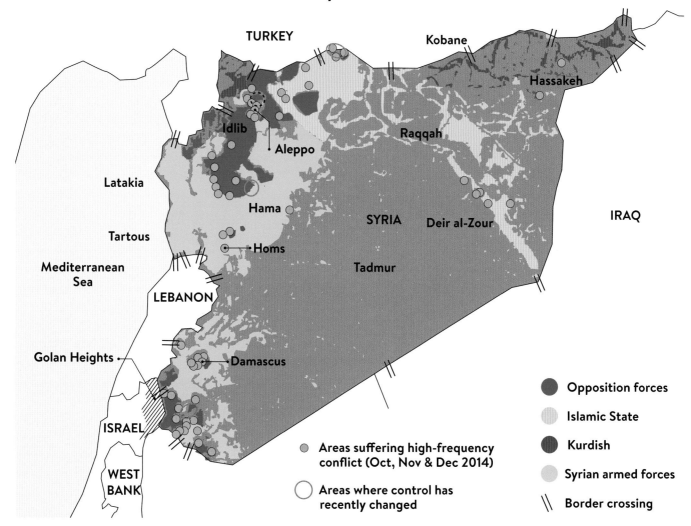

TURKEY

Kobane

Hassakeh

Idlib

Aleppo

Raqqah

Latakia

Hama

SYRIA

Deir al-Zour

IRAQ

Tartous

Homs

Mediterranean
Sea

Tadmur

LEBANON

Golan Heights

Damascus

ISRAEL

WEST
BANK

● Areas suffering high-frequency
conflict (Oct, Nov & Dec 2014)

○ Areas where control has
recently changed

● Opposition forces

░ Islamic State

● Kurdish

▢ Syrian armed forces

\\ Border crossing

Khaled called another Civil Defense team—there were four in Aleppo—to bring a dump truck so that they could load up the gear from the station.

As they were pitching equipment into the dump truck, they heard the roar of an incoming helicopter and, spooked from the night before, ran for cover. Two booms sounded in quick succession, and the team came back out, dusting themselves off and kidding about who had run away fastest.

A call came over their crackly, shoddy radio: Civilians had been hit. Khaled delegated his protégé Annas to take the rescue truck, and he and

several of the guys jumped in and raced toward the smoke, the siren wailing. The bomb site was on a main thoroughfare in Sakhour, near a park and an intersection that had been sliced in half by a high earthen barrier to protect against snipers. "Stop stop stop stop stop," shouted Annas when they'd reached a safe distance; the team jumped down and started running toward the site.

The helicopter had dropped two big barrel bombs: one cratering the road, and a second falling on the edge of the park, which set a large palm on fire. There were a number of cars scattered around, some of them now twisted hulks. A crowd of rebels and civilians, as well as several ambulances, had already gathered.

Ali ran toward a barely recognizable object on the sidewalk. It was a portly man who had been stripped of his clothes and powdered the color of concrete dust. He had been severed in half at the navel; his intestines were scattered behind him and one of his legs was folded up over his shoulder. He lay face down, and his eyes were closed, but as Ali ran up, his chest rose

and fell a single time. Then he was still. Ali pulled on a pair of white latex gloves. There was nothing to be done for him. Taking a blanket, he gathered up the pieces as best he could, and then bundled him into the back of an ambulance, where bodies were accumulating.

A rebel shouted from the road: "There are children in that car." Annas ran over to a little blue sedan that lay crumpled near the site of the second bomb; it looked as if it too had fallen from the sky. He started prying frantically with a crowbar at the rear door; a mother and her children were still in the back seat. The mother had been decapitated by the blast, and the children were pale and immobile. As he hefted their small bodies out, he saw why. The little boy was missing his right leg below the knee, and had bled to death. His sister had taken a fatal piece of shrapnel through her chest.

The site was close to several hospitals, and the wounded—including the driver of the sedan, the children's father—had already been carted away. The team realized they were just recovering bodies from the wrecks. They worked urgently; the site was wide open and exposed and the helicopter might return at any minute. It was hot and there was a sharp stench in the air, more acrid than blood. Someone yelled that a plane was coming, and the crowd broke and ran in a panicked herd. But it was a false alarm. When the last body was out, the team climbed back into the truck; the whole affair had taken fifteen minutes.

Back at the station, there wasn't even water to wash the blood from their hands. The bathroom had been destroyed in the blast the night before. No one had slept for twenty-four hours, but everyone dug in to help empty the ruined station of its cargo: the beds and desks, all the donated

3.5 MILLION

MORE THAN 3.5 MILLION PEOPLE HAVE FLED THE FIGHTING IN SYRIA AND ARE NOW REFUGEES IN NEIGHBORING COUNTRIES: IRAQ, JORDAN, LEBANON, EGYPT, AND TURKEY.

rescue gear from the West. Surkhai and Ahmed came out carrying the old couch from Khaled's office, but as they lifted it upward it let out a plaintive mewling. "Lulu!" said Ahmed. They tilted the couch and shook it as if they were tipping out spare change; after a moment the calico sprung onto the concrete and began rubbing herself against their legs, another survivor.

In contrast to the Hanano station, their new home was a sturdy, three-story, L-shaped fortress made of thick concrete and stone. It had been an elementary school before the war. Since then, like many government buildings, it had held a succession of tenants. The markings on its walls served as a history of the revolution's stalled arc. Atop the original paintings of flowers and butterflies were several layers of graffiti: a perhaps prerevolutionary "A♥M," "Free Syria," the slogan of the demonstrators; the names of a few of the hastily formed rebel militias, or "katibas," that had taken over the area; and finally, the sinister black flag of ISIS. The Islamic State had been

a menace in Aleppo and the northern countryside; last October, when Khaled had gone to pick up a big shipment of five fire trucks donated by the West, an ISIS commander at the border had arrested him and impounded the vehicles. ISIS was finally forced out of the city by the rebels in January, but now they were on the rise again, their forces less than twenty miles to the east, and advancing.

Though they all considered themselves faithful Muslims, most of the team wasn't interested in the Islamic fundamentalism that had come to dominate the rebel fighting groups. Fed up with the corrupt, repressive regime of Bashar al-Assad, they had participated in the peaceful demonstrations that began during the Arab Spring in 2011. But after the murderous regime crackdown on the demonstrations, the movement turned to armed rebellion. By July 2012, the rebels had seized half of Aleppo, settling into a stalemate along front lines that had largely been unchanged since then.

At first, life in the rebel-held part of the city had been full of hope. Rebel advances in the countryside had opened up the supply lines to Turkey, and many refugees from the initial fighting had returned. The markets were bustling and full of goods, and many civilians had volunteered to keep the city running. Khaled himself joined a rebel office that distributed food to the needy, and then volunteered as a schoolteacher. But the bombardment by jet and helicopter intensified, much of it targeting ordinary people. In February 2013, several giant Scud missiles landed in rebel-held neighborhoods, each leveling dozens of homes and killing hundreds.

By then the need for some kind of urban rescue team had become apparent. The bombs didn't just kill or maim people; they trapped them under the rubble. Each strike was like a pinpoint earthquake. When a building collapsed, the whole neighborhood would turn out, swarming the rubble, frantically picking at the concrete. In the pandemonium, you couldn't hear anyone buried or calling for help. Sometimes someone would come along with a backhoe and start tearing at the rubble pile, often killing those who were still alive inside. It was possible to save those who were trapped—if they weren't badly injured, they could stay alive for days—but it required trained rescuers.

The Hanano team was the first to form in Aleppo City, out of locals who were already involved with the civilian side of the resistance. Surkhai and his twin brother, Shahoud, were among the founding members. Khaled came along soon after.

Around the same time, ARK, an international contracting firm based in Istanbul, had received a mix of U.S.

44 YEARS

THE AL-ASSAD FAMILY HAS BEEN IN POWER IN SYRIA FOR 44 YEARS. HAFEZ AL-ASSAD WAS PRESIDENT OF THE COUNTRY FROM 1971 TO 2000. HIS SON BASHAR, THE CURRENT RULER, BECAME PRESIDENT AT HAFEZ'S DEATH IN 2000 AND REMAINS IN POWER DESPITE THE OPPOSITION TO HIS REGIME.

AT THE TOP OF THE PILE, ALI COULD HEAR THE SOUND OF THE LITTLE BOYS' VOICES CALLING FOR HELP, AND THEY REDOUBLED THEIR EFFORTS

and British funding intended for "non-lethal aid" to the Syrian opposition, and had identified the rescue teams as a priority. The scale of Assad's bombardment paralleled conventional wars in Europe, and ARK resurrected a Blitz-era doctrine called Civil Defense. Partnering with a Turkish organization, AKUT, that specialized in earthquake response, they established a training center in southern Turkey for the new teams. There, the boys from Hanano learned basic urban search-and-rescue techniques, along with first aid and firefighting. They were issued trucks, uniforms, and equipment, and then sent back to Syria.

Their training came just in time. In the fall of last year [2013], the momentum of the war began to shift in favor of Assad. After the regime killed over a thousand people with sarin gas on the outskirts of Damascus on August 21, 2013, and the West declined to intervene, Assad renewed his offensive. Aleppo, the linchpin city of the north, was among the regime's key objectives. And to break the rebels' grip on the eastern half, the regime turned to

a tool it had been testing in other cities: the barrel bomb.

Last November [2013], the campaign began in earnest. Dozens of bombs rained each day and night on crowded markets and apartment buildings. In one two-week span, over five hundred people were killed, almost all of them civilians. The Hanano team worked the sites nonstop, massacre after massacre, from early morning until late at night. There was hardly time to eat.

And yet through it all, they stuck together. In the last year, only two members had quit, one at the insistence of his family. *The people are waiting for us*, Khaled would tell the team each time there was a blast. *We know that they are waiting for us.* They cited as their motto a Koranic sura: "And whoever saves a life, it will be as if he has saved all of humanity." For all their gallows humor, they held it in earnest. They were there to stand beside the weakest and the most helpless, even at the cost of their own lives, even after losing three teammates, even after the destruction of their station. So that others might live....

"We should have told them we were all killed in the blast, then maybe Bashar would leave us alone," said Ali.

Shahoud, the elder twin, came in with a platter of fresh vegetables and *mezzes*, little dishes of tapenade and hummus, along with flatbread. "You think we're going to live a long time?" he said, slapping his belly. "We're eating so that we don't miss anything." And they all tucked in....

It had been another sleepless night in the basement of the school. Latif, the Al Qaeda fanboy, had gone to bed with a pop song endlessly looping on his phone. The shelling had been particularly loud and intense, but worse

RAPE AS A WEAPON OF WAR

In Syria, the repression waged by Bashar al-Assad has been accompanied by campaigns of humiliation and the raping of women and prisoners. Witnesses give accounts of women and young girls being raped in front of their families. Today, the Islamic State of Iraq and Syria (ISIS) resorts to rape. It abducts women to sell them as sexual slaves. These crimes have as their objective the disruption of communities and the denigration of honor in cultures where women's virginity must be protected. The consequences of these rapes are drastic: They cause unwanted pregnancies, honor killings, and suicides. Far from being an isolated act, rape constitutes a weapon of war and a deliberate strategy. In the Congo, at least 200,000 women have been raped since 1998. During the Rwandan Genocide, in 1994, between 100,000 and 250,000 women were raped. And 60,000 rapes have been tallied in the former Yugoslavia. "Sexual violence in conflict needs to be treated as the war crime that it is; it can no longer be treated as an unfortunate collateral damage of war," states Zainab Hawa Bangura, Special Representative of the United Nations Secretary-General on Sexual Violence in Conflict. Since 2008, the UN Security Council Resolution 1820 has recognized sexual violence as a crime against humanity. Yet, these sexual brutalities are rarely acknowledged in the courts.

DROUGHT AND CIVIL WAR IN SYRIA

Several studies demonstrate the role of climate in triggering the Syrian conflict: In fact, between 2007 and 2010, the country suffered the most significant drought recorded in the region in decades. Close to 60 percent of cultivated land in the country has suffered from drought, causing food insecurity and extreme poverty. Consequently, numerous stockbreeders have lost their herds and farmers their crops. In a period of just a few years, 1.5 million Syrians from the north left the countryside for cities. This rural exodus and spiking food costs have stoked the population's resentment. Bashar al-Assad's regime was not able to confront the discontent, which has subsequently become confrontational. Concurrently, in other countries in the region, the Arab Spring brought about the fall of regimes in Libya, Egypt, and Tunisia. For several years, military forces have been interested in the consequences of climate change on security. But the impact of climate is nothing new: The French Revolution, too, began with a bad harvest!

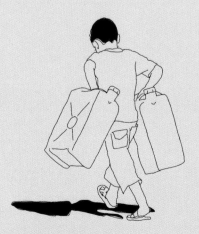

still were the famished mosquitoes. The first bombs at dawn were almost a relief.

The team, led by Surkhai, one of the twins, pulled on their clothes and ran upstairs to the truck, breakfasting on cigarettes as they rattled through Aleppo's broken streets. For once Surkhai, the team jester, was silent. It was the fifth day in the new station.

They found the site down a narrow side street. A bomb had come sailing down in the clear morning air and struck a small apartment building, partially collapsing it. Most of the extended family who lived there had made it out and were standing anxiously in the street. There were two sisters in headscarves holding each other and weeping; men were digging angrily at the rubble. Surkhai got down from the truck and ran up to an old man, still in his pajamas, who was powdered with dust. "There are two boys trapped inside," he said.

According to the training they received in Turkey, the rescue technique they chose depended [on] the kind of structure and the degree to which it had collapsed. When multilevel concrete buildings fail—whether from a bomb strike or an earthquake—[their] floors tend to pancake on top of each other, crushing those inside. However, small spaces will often remain around columns, stairwells, or pieces of heavy furniture, allowing people to survive. The key was to get to them in time, without getting caught by a further collapse of the building.

The first step was to locate the victims. The family knew that the kids had been in their bedrooms, sleeping, so the team had an idea of where they should be.

Now there were two possible approaches. The first was known as a horizontal rescue, where the team tunnels parallel to the floor layers, shoring with pieces of wood as they went. The second was a vertical rescue, where they would dig from either above or below to the victim. In this case, the team went for both approaches simultaneously. Surkhai went into a one-room shop on the ground floor of the building and started smashing at its back wall with a pick. Meanwhile, whippet-skinny Ali got up on top of the rubble pile and, aided by the boys' father, started digging downward toward where the bedroom had been.

The old man and the women stood in the street, watching helplessly as the men swarmed atop the pile that had been their home. They were simple tailors who were trying to eke out a living in Aleppo. Why should they leave their homes for Bashar al-Assad?

At the top of the pile, Ali could hear the sound of the little boys' voices calling for help, and they redoubled their efforts. The closer they got to their target, the slower they went, even as the pressure mounted—a frantic search turned archeological excavation. Smaller chunks of concrete were picked away, larger ones levered free, webs of rusted rebar were sawed in half. Finally, they opened a hole through the floor, and there they were: The brothers crouched down by their beds, chalk-white but seemingly unharmed. It was as if they had been etched back into the world.

Ali and Surkhai carried the children down to a waiting ambulance. Their mother ran to them, sobbing in relief at a kind of second birth. Watching the reunion, even Surkhai got a lump in his throat.

The team returned to the station elated. But there was only time for a cup of tea before a second call came in—the firefighting team needed their help.

BRINGING AID TO VICTIMS OF CONFLICTS

ICRC

The International Committee of the Red Cross (ICRC) is a humanitarian intergovernmental organization. Founded in Switzerland in 1863, it has as its mission to protect and assist the victims of conflicts while maintaining neutrality. It is active in more than eighty countries and has thirteen thousand employees. The organization tries to enforce basic humanitarian principles among combatants. It brings aid to the injured and helps prisoners of war. Its volunteers visit them and guarantee their safety or help maintain contact with their families. The ICRC intervenes in conflicts all over the world, notably in Syria, Iraq, Israel and the Palestinian territories, the Republic of South Sudan, and the Central African Republic. The ICRC represents the federation of all national Red Cross and Red Crescent societies, working in the spirit of the International Red Cross and Red Crescent Movement.
www.icrc.org

LANDMINE REMOVAL: SAVING LIVES

APOPO

Conflicts continue to injure and kill long after they have ended, because of explosions of munitions and land mines left in battle sites. Numerous organizations, such as Handicap International or Halte aux mines antipersonnel (HAMAP), denounce the sale of these weapons and work to have them banned. They also conduct demining operations. The Belgian nongovernmental organization APOPO (Anti-Persoonsmijnen Ontmijnende Product Ontwikkeling, or Anti-Personnel Landmines Detection Product Development) raises, trains, and uses rats to demine: The rats learn to recognize the smell of explosives, the sound of a mine engaging, and to walk in file to facilitate their work with deminers. They already have proven themselves by locating thirteen thousand mines in Mozambique and are active in other former conflict areas, including Angola, Tanzania, Cambodia, Vietnam, Laos, and Thailand.
www.handicap-international.org
www.hamap.org
www.apopo.org

HELPING CHILD SOLDIERS REINTEGRATE

UNICEF

Since 1998, UNICEF has come to the aid of more than one hundred thousand former child soldiers. Innumerable children have been forcibly enlisted in armies and militias, whether in Africa (e.g., Angola, Ivory Coast, Democratic Republic of the Congo, Liberia, Sierra Leon, Somalia), Asia (e.g., Nepal, Afghanistan, Sri Lanka) or Latin America, and they continue to be so. These minors serve as messengers or carry munitions or food to combatants, sometimes even using light weapons themselves. They are both the actors and the victims of war. Liberating them from the clutches of armed groups isn't enough; they have to learn to live again. That is why UNICEF and numerous other local NGOs offer these children psychological support and help them get back to school or train them for a profession.
www.unicef.org

HELPING REFUGEES COMMUNICATE

INTERNEWS

Internews is an international NGO that supports the media, especially in conflict areas. It helps Afghans to follow the parliamentary elections to strengthen transparency, allows almost a million Ukrainians displaced by the war to have information on the areas occupied by rebels, provides radios in refugee camps, such as those in South Sudan or Kenya, and sends first-aid information such as medical advice or information on the distribution of water or food. To date, Internews has done work in nearly ninety countries.
www.internews.eu

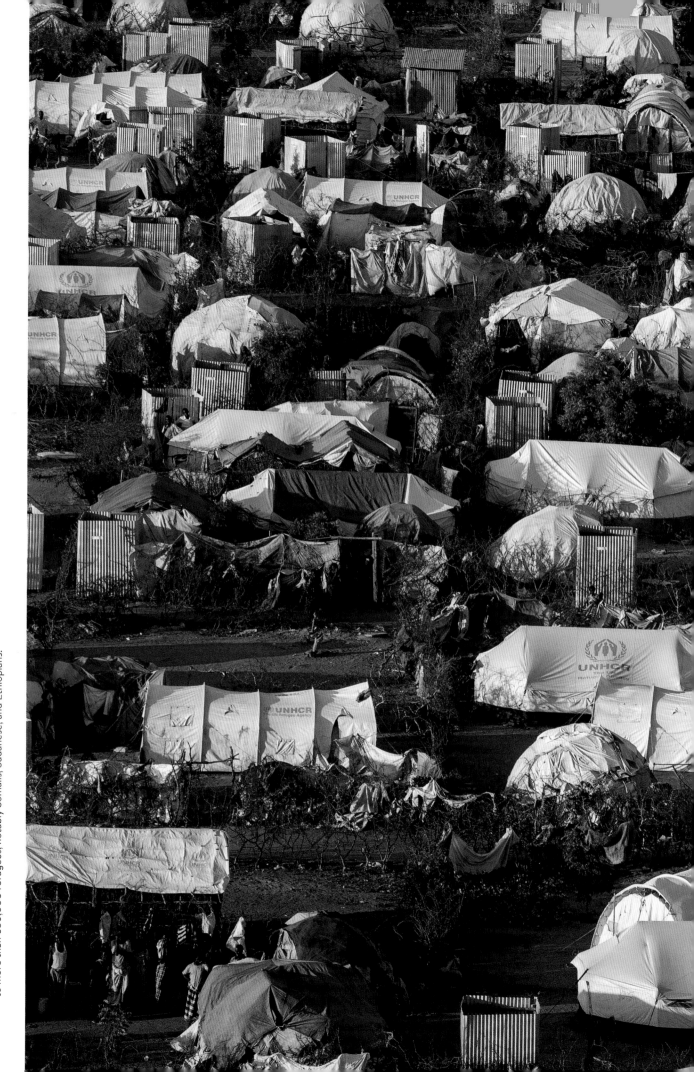

SOMALI REFUGEE CAMPS, KAMBIOOS, DADAAB, KENYA 0° 02' S – 40° 24' E

Dadaab is the largest refugee camp in the world. A complex of several camps, it was built to receive Somali refugees in the early 1990s. But exile has become perennial. In January 2015, Kenya was home to more than 650,000 refugees, notably Somalis, Sudanese, and Ethiopians.

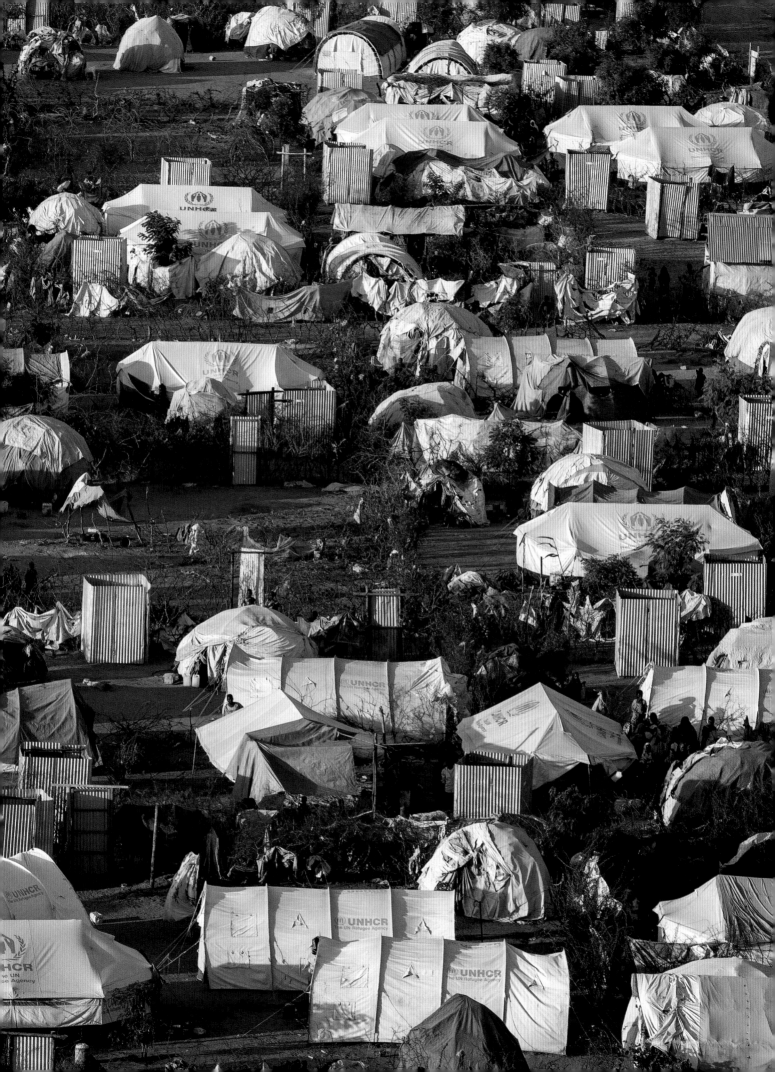

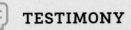
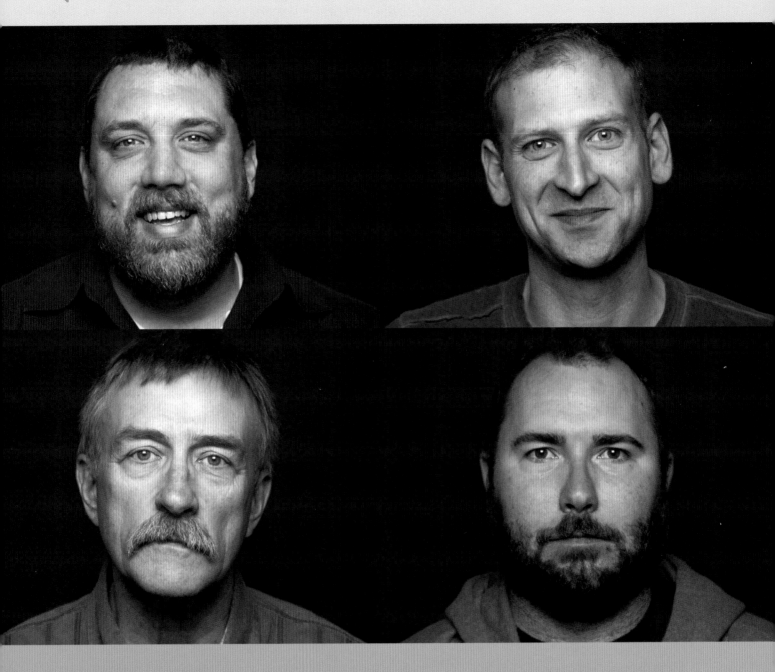

THE COLD SENSATION OF DEATH

WAR CHANGES SOMETHING IN THE DEPTHS OF OUR
HUMANITY. AMERICAN VETERANS TELL HOW THEY
WERE SURPRISED AT HAVING BECOME KILLERS.

When Alex was sent to Iraq at age nineteen, he had only just come out of training. "You can never really train for the kind of violence you see over there," he states. But as with most veterans, in his story of war Alex skips over anything bloody: He comes back, instead, to the changes he progressively felt inside himself. "I didn't realize that my feelings had turned off until it was way beyond normal. I noticed it when, on the phone with my family, I wasn't reacting anymore to things that would otherwise have angered or excited me," he tells me. On the ground, his emotions seemed asphyxiated. And he isn't the first veteran to share this feeling with me. Sean, a sergeant first class in Iraq, tells me, "In combat, your emotions explode, they shatter and you need to relearn how to use them again." How can anger, joy, and sadness disappear? What remains that is human?

Doc Martin, a Vietnam veteran and psychology professor and counselor to veterans at the University in Pasadena, California, takes it even further. For the time he spent on the battleground, he considered himself a dead man: "What allowed me to be efficient and even very efficient as a combatant and soldier, is that I gave up on life. I convinced myself that I wouldn't survive and since I thought that, I was furious and I became a killer.... Giving up the idea of living is a hell of a price to pay. There's something that leaves you, and you know you're turning bad when you become more and more

> I'D BE HAPPY TO HAVE THE OPPORTUNITY TO KILL AGAIN, LEGALLY AND AS A LEGITIMATE DEFENSE. SO I DO HOPE THAT SOMEONE WILL GIVE ME THE CHANCE ONE DAY

mean and more and more cold and turned off, distant from others." His description sends chills up my spine.

His tears flowed during our interview. And I felt a deep discomfort seeing the tenacity of his pain, the discomfort of admitting to his dehumanization.

I am concerned for all the lost souls of this world who no longer feel alive.

But the words of Peter, also a veteran of the Iraq War, leave me paralyzed. With blank blue eyes and a pale complexion, he explains to me in a monotone, "The sensation of killing isn't like any other thing that you might experience in your life. And unfortunately, once you've experienced this feeling a first time, your body will want to feel it again." His confession opens up for me the abysses of an addiction usually attributed to rapists or serial killers. It is cold as death, cold as the absence of emotion in his speech.

"Today, I keep a loaded gun in my room," he continues, "and I admit I'm hoping someone breaks in. I'd be happy to have the opportunity to kill again, legally and as a legitimate defense. So I do hope that someone will give me the chance one day...to kill again."

Peter shows me the all-powerful perversity of war, its capacity to dehumanize. I then can grasp the urgency of treasuring our emotions: our fears, our joys, our sadness, and why not, our anger. But above all, I grasp the urgency of psychological and psychiatric support for veterans.

—Mia Sfeir

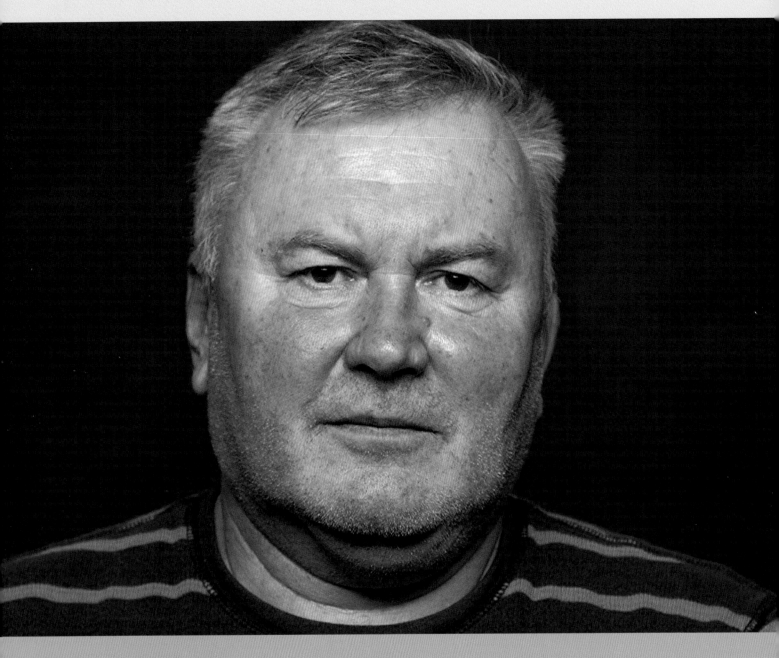

FATHER COURAGE

MINES KILL AND MAIM EVEN AFTER THE END OF THE WAR. AND
REINVENTING A LIFE AFTER AN AMPUTATION IS ANOTHER FIGHT.
BUT WE MUST ALSO OVERCOME THE SILENCE.

Sometimes, it's through what is not said, through what people aren't able to express, that one understands a country. Such is the case in Bosnia-Herzegovina, where land mines, those remnants of war, continue to kill and injure. More than seven thousand victims have been recorded in this small country of four million inhabitants.

On the road from Sarajevo to Doboj, where we're going to film some of our interviews, the surrounding fields are covered with red signs stamped with skulls and a single word in capital letters: MINE. Land mines are everywhere, invisible, hidden underground, forgotten after the war. Some regions have been demined, but they continue to kill. Why? The many floods the country has recently experienced have displaced soil, and mines along with it. But it's also because of corruption: The money for demining programs has disappeared. It is to talk about all of this, to stand up against this injustice, that we've come here. But it is especially to give voice to the victims, to listen to their stories, and to give them the chance to send a message to the rest of the world.

Janja arrives with her eighteen-year-old son; she helps him climb the short staircase of the hotel because the young man walks with crutches. They both look weary, their eyes full of pain. Janja's husband stepped on a mine three months ago when going to get wood in the forest. His son was with him that day. He was injured by the explosion, but worse than the injury, he saw his father die, and he couldn't do anything to save him. As for Janja, she hasn't slept well for three months; she feels that her life stopped the day of the explosion. She's present physically, but doesn't speak or look at anyone. It is as if her soul was taken the day her husband's was. She tells me that mostly she's afraid for her son, because after the accident, he has shut himself in; he doesn't want to go to school or see his friends. He stays at home, prostrate, like on the day of our meeting. But Janja doesn't mention any of this during our interview. In front of the camera, she freezes, incapable of reliving, of speaking about her loss; the pain is too big.

Over the next few days, we meet Jasminka, Petar, Drago, and others. All of them have lost someone or a part of their bodies in the explosion of an antipersonnel mine. But none manage to talk about it. Resigned, they all ask me: What for? They don't believe that someone could be touched by their story, that their injury could affect someone, that it could change things. Because here, after the end of the war, nothing has changed.

At the end of a few days and faced with people who have given up, I also begin to feel resigned, to feel that it isn't worth pushing to speak those who don't wish to. But at the same time, I feel like screaming out their stories, that they might become known by the whole world.

It's our last interview. You can hear Miralem Malkic, a loud guy, in the hallway before he's even come into the room. I can tell he's proud, but I don't yet know of what or whom. He settles down in the chair and tells me his story, or rather his son's—a little boy who stepped on a mine at the age of nine, when there was still war in Bosnia. He lost both arms and a leg in the explosion. This father, six and a half feet (two meters) tall and weighing more than 220 pounds (100 kg), breaks down in tears remembering the day when his son woke up at the hospital after the accident and begged, "Papa, don't abandon me; I don't want to die." And Miralem never abandoned him. He fought, and as a result, his son was cared for in the United States, where he was able to receive prostheses. He leads an extraordinary life: Gifted in information technology, he has a good job in Manhattan, drives a car, plays sports, has a partner. Looking straight into the camera, Miralem sends a message of hope to those who no longer believe in hope. He tells them loud and clear that there is life after the mine, there is life after the war.

—Anastasia Mikova

> HE TELLS THEM LOUD AND CLEAR THAT THERE IS LIFE AFTER THE MINE, THERE IS LIFE AFTER THE WAR

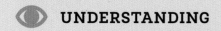
REFUGEES WORLDWIDE

POPULATION DISPLACEMENT FOR 25 YEARS (1989–2013)

In millions

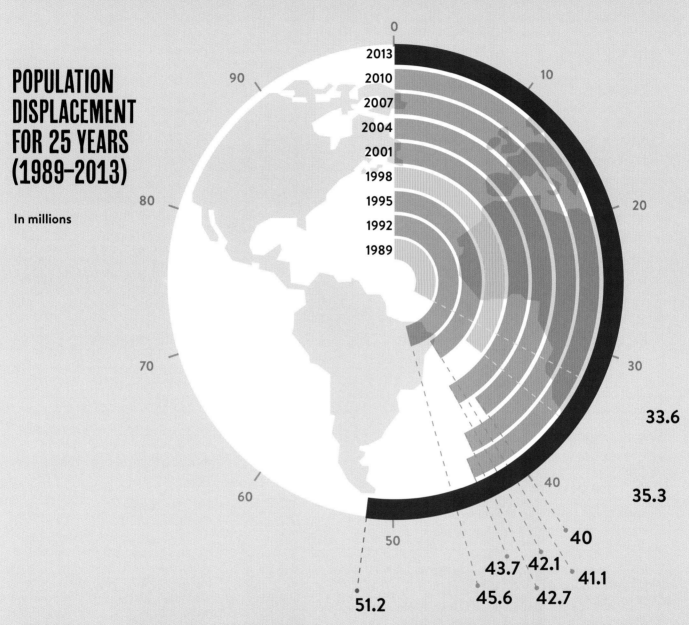

2013
2010
2007
2004
2001
1998
1995
1992
1989

0
10
20
30
40
50
60
70
80
90

33.6
35.3
40
41.1
42.1
42.7
43.7
45.6
51.2

REFUGEES — IN AND OUT OF CAMPS

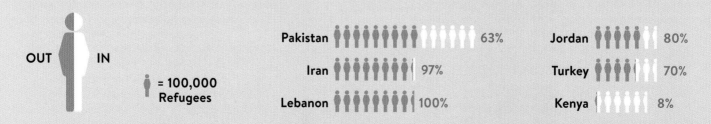

OUT   IN

👤 = 100,000 Refugees

Pakistan 63%	Jordan 80%
Iran 97%	Turkey 70%
Lebanon 100%	Kenya 8%

WHERE DO SYRIAN REFUGEES GO?

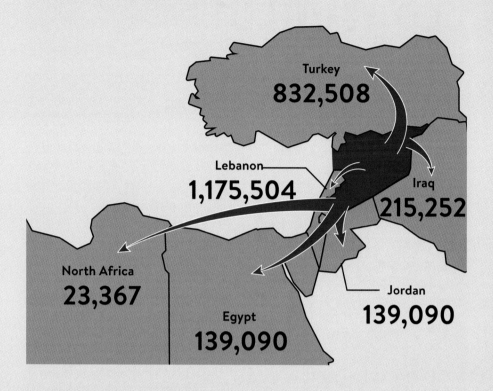

Turkey
832,508

Lebanon
1,175,504

Iraq
215,252

North Africa
23,367

Egypt
139,090

Jordan
139,090

25 YEARS OF CONFLICTS AND REFUGEES

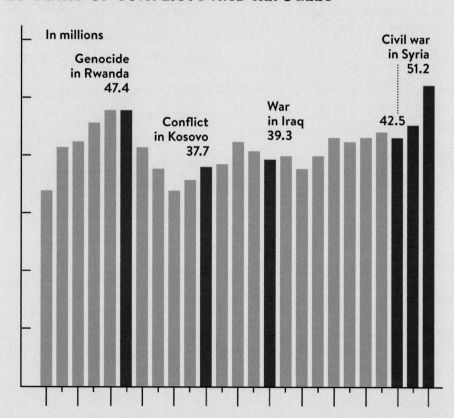

In millions

Genocide
in Rwanda
47.4

Conflict
in Kosovo
37.7

War
in Iraq
39.3

Civil war
in Syria
51.2

42.5

KEY FIGURES

The five largest armies in the world are, in terms of manpower, those of China (2.2 million soldiers), the United States (1.8 million), India (1.3 million), North Korea (1.1 million), and Russia (1 million).

Twenty-two countries do not have militaries. Not surprisingly, these include seven of the world's ten smallest independent countries by land area (which traditionally haven't been subject to invasion).

At least 16,400 nuclear weapons can be tallied in the world, owned by nine countries: the United States, Russia, China, France, United Kingdom, India, Pakistan, North Korea, and Israel. More than 2,055 nuclear tests have been reported. But a nuclear weapon has been employed only twice, in 1945, in Hiroshima and Nagasaki.

Some 8 million "light" weapons (such as machine guns) are manufactured each year, as well as 12 billion bullets. Light weapons kill a person every 2 minutes, and 12 billion bullets are almost enough to kill everyone in the world twice.

There is thought to be about 250,000 child soldiers in the world. Thanks to the efforts of UNICEF and multiple other organizations, more than 100,000 children have been liberated and reintegrated into their communities since 1998.

In 2013, worldwide military expenditures reached $1.747 trillion, or 2.4 percent of the planet's Gross World Product (GWP).

TIMELINE

1864
The First Geneva Convention, which addressed those wounded on the battlefield, opens the way for other humanitarian conventions.

1939–1945
The Second World War; more than 50 million dead.

1945
The atomic bombings of the Japanese cities of Hiroshima and Nagasaki.

1945
The creation of the United Nations (UN).

1947
Start of production of the AK-47. More than 70 million copies of this rifle, also known as the Kalashnikov after its inventor, have been produced. It is still commonly used in current conflicts.

1948
The first dispatch of a peacekeeping force, the Blue Helmets, by the UN, during the conflict between Israel and its Arab neighbors.

1999
The Anti-Personnel Land Mine Convention becomes international law.

BOOKS AND ARTICLES

The Iliad
Homer, c. 760–710 B.C.
One of the oldest extant works of Western literature and one of the greatest classics of antiquity is a book about war, describing the ten years of conflict between the Achaeans and the Trojans. It underscores the centrality of war in our civilization.

All Quiet on the Western Front
Erich Maria Remarque, 1929
The disillusions of a young German soldier sent to the Western front during World War I are told in this novel that was first published in a German newspaper. Although Remarque says in the opening statement that the book was simply an attempt to describe the experience of a soldier, the work became a symbol of pacifism.

1984
George Orwell, 1949
This novel conveys not only a totalitarianism that engages in the surveillance and oppression of individuals but also how a state can use real or fictive enemies to subjugate its own people: Big Brother is watching, because we are at permanent war with our rivals. It is a reflection on emergency laws imposed during war that become perennial and harm individual freedom.

Anne Frank: The Diary of a Young Girl
Anne Frank, 1947
A young girl tells of the tragic and true-story destiny of her Jewish family who was forced to live in hiding in a house in Amsterdam during the Nazi occupation.

A Woman in Berlin
Anonymous, 1954
A memoir of a young German woman—now known to be Marta Hillers, who for a long time remained anonymous—in Berlin in 1945, when Soviet troops entered the city. Her story illustrates the horrors of war for women when battles take place near the home front.

Barefoot Gen
Keiji Nakazawa, 1973
In the spring of 1945, in the city of Hiroshima, the Nakaoka family is subject to discrimination by its neighbors because the father is a pacifist. The family is left to deal with the atomic bombing and the aftermath of war. This manga is based on autobiographical experiences and is at once an informed account of Japan's role in World War II and a powerful anti-war statement.

Maus
Art Spiegelman, 1980
In the first graphic novel to win a Pulitzer Prize, the cartoonist Spiegelman masterfully recounts the story of a Polish Jew and survivor of Auschwitz and his son as he comes to terms with his father's wartime experiences.

"Rules of Engagement"
William Langewiesche, 2006
(in *Vanity Fair*)
This report investigates a massacre that occurred in Iraq in 2005, in a zone occupied by the armed forces of the military coalition. In Haditha, a bomb exploded under a convoy of American marines, causing one death. In retaliation, the marines killed twenty-four civilians in the area. The author shows how uncontrolled violence becomes a norm. He analyzes the causes of the carnage: the incomprehension, the noncommunication, the dehumanization, and the disproportionate means to kill placed at the disposal of young marines.

FILMS AND TELEVISION

Paths of Glory
Stanley Kubrick, 1957
This classic film, which takes place during World War I, shows the irony and futility of war in the trenches. Using promotion as enticement, a French general orders his subordinate, who in turn commands his own subordinates, to attack a German trench position even though the mission is suicidal. When the charge ends in mayhem, three luckless soldiers are executed so their superior can save face.

Johnny Got His Gun
Dalton Trumbo, 1971
Probably the most horrific of antiwar films, this picture follows a soldier who has his four limbs amputated and becomes blind, deaf, and dumb after a mission during the First World War.

The Deer Hunter
Michael Cimino, 1978
Russian roulette is a metaphor for war in this film about the psychological aftereffects combat has on soldiers.

First Blood
Ted Kotcheff, 1982
The first and best in the famous five-part series. It paints the portrait of Vietnam veteran John Rambo (Sylvester Stallone), who cannot reintegrate into American society.

Grave of the Fireflies
Isao Takahata, Studio Ghibli, 1988
One of the most moving animations ever made, this film inspired by an autobiographical novel narrates the tragic destiny of two orphans after the bombing of Kobe by the Americans, in 1945.

Warriors
Peter Kosminsky, 1999
This British television series tells of the involvement of British soldiers in Bosnia-Herzegovina at the beginning of the 1990s. Mandated to maintain peace, these young recruits helplessly stand by as atrocities are perpetrated against civilians.

Enemy at the Gates
Jean-Jacques Annaud, 2001
This film presents the duel of two snipers during the massive Battle of Stalingrad between Soviet and German forces. The opening scene underscores the absurdity of massacres and what little regard a great patriotic war holds for human life. Barely trained and inadequately armed men (one rifle for every two) are reduced to cannon fodder; if they retreat, the political commissar will kill them.

War Photographer
Christian Frei, 2001
The camera intimately follows one of the most important war photographers of his time, the American James Nachtwey. This documentary raises questions about how journalists should give account of war and its atrocities.

Waltz with Bashir
Ari Folman, 2009
An Israeli film on the Sabra and Chattla massacres, and the search for lost memory. An eponymous book followed.

The Gatekeepers
Dror Moreh, 2012
This documentary interviews six former heads of the Israeli security agency. They cast a very critical eye on political decisions and the capacity of successive governments to truly obtain a viable peace plan with Palestinians.

GAMES

This War of Mine
11 bit studios, 2014
Applauded by critics, this video game offers players the experience of war, not as a super soldier or general but as a civilian. Entrenched in his shelter, the player has to survive day-by-day, find water, food, and medicine, and ensure the survival of his companions in misfortune.

Valiant Hearts: The Great War
UbiSoft, 2014
Produced for the centennial commemoration of the First World War, this game, which unfolds like a comic book, lets you experience four characters facing the violence of war. Puzzles are favored over blood, and everything is accompanied by historical documents that help players to better understand what the men and women of that epoch lived through.

My Life As a Refugee and Against All Odds
These serious games let players experience what it's like to be a refugee. Will you make the right choices to survive?
www.mylifeasarefugee.org
www.playagainstallodds.ca

WEBSITES

The UN Refugee Agency
www.unhcr.org

Stockholm International Peace Research Institute (SIPRI)
www.sipri.org

IRIN
Humanitarian news and analyses throughout the world
www.irinnews.org

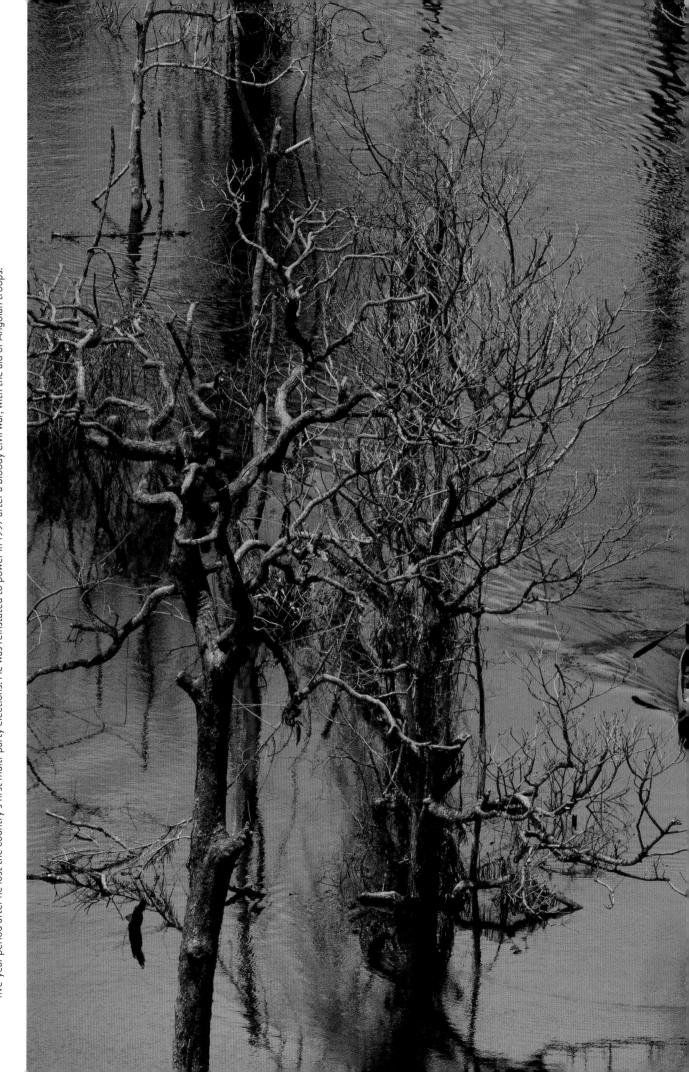

IMBOULOU DAM ON THE LÉFINI RIVER, REPUBLIC OF THE CONGO [CONGO-BRAZZAVILLE] 2° 56' S – 16° 02' E

Since the 2000s, the Congo has been reaping profits from the region's prosperity and relative calm. The country is headed by Denis Sassou-Nguesso, its president since 1979, with the exception of a five-year period after he lost the country's first multi-party elections. He was reinstated to power in 1997 after a bloody civil war, with the aid of Angolan troops.

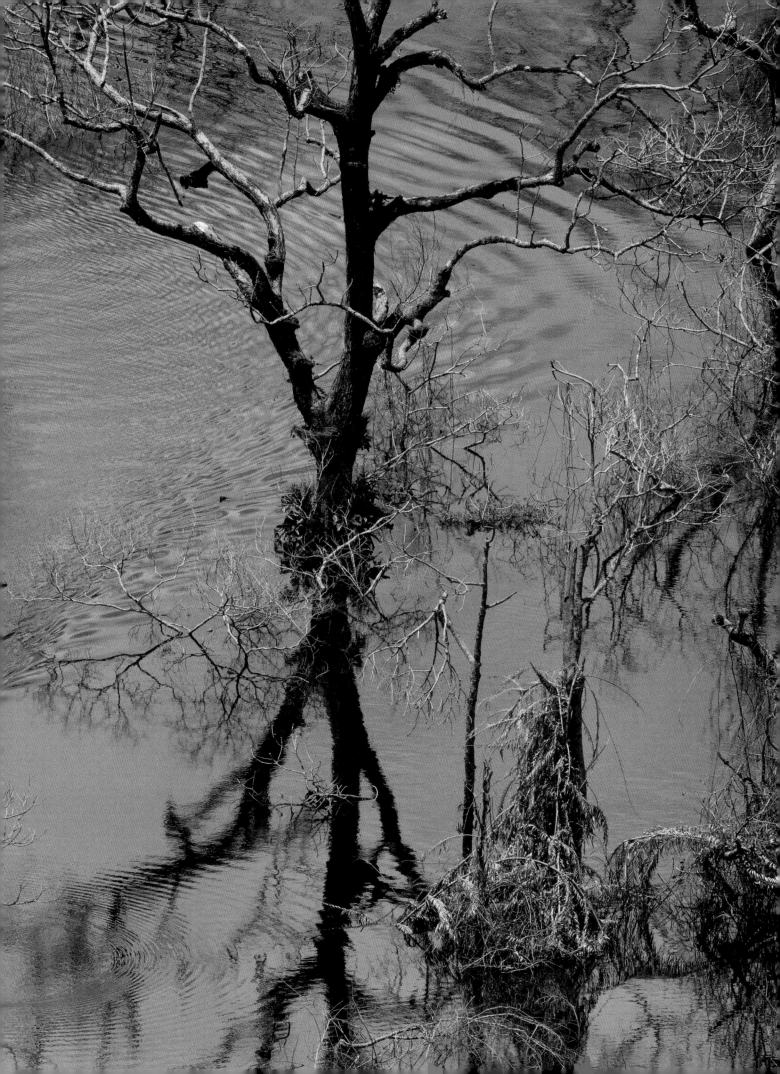

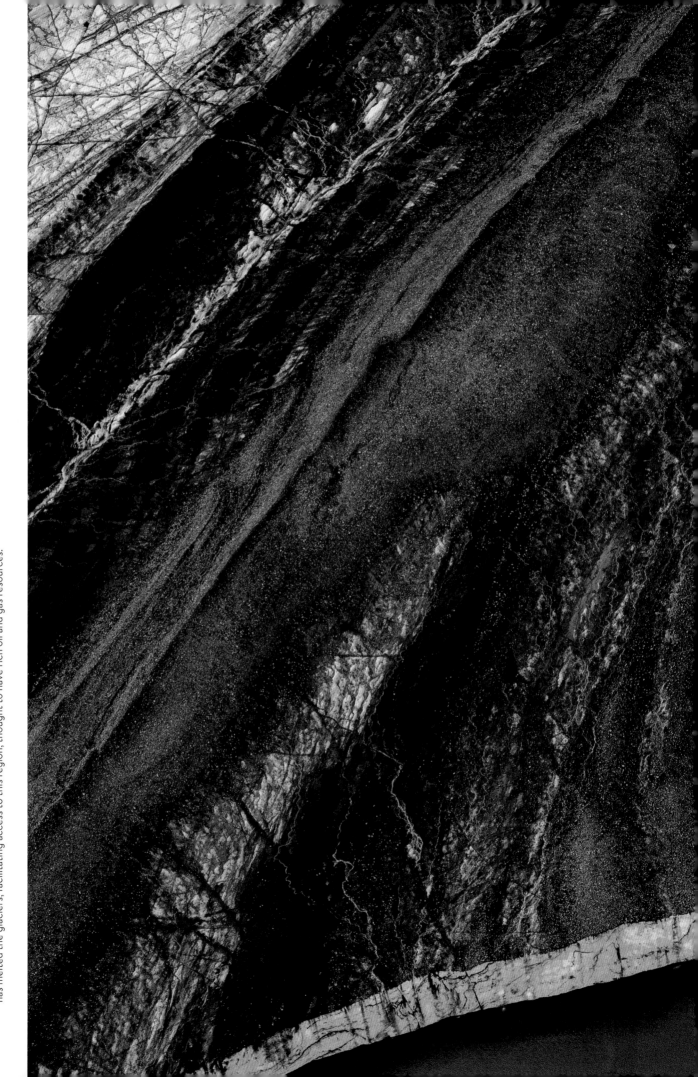

STRONGBREEN GLACIER, KVALVAGEN FJORD, SPITSBERGEN, SVALBARD, NORWAY 77° 34' N – 17° 35' E

The Svalbard archipelago, situated within the Arctic Ocean, about midway between continental Norway and the North Pole, is very sparsely populated. Glaciers cover most of the land. Climate change has melted the glaciers, facilitating access to this region, thought to have rich oil and gas resources.

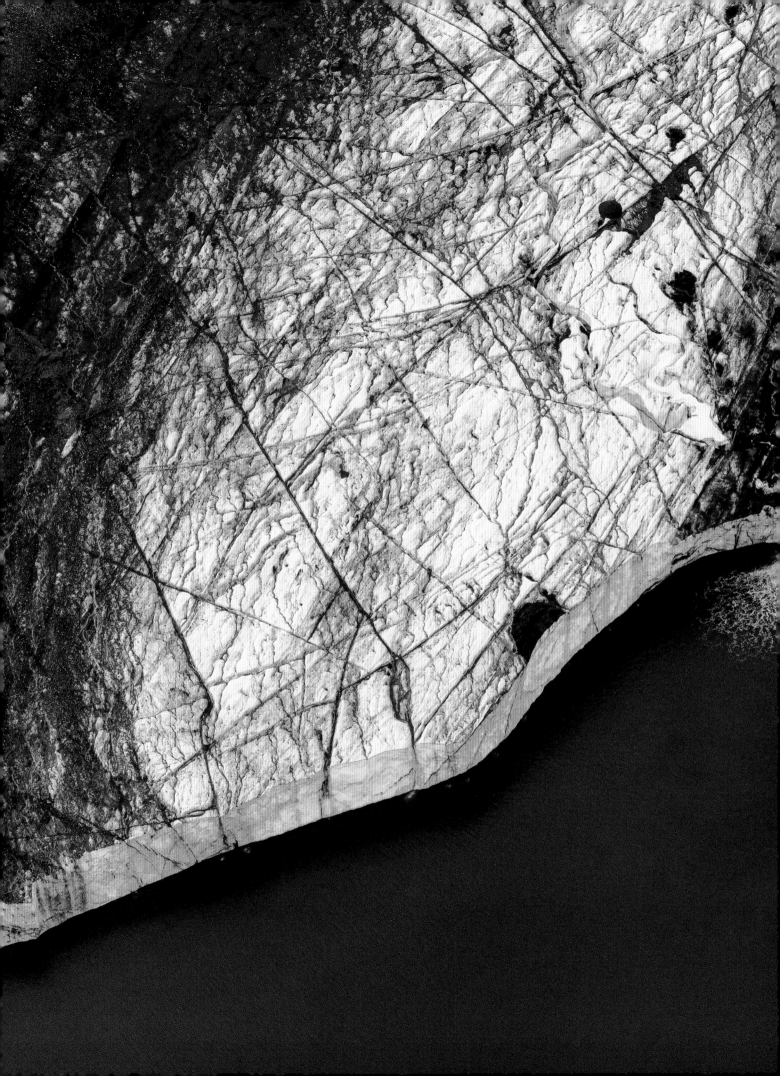

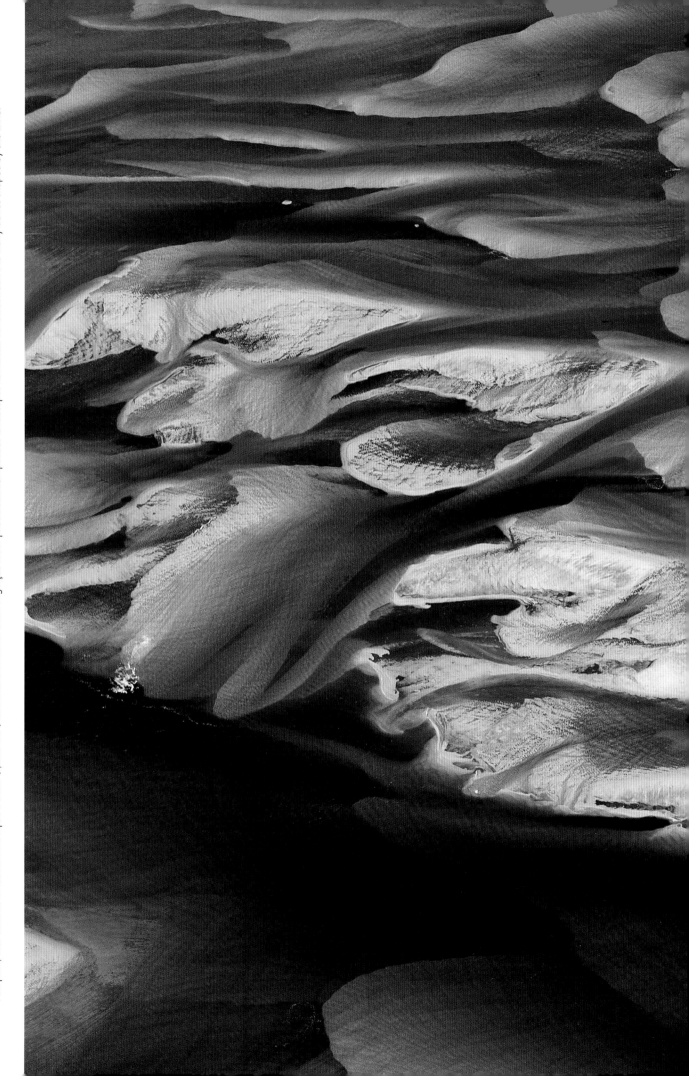

LENÇÓIS MARANHENSES NATIONAL PARK, MARANHÃO, BRAZIL 2° 32' 00 S – 43° 07' 00 W

This park, with an area of about 600 square miles (1,500 km²) between the ocean and Preguiças River provides a sumptuous landscape. Rainwater runs between the many dunes shaped by the wind.

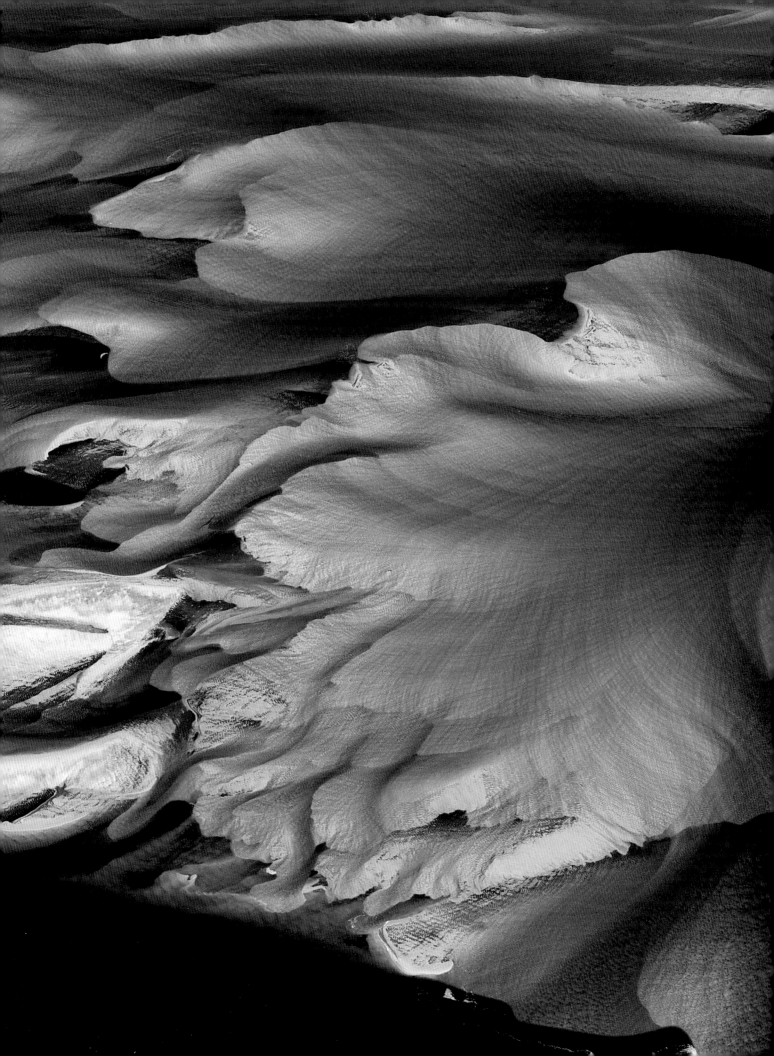

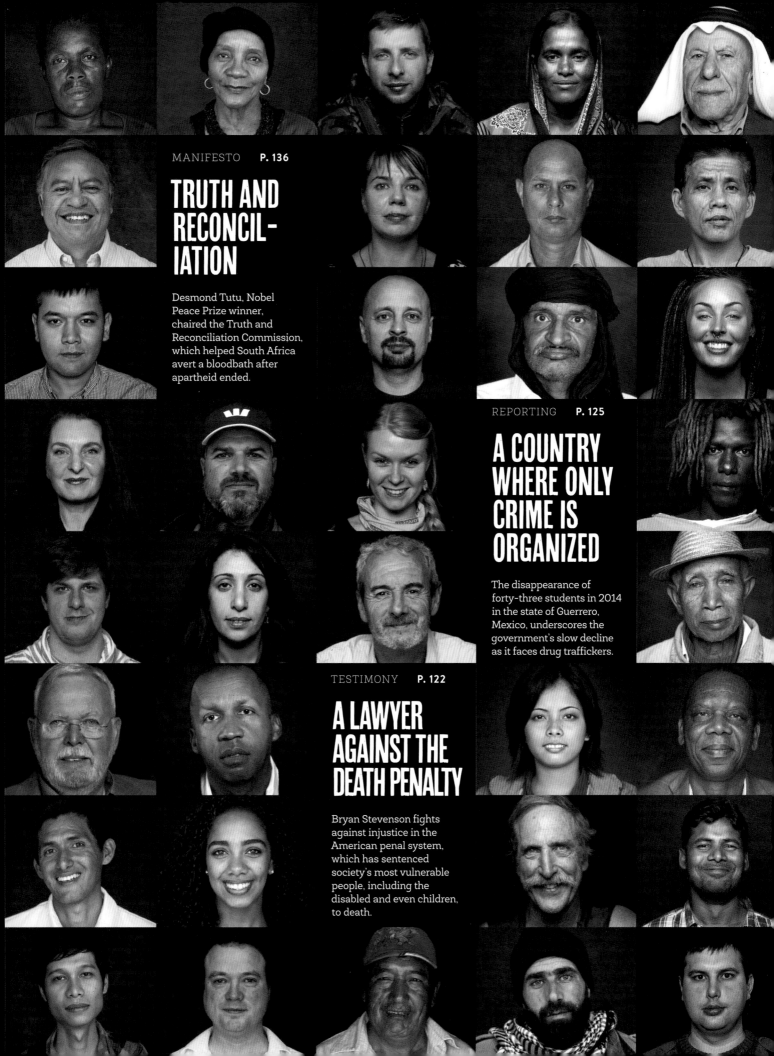

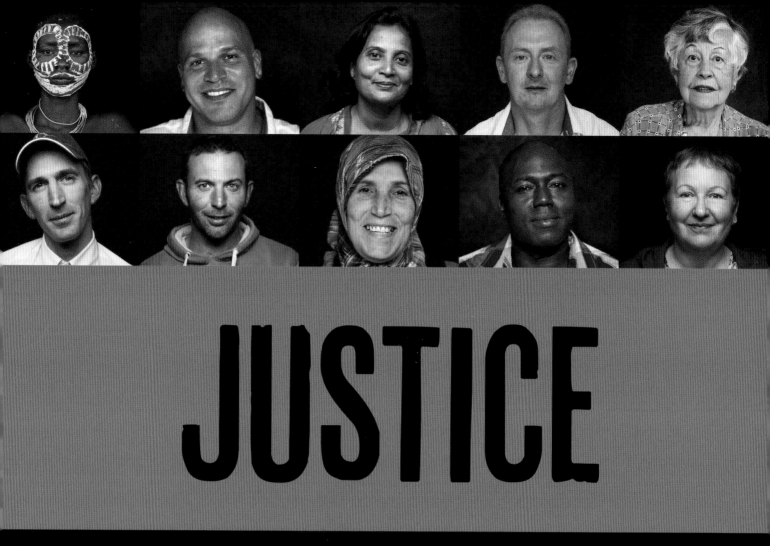

JUSTICE

When justice disappears, when it's eroded by corruption, when it strikes innocent people or protects the powerful, our ability to live together is affected. In the end, there are few ideas and few institutions that are as indispensable. But justice is not necessarily vengeful. It can heal those accused of the worst crimes and countries in their darkest hour, as examples in South Africa and beyond demonstrate.

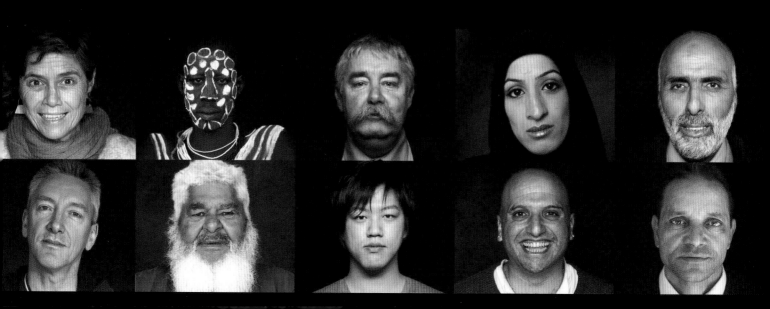

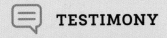
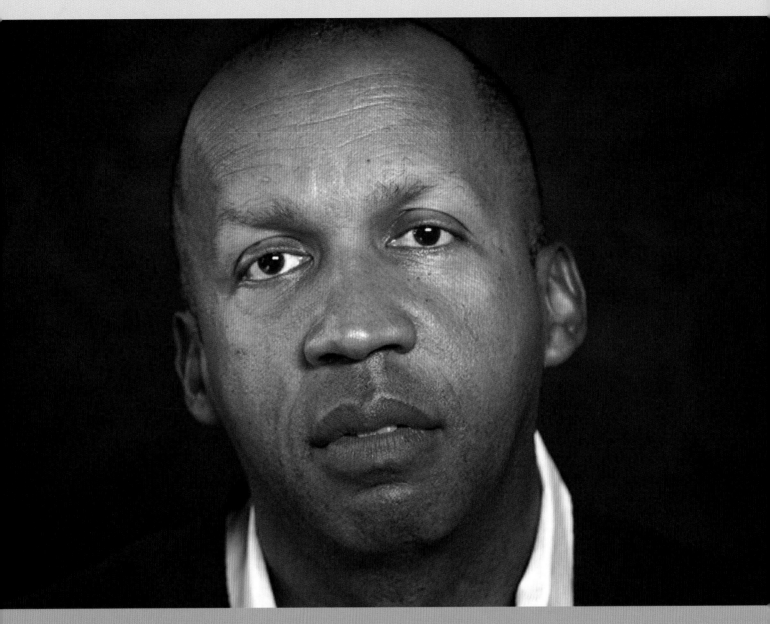

A LAWYER AGAINST THE DEATH PENALTY

BRYAN STEVENSON FIGHTS AGAINST A SYSTEM THAT KILLS THE MOST VULNERABLE INSTEAD OF HELPING THEM OUT OF THEIR PLIGHT.

A few years ago, I represented a fourteen-year-old child who had been assaulted on many occasions and who had shot the man who was abusing him. He was sent to a prison for adults and when I went to see this boy, he didn't talk and didn't answer any of my questions. I couldn't discuss anything with him until I came closer. When I leaned in toward him for a moment, he leaned in too. I placed my arm around his shoulders and he began to cry, then to talk. But not about what had happened with the man he was accused of shooting. He began talking about what had happened to him in prison. He told me that every night, he was being raped by several men and that the night before I came, he had been assaulted by more people than he could count. I listened to this boy crying his eyes out, and I was left speechless.

When I left the prison, I asked myself, "Who's responsible for this? Who did this?" And I think the answer is that we are, we did. We're all responsible. Our inability to answer to the needs of people, even people accused of crimes, while respecting their dignity and fundamental human rights, creates this kind of unjust situation.

It's what leads to the sentencing of youth to die in prison when they're only thirteen or fourteen years old. Forcing any thirteen-year-old child to die in prison is cruel! It can't be reconciled either with morality or with children's rights.

I observed the same thing with the disabled: A great number of my clients suffer from mental illnesses that have never been treated because they're poor. Punishing a disabled person—convicting and executing him or her—is, to me, cruel and barbarous, and goes against human dignity and human rights.

On this point, my work has taught me simple principles. I've defended people who have committed terrible crimes, but who have come through, who have changed—incredible people full of hope, grace, gratitude, and love. I've learned that we cannot be summed up by the bad actions we've committed: We're more than that.

I think that a person who lies can't simply be summed up as a "liar." Someone who steals is not just a thief. Even if someone kills, he or she is not simply a killer. There's a fundamental human dignity. And it must be respected through the law.

I've met many people who I could have said would maybe never get out [of prison], that they'd always be a threat to themselves or to others, but I never met someone who I could say was beyond redemption, beyond hope. And that's why I don't think we should accept the death penalty.

One of the first cases I worked on resulted in an execution. It was a matter in which we intervened at the last second because this man couldn't find a lawyer. I tried to stop the execution but every court I went to said,

> I'VE DEFENDED PEOPLE WHO HAVE COMMITTED TERRIBLE CRIMES, BUT WHO HAVE COME THROUGH, WHO HAVE CHANGED— INCREDIBLE PEOPLE FULL OF HOPE, GRACE, GRATITUDE, AND LOVE

● ● ●

● ● ● "too late." The night of the execution, I went down to be at his side.

The conversation we had is one I'll never forget. He said to me, "It was such a weird day, Bryan, it was on loop. When I woke up this morning, the guard asked me what I wanted for breakfast; at noon they came and asked me what I wanted for lunch; at night they asked me what I wanted for dinner. The whole day, people were saying, "What can I do to help you? Can I get you stamps, paper, can I bring you water? Coffee?" I'll never forget this same man confiding in the final minutes of his life, "Bryan, more people asked me what they could do for me in these past fourteen hours than in the first nineteen years of my life."

Holding his hand, I couldn't help but wonder, "But where were they, those people, when you were three years old and being abused? Where were they when you were seven and being sexually abused? Where were they when you were nine, ten years old and getting hooked on drugs? Where were they when you were fourteen, when you were homeless, wandering the streets not knowing where to go?" As all these questions filled my mind, this man was brought to the electric chair to be executed.

There was no doubt; I'm convinced of it, that we were doing something that was profoundly immoral, profoundly unjust, and profoundly against human dignity and human rights

The death penalty is the destruction of a very important human course, one that brings us closer to one another and leads us to compassion and understanding. It's the elimination of a new bit of road towards the destination, which, I think, we must reach and which is this: more justice, more gratitude, more compassion.

On this path, I was influenced by my grandmother, who was the matriarch of our family. She was the daughter of people who had been made slaves, and she always pushed us to believe in something. I was a little boy, and if I went out or if I was hanging out with kids she thought I shouldn't be hanging out with, she would say to me, "Bryan, watch out! People will judge you based on the people you're with." My grandmother died a long time ago but if I could tell her something today, I'd tell her this: "I've been lucky enough to find myself alongside very impressive people, really incredible, really considerate people, but I've also been lucky enough to be alongside people who, even though they had been convicted, had a heap of hope in them. People who, even though they had been incarcerated, showed great compassion. People who, even though they had been wounded by different kinds of abuse, by violence and discrimination, had great love. These people are my community, these are the people I spend time with." I'd tell my grandmother, "I hope you're right, Mama, that people will judge me based on the people around me, because there's no one better in my mind to be with than them: the convicted, the bullied, the abused, people who try and try again, who continue to seek out redemption, to seek out justice."

> ## AS ALL THESE QUESTIONS FILLED MY MIND, THIS MAN WAS BROUGHT TO THE ELECTRIC CHAIR TO BE EXECUTED

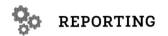

A COUNTRY WHERE ONLY CRIME IS ORGANIZED

By Alejandro Almazán
First published in the *Gatopardo*, December 2014

The brutal disappearance of forty-three students on September 26, 2014, caught the attention of the world, casting a sinister light upon the state of Guerrero in Mexico. And yet, violence, drug trafficking, corruption, and legal system failures have a long history there. Alejandro Almazán, a journalist and novelist, won the Gabriel García Márquez Award for his reports on drug trafficking. In this excerpt from his December 2014 *Gatopardo* article, he recounts his experience of going to Guerrero to meet the ordinary people who have to live with extreme lawlessness every day.

In Chilpancingo [the capital of the state of Guerrero] half the stores have been forced out of business, and 70 percent of businesses close at 7:00 p.m. A dozen currency exchange offices have been closed by court order; they've been laundering drug money for two or three years now. The drug dealers own 250 taxi licenses, awarded by the state government, and 120 garbage trucks belong to criminal organizations. The operators have to turn over the equivalent of 10 percent of work costs to elected officials and to drug dealers. About three hundred well-off families have fled the city. Three hundred houses have been put up for sale, but only two of them have actually been sold. In order to avoid being kidnapped and in order to be able to work, a bar owner has to pay out 3,500 pesos per week, a hardware store owner 5,000 [10 pesos = $0.65]. Organized crime receives fifty pesos for every pig sold to a slaughterhouse. It demands twenty-five pesos per day

from taxi drivers. In Iguala, criminals can demand up to twenty thousand pesos per month from a jewelry store owner, simply to leave him alone. Twenty thousand farmers lose 50 percent of their social subsidies and half the return from their harvests to organized crime. Drug dealers demand two pesos per chicken from the poultry farmer and fifty centavos for each slaughter.

Initially, I jotted down every figure furnished by Jaime Nava, president of the Employers Confederation of the Republic of Mexico (Coparmex) at Chilpancingo. I stopped when he tells me that the only economic sectors that have prospered since the increase of violence in Guerrero were private security services and money lenders. The former owe their success to abductions, protection rackets, and robbery. The latter make their living from the results: People go into debt to pay a ransom, to pay the weekly extortion fees demanded by the mafia, or simply to move away. Nava laments,

"Two years ago there were five pawn shops in Chilpancingo. Today there are more than sixty." He tells me that he owns a printing company and that in the fifteen years he has owned it he has never produced as many signs with words such as "For Sale," "For Rent," and "For Sublet" as he does today.

I remark, "The funeral business must also be doing pretty well."

"Oh that. That always does well. That's why I didn't even bother mentioning it."

During these last ten years Guerrero has been a death machine: 14,518 people have been murdered, according to National Public Safety statistics....

I met Javier Monroy in 2010. At the time, assassins were watching his house on the outskirts of Chilpancingo. Today he tells me that the Templarios or Knights Templar, the cartel from Michoacán that sells drugs in Guerrero as easily as oranges, abducted him a few months ago and brought him to one of their bosses. Javier told me: "He wanted me to help him clean up his reputation. Can you believe that?" To tell the truth, I could hardly imagine the scene.

Javier is an activist. For twenty years now he has directed the Community Development Workshop (Tadeco), an organization that over the years has become an itinerant legal aid bureau that deals with cases of disappearance, abduction, and murder that have occurred in Guerrero.

The activists began to work on such cases in March 2007, after the abduction of one of their colleagues, Gabriel Cerón. Gabriel was an architect and was about to get married. In order to save money to pay for the wedding, he had designed architectural plans for Francisco Cortés, a protected witness, who had always been a member of the mafia. When Gabriel went to deliver his plans to Cortés, the police took them both away. Since then, Tadeco has built a small tent in the main square of Chilpancingo, where hundreds of people from all the communities of the state come to tell Javier their terrible stories.

It was from this moment that threats began to rain down upon him....

"One day, someone called to tell me that I should buy my coffin," Javier said.

"Who do you think it was?"

"Tadeco disturbs the authorities of Guerrero, the military leaders, the local elites, and the drug mafia. It could have been any one of them. We have accused all of them of these forced disappearances."...

The Missing Persons Committee of Guerrero lists more than 6,500 victims of forced disappearance or of murder between 2005 and December 2013. Tadeco has dealt with six hundred cases during approximately the same period....

On one of the hills that surround Iguala...I ask an elderly farmer about when things began to go down the drain in Guerrero. "Well now, you're a bit late," he answers. There's no trace of reproach in his voice, but I still feel the need to excuse myself. He's right: We're all coming to this really late, all of us, except for crime. As always, crime was the first to arrive.

DURING THESE LAST TEN YEARS GUERRERO HAS BEEN A DEATH MACHINE: 14,518 PEOPLE HAVE BEEN MURDERED

Crime perhaps arrived in Guerrero during the 1970s, when Alberto Sicilia Falcón, a Cuban drug dealer, entered an alliance with army officers to manage the production of marijuana and heroin poppies. Today 60 percent of Mexican heroin production is concentrated in Guerrero. Crime perhaps also arrived with politicians who thought the state was their own personal property (I'm referring to the Figueroas, the family that governs Guerrero and today controls the fertilizer trade). Maybe it arrived on January 1, 2001, the day the Torres and the Arizmendis, two groups that controlled a large part of the drug traffic in Guerrero, killed each other near Acapulco....

Maybe crime arrived in November 2009, on the day when Commandant Ramiro of the ERPI [Revolutionary Army of the Insurgent People] was assassinated by paramilitaries on the payroll of the army and the federal government. Ramiro was famous for organizing the people, carrying out community projects, and standing up to the drug cartels. Or maybe crime arrived a month later, in December, on the day that Arturo Beltrán Leyva was killed by the Mexican Navy. His cartel, which enjoyed hegemony in Guerrero,

162 MILLION

BETWEEN 162 AND 324 MILLION PEOPLE USED AN ILLEGAL DRUG AT LEAST ONCE IN 2011.

broke up into two groups, the Reds and the United Warriors.

Maybe crime arrived on the day that the political parties decided to support any candidate who could afford to pay for his own campaign, such as José Luis Abarca, the former mayor of Iguala who was indicted for the abduction of forty-three students from a rural teachers' college. He was not the first such candidate, nor will he be the last. Or maybe crime arrived on the day when drug traffickers began to infiltrate the municipal police forces. In Iguala, for example, Abarca's brothers-in-law, the local bosses of the United Warriors drug cartel, controlled the police and even created an antikidnapping unit, which they called Los Bélicos (the warriors)....

Crime could have arrived at any one of these moments, but it had taken me all this time to come. "Forgive me," I said to the elderly farmer before I went on my way....

A scrap dealer in Chilpancingo says that drug dealers kidnapped his twelve-year-old son and are forcing him to operate as a lookout. A fellow journalist tells me about his brother, who was kidnapped in 2012. A young entrepreneur tells me he never drives the luxury 4x4 he bought six months earlier. In Zumpango, a woman tells me she frequently sees trucks drive

A WOMAN TELLS ME SHE FREQUENTLY SEES TRUCKS DRIVE BY, FILLED WITH CORPSES

by, filled with corpses.... And in Iguala I saw the army, the federal police, and local police dramatically take over the entire town.

I'm at the point where I wonder if there's any hope in all this barbarism. I've gone in search of that hope with the members of the Union of Peoples and Organizations of Guerrero State (UPOEG). They arrived in Iguala at the beginning of October to search for the forty-three students whom the police and the hired killers of the United Warriors had caused to disappear on September 26, 2014.

The UPOEG is a group that splintered away from the Regional Coordinating Body of Community Authorities (CRAC), an indigenous group created in 1999 to protect villages from the drug cartels, the military, the police, and paramilitary forces. Members of CRAC say that the UPOEG is an armed force of the state of Guerrero, and that one of its directors, Plácido Valerio, is connected to the former governor, Ángel Aguirre. "We've accepted that the government provides us with weapons, radio transmitters, trucks and uniforms, but we're not on its payroll," Crisóforo García, another leader of the UPOEG, assures me. I let him continue because one shouldn't nourish too much hope in a state like Guerrero:

Ayutla was a real mess: the police protected the criminals; the criminals abducted our wives and daughters. The soldiers and police made people disappear; the farmers' land was confiscated in order to grow heroin poppies on it. A mess. It's the same situation at Tierra Colorada, at Tecoanapa, and in the Ocotito Valley. The population organized quickly, we had experience from the CRAC, and we started acting as the police ourselves. We were born on January 4, 2013. In Ayutla, we arrested 53 criminals within two months. We turned them all over to the legal system, which then set them all free again. That's why, when we catch a criminal now, we rehabilitate him ourselves. He's convicted to a sentence of between six months and five years of labor for the public welfare. Many of those we rehabilitated still live among us; they've become

THE FAILURE OF THE WAR ON DRUGS

Many countries have become involved in the war on drugs. The Single Convention on Narcotic Drugs was adopted in 1961 and has been signed or ratified by 154 countries. Between 1991 and 2000, the United Nations observed the Decade Against Drug Abuse. But the efficacy of these initiatives is in doubt. The United Nations Office on Drugs and Crime estimated that as of 2012, for example, between 162 million and 324 million people used an illegal drug in the previous year.

The U.S. Drug Enforcement Administration (DEA), whose annual budget exceeds $2 billion, intervenes in many countries and regions, including Afghanistan, where opium culture has been on the rise since the fall of the Taliban in 2001, and the Andean region, where cocaine is produced. But these means remain derisory in comparison to what drug trafficking brings in worldwide: some $300 billion per year! And these sums enrich powerful mafias. In 2009, it is estimated that the cocaine produced in the Andes alone commanded $85 billion, only $1 billion of which reached the growers. The rest went into the traffickers' pockets.

More and more countries are passing legislation to decriminalize or authorize soft drugs such as cannabis. What's more, in 2014, the Organization of American States, observing that the war on drugs waged by the United States was harming their interests, passed a resolution calling for new strategies to fight narcotrafficking. Among the avenues to be explored are the legalization of unlawful substances and the classification of drugs as no longer a matter of criminal justice but of public health. These questions will be debated in 2016 during a special session of the United Nations General Assembly on the World Drug Problem.

good people. You see, for example, a kid who turned himself in voluntarily. He told us that he had killed people, so the elders spoke with him. Today he's here helping people....

On that day, in Iguala, the people from the UPOEG climbed up a hill called Loma del Zapatero. There, they found six common graves, two of which were ready to be used. They wanted to dig but had only a single shovel with them. "This damned government. If they wanted to find those students, they would give us a hand. But they won't even lend us any shovels," Crisóforo complains.

Then an old man arrives with a shovel and a trowel. "My son was killed by the Iguala police. They shot him down—just like that—at the school entrance. But at the trial they claimed it was done by a paid killer who was later killed himself during a showdown.... That's why I'm here because if I help find those students, I'll be helping to serve justice," the old man explains before starting to dig....

Ultimately, the UPOEG would open up three of four common graves. They find sandals, a glove, and something that Crisóforo says is a knuckle bone. At this point, I can hardly describe

ONE DAY,
SOMEONE
CALLED TO TELL
ME THAT
I SHOULD BUY
MY COFFIN

PRINCIPAL AREAS OF CARTEL INFLUENCE

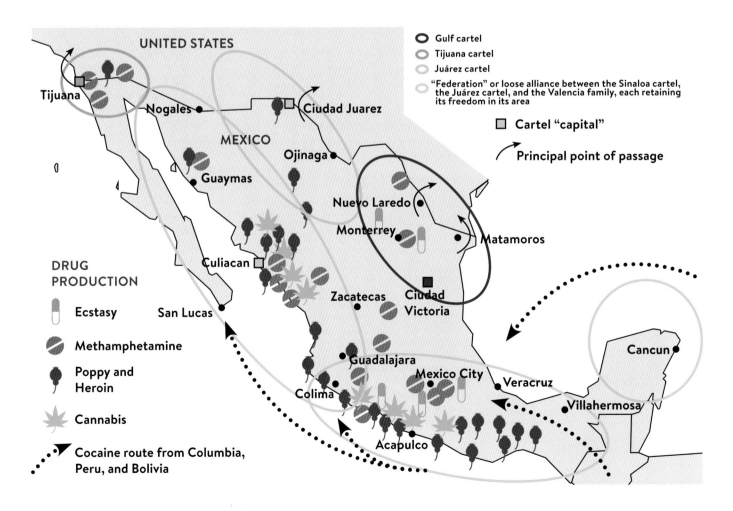

what the odor was like, but it impregnated my clothing and my hair for the entire day.

Eighty residents of a hamlet in the municipality of Teloloapan live in the small reception hall called "Calipso," not far from the center of Chilpancingo. They arrived in the state capital nine months ago after receiving an ultimatum: "If you don't get out, we'll take your daughters."…Two women approach us and make accusations against the drug dealers, the military, and the police. "They want our land to plant drugs," one of them protests.

A few minutes later, at the door of the Calipso, I find myself surrounded by women and children. At their request, I don't write down their names, but I do listen to their stories. "In the mountains you can't go around alone anymore. They do things to us. That's why we always accompany each other, so that there's always someone who can run and get help."

"Up there in the mountains, there are shoot-outs all the time. They last a long time and the authorities don't even bother going," says another woman.…

A young man interrupts: "The mafia strips us of everything: our lives, our animals, our food. When the mafiosi are hungry our wives have to cook for them. And what happens after that? The other mafiosi, the guys from the other camp show up, and they knock you around because you gave food to the other bastards."

Last August [2014] the Guerrero State Secretariat for Public Safety and Civil Protection counted a total of 2,897 persons who had been displaced because of violence between January 2013 and July 2014. According to the Quadratín Guerrero, which had made its own calculation, more than four thousand persons had been forced to leave their villages between July 2013 and July 2014. The majority came from the region of Tierra Caliente, like the eighty displaced persons being sheltered in the Calipso.…

An elderly taxi driver from Tixtla complains about the lack of customers and blames the students from Ayotzinapa for it. A customer representative of the Bancomer Agency, located on the main plaza of Chilpancingo, tells me that no one is setting foot in the bank anymore because of all the teachers who are camped out on the plaza. She has to contact her customers by telephone to suggest mortgage loans or credit cards in order to fill her monthly quota. And in Iguala a merchant endowed with an extraordinary capacity for indifference tells me the vanished students were agitators.

THE MEXICO OF WEAPONS FEARS THOSE WHO TEACH PEOPLE HOW TO READ

I wanted to make everyone I spoke to understand that the disappearance of the forty-three students represented a breaking point in Mexico. I believe I told them that we could recover our dignity, that the government had always criminalized teacher colleges.…that students are young, that they're the children of peasants, and that they're on our side.

But I digress. I just want to say a few words about the students of Ayotzinapa.

MEXICO: THE DEGENERATION OF THE STATE

The disappearance of forty-three students in 2014 is perhaps the event in recent years most covered by the media in the war between Mexican drug-trafficking gangs and the federal state. And it is a genuine war that is being waged. Between 2006 and 2012, an estimated fifty thousand people were killed.

The conflict took on a military dimension when Mexican president Felipe Calderón (whose six-year mandate ended in 2012) entrusted the army with the mission to put an end to the criminal activities of gangs. But the task has proved more difficult than predicted: Heads of cartels who are arrested or killed are quickly replaced, and the elimination of one criminal group makes room for another.

The violence has assumed massive proportions. In addition to the thousands of civilians killed and kidnapped by the cartels, violence has increased on the military side. According to an Amnesty International 2012 report, *The State of the World's Human Rights*, the Mexican human rights commission has received more than two thousand complaints of human rights violations committed by the Mexican army. It further revealed that 8,898 bodies housed in morgues across the country have yet to be identified and that 5,397 people have been reported missing since 2006.

The Mexican novelist and journalist Juan Villoro wrote in *El País* on October 30, 2014:

A literate culture is a provocation, an act of defiance, in a region where conflicts are settled with firearms. In the 1960s two-thirds of the population of Guerrero was illiterate. The teachers training college of Ayotzinapa was created in order to help overcome this backwardness, but it could not remain indifferent to ills that were even worse: social inequalities, the power of the elites, the corruption of local authorities, the idea of repression as the sole answer to discontent, the impunity of the police and the growing penetration and presence of the drug traffic.... The teachers training college is a center of opposition and protest.... On September 26 there were four separate shootings but only one target: the young. With the help of organized crime, Mayor José Luis Abarca sowed terror so as to frighten the students who had mobilized to honor the memory of the victims of the massacre of Tlatelolco (a student demonstration that was bloodily suppressed in 1968). Once the machine of repression began to roll, a soccer team was sprayed with bullets. The team's crime? It was made up of youngsters, in other words, potential rebels.... Che Guevara spent his last night in a rural school. Already wounded, he read a sentence written on the blackboard and said to the teacher: "It's missing the accent mark." The sentence was "Yo sé leer" (I know how to read). Knowing he had been defeated, the guerrilla turned to another way to correct reality.... Forty-three future teachers have vanished. The dimension of the tragedy revolves around a single phrase that is opposed to impunity, disgrace and injustice: "I know how to read." The Mexico of weapons fears those who teach people how to read. This country lacks an accent mark. The time is coming when it will have to be added.

Felipe Arnulfo Rosa speaks Tu'un Savi, a variant of the Mixtec language. He's learning Spanish. He works as a day laborer in his village, Rancho Ocoapa, in the municipality of Ayutla. He wants to continue his studies, so he divides his days between fieldwork and school. He passes the entrance exam for the teacher training college at Ayotzinapa. He wants to earn a teaching diploma with a bilingual intercultural specialization. There are only forty spots. He is accepted.... One day he goes to take up a collection with his first-year colleagues. They're shot at. They disappear.

Dominga Rosa, Felipe's mother, doesn't speak Spanish, but Kau, a fellow journalist from Chilpancingo, serves as translator on the morning of October 30. "If I haven't dreamed about him, it's because he's still alive," Doña Dominga tells me via Kau. "The worry is killing me. Down there, in the village, the corn field has been abandoned because, without Felipe, what's the point?"

Doña Dominga is sitting at one end of the basketball court at the teacher training college. Since the disappearance of the students, this spot has become the epicenter of absence:

Parents spend hours there waiting for news, but they hear nothing.

Doña Dominga doesn't understand why the federal government has been unable to find Felipe and the other forty-two students. "They're hiding something from us," Kau translates. "I'm going back to the village for All Saints' Day and I'll ask my older brother to bring back Felipe."

"Your older brother is dead?" Kau asks my question. They talk for a moment, then Kau says: "He was killed two years ago. He was heading to the sugarcane fields when he was attacked. He died on the spot."...

Until a few days ago, the United Warriors were tyrannizing Cocula. But this is not a triumph. They preferred to leave the city because the municipal landfill has become world news. If you believe the federal government, that's where they burned the bodies of the forty-three students.

"When everyone has left, the mafia will come back," a man who wants to stay anonymous says to me. "This

516,000

THE LAND CULTIVATED TO GROW POPPIES FOR OPIUM EXCEEDED 516,000 ACRES (209,000 HECTARES) IN 2013.

has been going on for years, the violence, the rackets, the robberies. But last year I understood that things had reached the point of no return with the abduction of seventeen young people in one night."

That occurred on July 30, 2013. An armed group raided three locations. Among those kidnapped were two high school graduates and three women. No trace of them has been found, even though people in Cocula say the girls reappeared but left to live elsewhere.

A month earlier they tried to ambush the mayor, César Peñalosa. He managed to escape the attack. Six months before that, in November 2012, they murdered Tomás Biviano, who had just been appointed director of the municipal police.

"Cocula fell apart from one day to the next," I was told by the wife of the man whose name I can't give. "Shootings, kidnappings, disappearances. Everything that happened at Iguala also happened at Cocula, and worse things still. I'm an engineer and I work at the Nuevo Balsas mine. I quit because the mafia was demanding up to half of the workers' salaries. I opened a store here but I had to close again due to extortion."

Later, in the square in front of a church, I come across four women who have attached a banner showing the faces of four men to the church entrance. They're three professors and a young man. They were arrested and beaten up by the federal police, who are trying to implicate the men in the disappearance of the students.

"These are our loved ones. Some of them were arrested at a police roadblock, others were taken at home," one of the women tells me. She tells me the whole story of police abuse and when she's done I ask her to talk to me about violence in Cocula. "No, sir," she replies. "The village is peaceful. I don't understand why people say the students were brought here."...

It's almost midnight when I hail a taxi. "The bus station," I tell the driver, but he isn't listening to me. "I'm not myself," he apologizes. "I just dropped off a woman. I drove her all over the place to collect money but then I made her get out." I had no idea what he was talking about until he told me the story from the beginning. The woman owned a clothing shop and her husband, a high school teacher, had been kidnapped. The woman had to collect one hundred thousand pesos to prevent her husband from being tortured, and two hundred thousand more to get him released. "She wanted me to take her to pay the ransom," the driver told me. "Would you have gone with her?" he asks. "I don't think so," I tell him and immediately am ashamed of myself. And that's exactly why I had to tell the story.

> THE WOMAN HAD TO COLLECT ONE HUNDRED THOUSAND PESOS TO PREVENT HER HUSBAND FROM BEING TORTURED, AND TWO HUNDRED THOUSAND MORE TO GET HIM RELEASED

AN ORGANIZED CRIME EXPERT

In 2013, Alejandro Almazán received the prestigious Gabriel García Márquez award in journalism for a report published by the magazine *Gatopardo* on drug traffickers in the La Laguna region of northern Mexico. Almazán, who had always wanted to report on organized crime, has worked with the daily newspapers *Reforma* and *El Universal* and is one of the founders of the newspaper *Milenio*. In 2012, Almazán published a novel, *El más buscado*, inspired by the story of Joaquín Guzmán, the drug lord known as El Chapo. *Gatopardo*, which published the award-winning article, was founded in 2000 and is distributed throughout Latin America. *Gatopardo* features long investigative reports authored by the best journalists on the continent, including Alma Guillermoprieto and Ernesto Sábato (1911–2011), both from Argentina. The monthly magazine was originally based in Bogotá, Colombia, but moved its headquarters to Mexico City in 2006.

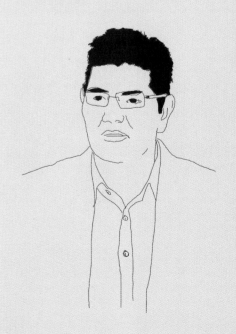

MARKET IN THE NEIGHBORHOOD OF XOCHIMILCO, MEXICO CITY, MEXICO 19° 27' N – 99° 16' W

More than twenty million people live in the Mexico City metropolitan area. The Xochimilco market is one of the most famous in Mexico City, which is the political and economic capital of Mexico.

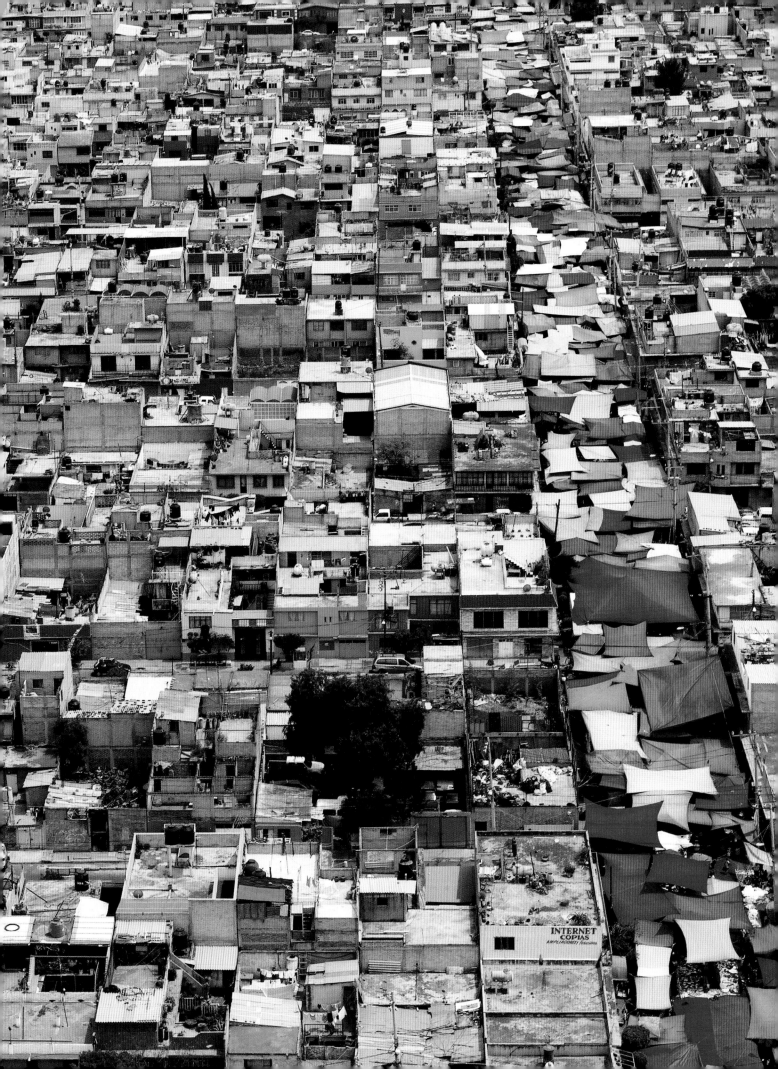

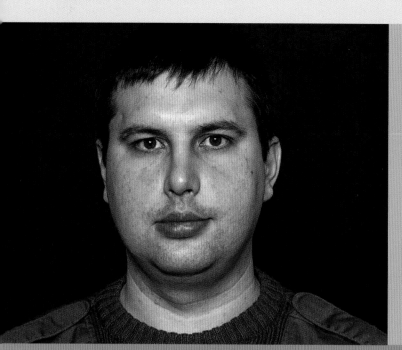

FREEDOM GAINED

SERGEY EXPLAINS WHY HE JOINED THE MAIDAN REVOLUTION IN THE UKRAINE.

I participated in the revolution in the Ukraine from day one. Why? Because I could no longer answer the questions my son was asking me. He is very young, but he sees everything. He asked me, for example: "Why did that policeman ask us for money even though we didn't do anything wrong? Why are old, retired people begging on the street or picking up empty bottles for the deposit?" And I didn't know how to answer him. I didn't know how to explain to him why I always carried a knife on me or why the streets were dangerous. So, when the revolution started, I decided to participate so that I could answer my son and tell him why things were the way they were.

At the beginning of the revolution, in November 2013, when I arrived on Maidan Nezalezhnosti [Independence Square], I noticed that a great many people thought as I did. Despite the cheerful ambiance, despite the music and concerts, people looked serious. You could read on the signs and in the eyes of protesters the message, "We've had enough!" Everyone was ready for change, any kind of change.

When the clashes began on Maidan Nezalezhnosti, we were scared. We saw more and more special forces in front of us. Elite riot police could be hiding anywhere on the rooftops of the big buildings surrounding the square. Anyone could become their target, and it was terrifying. The wounded and dead were generally not sent to the hospital, and if they were taken way, it was to forests, prisons, parking lots, where they would be made to disappear, temporarily or forever.

Now that the revolution is over, I feel free. Before, we considered the police our enemies. Now, we have taught them a big lesson, and some even bear the Ukrainian flag: They're with the people. We've changed our opinion of them, because now they're at our service; they work for us. For example, yesterday, I saw a police officer in the street who had thrown his cigarette butt on the ground even though there was a garbage can right next to him. I was in a hurry and didn't have time to say something this time, but I will next time, and every time I have to. Because I now understand that they're men just like us, even if they wear a uniform; they're not prison guards. And they have come to understand that, too, and that's freedom.

> ## NOW THAT THE REVOLUTION IS OVER, I FEEL FREE

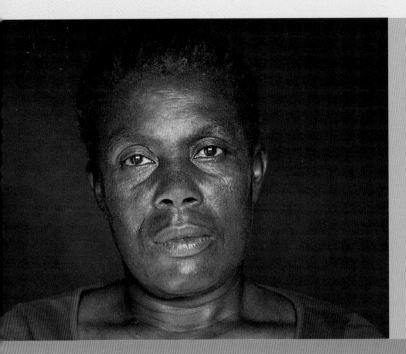

IMPUNITY FOR THE RICH

LUCIA'S EMPLOYER VIOLATED HER TWO DAUGHTERS AND MANAGED TO ESCAPE JUSTICE IN THE DOMINICAN REPUBLIC.

I live in complete desolation. Every day, when I wake up and think about my life, my head pounds. Life is impossible here. I think about it when I go to bed; I think about it when I wake up. What I'm living only God can understand.

Imagine that you are a woman, a mother, and that your circumstances have forced you to immigrate to the Dominican Republic. Imagine that the man who employs you sends you to work so that he can rape your two children. One of my young ones has already given birth; she's fourteen. The other is getting ready to give birth, and she's only thirteen. So there is my suffering. This man is a criminal. The biggest criminal there is in the world. His name is Juancho.

As it would be for any mother in the world, this terrible crime has been very painful. Imagine: You're already poor and then your employer leaves you with two additional children to take of. You find yourself twice as deep in poverty. When you think about that, a pain rises and the tears in your eyes never dry.

And when you file a report with the police, this man pays them 10,000 pesos and they tell me he's not around. And I go back again and again, and it's always the same thing until I don't have any more money for the transportation. The judge tells me, "The accused isn't here, he's moved abroad." That's a lie. He paid a bribe, and I wasn't served justice. My children's lives are ruined.

And there's no justice for me, because I'm Haitian. Because they say, "Haitians are dogs." Is this a life for us Haitians to live in Santo Domingo? No. But ever since I returned [to Haiti], I have had no father, no mother. I don't have anyone.

When I think about my children, about the situation they were in and about how they're spending their lives, my pain is endless; it brings tears to my eyes. I am constantly in pain, a pain that torments me. When I get to thinking about my life, I think it would have been better to die, to be done with it. And if there really is a God, then my death will be a deliverance.

So, when we're no longer here, I'd like for those coming after to not have to live in this poverty. I'd like you to hear us, to understand us, so that when we're not here anymore, when we're dead, our children can live a better life; I'd like your heart to be touched, so that in the future, the circumstances of the poorest change.

> ## THERE'S NO JUSTICE FOR ME, BECAUSE I'M HAITIAN

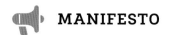
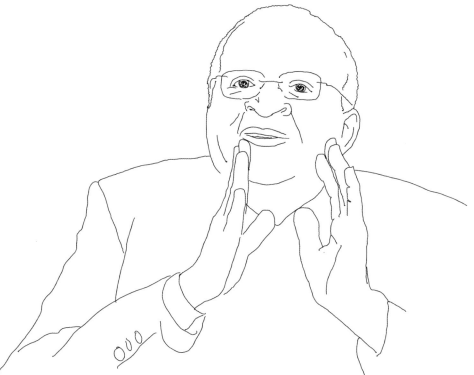

LET AFRICA SHOW THE WORLD HOW TO FORGIVE

DESMOND TUTU

Adapted from his speech at his acceptance of an honorary Doctorate of Laws degree, University of Toronto, 2000

Archbishop Desmond Tutu, winner of the 1984 Nobel Peace Prize, was chair of South Africa's Truth and Reconciliation Commission. This article was adapted from the speech he gave at the University of Toronto upon the receipt of an honorary doctoral degree.

If you asked even the most sober students of South African affairs what they thought was going to happen to South Africa a few years ago, almost universally they predicted that the most ghastly catastrophe would befall us; that as sure as anything, we would be devastated by a comprehensive bloodbath. It did not happen. Instead, the world watched with amazement, indeed awe, at the long lines of South Africans of all races, snaking their way to their polling booths on April 27, 1994. And they thrilled as they witnessed Nelson Mandela being inaugurated as the first democratically elected president of South Africa on May 10, 1994. Nearly everyone described what they were witnessing—a virtually bloodless, reasonably peaceful transition from injustice and oppression to freedom and democracy—as a miracle.

When the disaster did not overtake us, there were those who said, "Wait until a black-led government takes over. Then these blacks who have suffered so grievously in the past will engage in the most fearful orgy of revenge and retribution against the whites."

Well, that prediction too was not fulfilled. Instead the world saw something quite unprecedented. They saw the process of the Truth and Reconciliation Commission, when perpetrators of some of the most gruesome atrocities were given amnesty in exchange for a full disclosure of the facts of the offence. Instead of revenge and retribution, this new nation chose to tread the difficult path of confession, forgiveness, and reconciliation.

We South Africans have not done too badly. It is sometimes said of newly democratic countries that their first elections too frequently end up being their last. Well, we have already had a fairly uneventful second general election and have witnessed the transition from a charismatic, first democratically elected president, Nelson Mandela, to the more pragmatic, pipe-smoking Thabo Mbeki. The turmoil and instability that many feared would accompany these crucial events have not occurred. Why? Well, first, you have prayed for us and, if miracles had to happen anywhere, South Africa was a prime site for a miracle.

WITHOUT FORGIVENESS THERE IS NO FUTURE

And we have been richly blessed to have had at such a critical time in our history a Nelson Mandela. He was imprisoned for twenty-seven years; most expected that when he emerged, he would be riddled with a lust for retribution. But the world has been amazed; instead of spewing calls for revenge, he urged his own people to work for reconciliation—and invited his former jailer to attend his presidential inauguration as a VIP guest.

Wonderfully, Mr. Mandela has not been the only person committed to forgiveness and reconciliation. Less well-known people (in my theology no one is "ordinary," for each one of us is created in the image of God) are the real heroes and heroines of our struggle.

There was a Mrs. Savage who was injured in a hand-grenade attack by one of the liberation movements. She was so badly injured that her children bathed her, clothed her, and fed her. She could not go through a security checkpoint at the airport because she still had shrapnel in her and all sorts of alarms would have

been set off. She told us [at the Truth and Reconciliation Commission] that she would like to meet the perpetrator—she, a white woman, and he almost certainly, a black perpetrator, in the spirit of forgiveness. She would like to forgive him and then extraordinarily she added, "And I hope he forgives me." Now that is almost mind-boggling.

The daughter of one of four African National Congress activists, whom the police ambushed and then killed gruesomely—their mutilated bodies were found in their burnt-out car—came to tell her story. She said the police were still harassing her mother and her children, even after their father had died. When she finished, I asked her whether she would be able to forgive those who had done this. We were meeting in a city hall packed to the rafters. You could hear the proverbial pin drop, as she replied, "We would like to forgive. We just want to know whom to forgive."

Our country did not go the way of Nuremberg, to bring the perpetrators of such crimes to trial. After the Second World War, the Allies had defeated the Germans and could apply so-called "victor's justice." In our case, neither the apartheid government nor the liberation movements had defeated their adversary. Our country could not afford the exorbitant cost of trials, even if we could have held them and had the evidence to satisfy a court of law.

Our country rejected the other extreme of a blanket amnesty, as happened in General Augusto Pinochet's Chile. It victimized the victims a second time around and was really trying to let bygones be bygones, when in fact they never become bygones. Certainly, General Pinochet now knows you can't act with reckless impunity and hope to get away with it forever. This is a moral universe.

Our country chose a middle way of individual amnesty for truth. Some would say, what about justice? And we say retributive justice is not the only kind of justice. There is also restorative justice, because we believe in Ubuntu—the essence of being human, that idea that we are all caught up in a delicate network of interdependence. We say, "A person is a person through other persons." I need you in order to be me and you need me in order to be you.

The greatest good is communal corporate harmony, and resentment, anger, revenge are corrosive of this harmony. To nurse grudges and resentment is bad for your blood pressure. Psychologists have now found that to forgive is good for our personal, physical, psychic health, as well as our health as a community, as a society. We discovered that people experienced healing through telling their stories. The process opened wounds that were festering. We cleansed them, poured ointment on them, and knew they would heal. A young man who had been blinded by police action in his township came to tell us the story of that event. When he finished he was asked how he felt now, and he said, "You have given me back my eyes."

Retribution leads to a cycle of reprisal, leading to counter-reprisal in an inexorable movement, as in Rwanda, Northern Ireland, and in the former Yugoslavia. The only thing that can break that cycle, making possible a new beginning, is forgiveness. Without forgiveness there is no future.

We have been appalled at the depths of depravity revealed by the testimonies before the Truth and Reconciliation Commission. Yes, we human beings have a remarkable capacity for evil—we have refined ways of being mean and nasty to one another. There have been genocides, holocausts, slavery, racism, wars, oppression, and injustice.

WE DISCOVERED THAT PEOPLE EXPERIENCED HEALING THROUGH TELLING THEIR STORIES

But that, mercifully, is not the whole story about us. We were exhilarated as we heard people who had suffered grievously, who by rights should have been baying for the blood of their tormentors, utter words of forgiveness, reveal an extraordinary willingness to work for reconciliation, demonstrating magnanimity and nobility of spirit.

Yes, wonderfully, exhilaratingly, we have this extraordinary capacity for good. Fundamentally, we are good; we are made for love, for compassion, for caring, for sharing, for peace and reconciliation, for transcendence, for the beautiful, for the true and the good.

Who could have imagined that South Africa would be an example of anything but the most awful ghastliness? And now we see God's sense of humor, for God has chosen this unlikely lot and set us up as some kind of paradigm, as some kind of model that just might provide the world with a viable way of dealing with post-conflict, post-repression periods. We have not been particularly virtuous, anything but. We are not particularly smart—precisely. God wants to point at us as this unlikely bunch and say to the trouble spots of the world, "Look at them. They had a nightmare called apartheid. It has ended. Your nightmare, too, will end. They used to have what people regarded as an intractable problem. They are now resolving it. Nowhere in the world can people ever again claim that their problems are intractable." There is hope for all of us.

South Africa's Modern History in Six Dates

1910 – South Africa becomes independent

1948 – Establishment of apartheid

1984 – Desmond Tutu receives the Nobel Peace Prize for his nonviolent fight against apartheid

June 30, 1991 – Abolition of apartheid

1994 – First multiracial elections in the country. Nelson Mandela becomes South Africa's first black president

1995 – Creation of the Truth and Reconciliation Commission chaired by Desmond Tutu

DEFENDING HUMAN RIGHTS

AMNESTY INTERNATIONAL

Founded in 1961 by a British lawyer, the nongovernmental organization (NGO) Amnesty International defends human rights. Its first fight was pressuring Portugal to release students accused of drinking a toast to liberty. Since then, it has promoted the banning of torture, the defense of political prisoners, the eradication of the death penalty, and the right to control one's body. The NGO generates numerous petitions, which remains one of its preferred means of taking action.
www.amnesty.org

DENOUNCING INJUSTICE

HUMAN RIGHTS WATCH

The international organization Human Rights Watch is the result of a merger of several NGOs; today it is headquartered in the United States. The NGO publishes research reports on human rights violations.
www.hrw.org

PROTECTING JOURNALISTS

REPORTERS WITHOUT BORDERS

Although the news media is sometimes called the "fourth estate," freedom of expression is not guaranteed throughout the world. Journalists in some countries cannot exercise their profession owing to censorship, threats, attacks, and even execution. Reporters Without Borders has been promoting and defending freedom of information since 1985. The organization supports journalists who have been imprisoned, as well as ordinary citizens who have been convicted for expressing themselves. Every year, it prepares an index that ranks the press freedom records of countries around the world.
www.rsf.org

FIGHTING CORRUPTION

TRANSPARENCY INTERNATIONAL

The first step in fighting corruption involves the study of its breadth and its condemnation. Since 1993, this has been the difficult task on both the state and business level of the German nongovernmental organization Transparency International. The organization strives for transparency in political life and in business decisions; it publishes a Corruption Perceptions Index by country and reports on corruption in businesses.
www.transparency.org

DEATH PENALTY ACROSS THE WORLD

COUNTRIES THAT PRACTICE EXECUTION (2013)

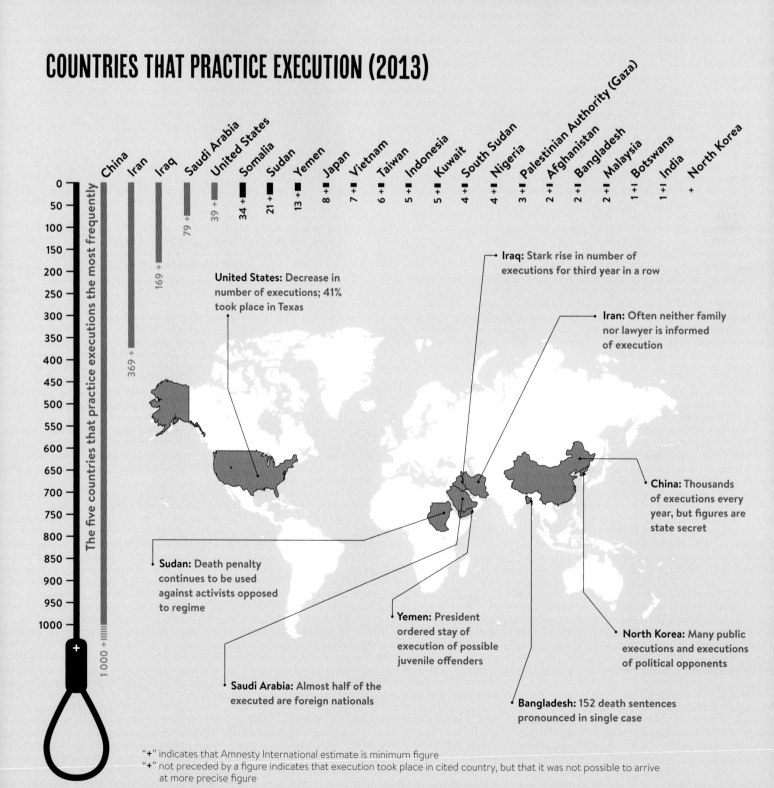

United States: Decrease in number of executions; 41% took place in Texas

Iraq: Stark rise in number of executions for third year in a row

Iran: Often neither family nor lawyer is informed of execution

China: Thousands of executions every year, but figures are state secret

Sudan: Death penalty continues to be used against activists opposed to regime

Yemen: President ordered stay of execution of possible juvenile offenders

North Korea: Many public executions and executions of political opponents

Saudi Arabia: Almost half of the executed are foreign nationals

Bangladesh: 152 death sentences pronounced in single case

"**+**" indicates that Amnesty International estimate is minimum figure
"**+**" not preceded by a figure indicates that execution took place in cited country, but that it was not possible to arrive at more precise figure

PRISON POPULATION ACROSS THE WORLD (2011)

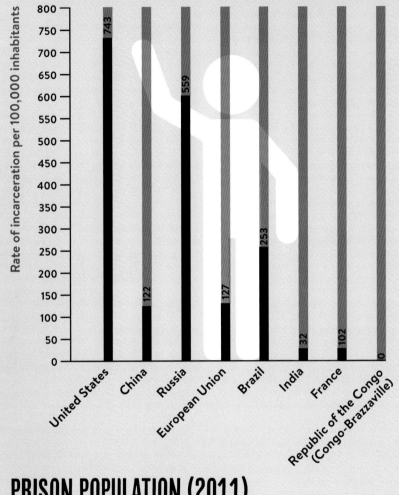

Rate of incarceration per 100,000 inhabitants

Country	Rate
United States	743
China	122
Russia	559
European Union	127
Brazil	253
India	32
France	102
Republic of the Congo (Congo-Brazzaville)	0

PRISON POPULATION (2011)

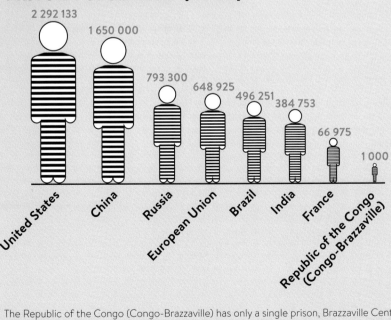

Country	Population
United States	2 292 133
China	1 650 000
Russia	793 300
European Union	648 925
Brazil	496 251
India	384 753
France	66 975
Republic of the Congo (Congo-Brazzaville)	1 000

The Republic of the Congo (Congo-Brazzaville) has only a single prison, Brazzaville Central Prison, constructed in 1943 to house 150 prisoners. Today over 600 prisoners are incarcerated there. This lack of resources allows the country to have one of the lowest incarceration rates in the world.

KEY FIGURES

551 million persons voted in India's legislative elections in May 2014, representing a participation rate of 66%. 814 million voters were called to polls for largest election in the world.

According to United Nations, international organized crime brought in $870 billion in 2009. This represents six times the amount devoted to international development assistance.

Largest types of trafficking, in order: Drug traffic: $320 billion per year. Human traffic (prostitution, migrants, etc.), arms traffic, traffic in wild animals and natural resources (some 10 billion per year), and traffic in counterfeit medications ($1.6 billion per year).

In 2014, 119 journalists were abducted worldwide, compared to 87 in 2013.

66 journalists were killed in 2014. Two-thirds died in areas of conflict.

47% of nations have laws condemning attacks upon religion or "religious sensibilities."

21 of 30 members of the Organization for Economic Co-operation and Development have established minimum wage for workers.

More than 2.8 billion persons live in one of 88 countries considered free by the Freedom House NGO. These are countries that respect a multiparty political system and freedom of opinion and expression, in addition to having free elections.

TIMELINE

c. 380 B.C.
Plato writes *The Republic* based on fictional conversations with Socrates. This book establishes the philosophical basis of justice.

1679
Adoption of habeas corpus laws in England, designed to end arbitrary arrest and imprisonment.

1690
John Locke, in *Two Treatises of Government*, establishes the principle of separation of powers, which Montesquieu would develop in *The Spirit of the Laws* (1748).

1804
Napoléon establishes the civil code in France.

19th century
Progressive income tax is introduced in several countries in Europe.

1894–1906
The Dreyfus affair: Wrongly accused of espionage, Captain Alfred Dreyfus was sentenced to prison. The affair divided French society; Émile Zola, defending Dreyfus, published his famous *J'accuse…!* Finally Dreyfus was declared innocent, acquitted, and rehabilitated.

2002
Establishment of the International Criminal Court, in charge of prosecuting war crimes and genocides.

BOOKS

The Prince
Niccolò di Bernardo dei Machiavelli, 1513, published 1532
This manual of sorts is a revolution in thinking about the exercise of power and political realism. For the prince, the state's reason overrides morality as the means to ensure the safety and freedom of citizens, who, out of their own will, are incited to act for the common good.

Discours de la servitude volontaire ou le Contr'un [Discourse on Voluntary Servitude]
Etienne de la Boétie, 1576
Is it tyranny that oppresses the people or is it the people that submit to the tyrant? De la Boétie opts more for the latter in an ironic text. He denounces the mass faculty that allows people to be subjugated and distracted, to the point that freedom is abandoned—but criticizes, in the final analysis, absolute monarchy.

Du contrat social [The Social Contract]
Jean-Jacques Rousseau, 1762
This philosophical treatise, which helped develop the idea of representative democracy, establishes the notion of the sovereignty of the people, the only legitimate body that can conceive of and decide on the laws of government.

Le Dernier Jour d'un condamné [The Last Day of a Condemned Man]
Victor Hugo, 1829
In this veritable plea for the abolition of the death penalty, readers follow the last days of a condemned man, about whom they know nothing except his anxiety and thoughts about facing capital punishment.

The Trial
Franz Kafka, 1925
In this story of a judicial machine that is bureaucratic, unbearable, and inhumane, Joseph K. has been arrested but knows not why, even though he must appear at his trial. Innocent, he does everything in his power to be acquitted.

The Gulag Archipelago, 1918–1956: An Experiment in Literary Investigation
Aleksandr Solzhenitsyn, 1973
A masterful book, written in secret, which denounces the system of prison repression established in the Soviet Union and which gives voice to the men and women imprisoned in it.

Surveiller et punir: Naissance de la prison [Discipline and Punish: The Birth of the Prison]
Michel Foucault, 1975
An essential book for understanding the modern prison system. The French philosopher takes a look at the invention of the modern prison, which has gradually replaced public punishment. He shows that the modern prison is based on the idea that the detainee can be observed at all times and reprimanded, in order to obtain his subjugation.

No Future without Forgiveness
Desmond Tutu, 2000
The renowned Anglican archbishop from South Africa recounts his experiences chairing the Truth and Reconciliation Commission, which was founded to shed light on the exactions and crimes committed under the apartheid regime.

Escape from Camp 14
Blaine Harden, 2012
Shin Dong-Hyuk was born in an internment camp in North Korea. This book is the incredible story of a man who was able to escape one of the worst dictatorships in the world where oppression, arbitrary detention, and poverty establish the power of a ruling minority.

FILMS

12 Angry Men
Sidney Lumet, 1957
A jury is assembled for the trial of a man accused of murder, a crime punishable by the death penalty. Only one juror votes not guilty. Summoned to argue for his doubts, he sets out to convince the other eleven jurors.

Down and Dirty
Ettore Scola, 1976
This grotesque comedy explores the poverty in an Italian shantytown and the psychological ravages its brings about.

Midnight Express
Alan Parker, 1978
A film about the horror of incarceration, written by Oliver Stone. It tells the true story of a young American who is arrested and imprisoned in Turkey in 1970.

Erin Brockovich
Steven Soderbergh, 2000
Based on a true story: A woman discovers that a corporation is polluting a small town's water, causing multiple cases of cancer. Once the scandal is uncovered, she fights for compensation. Erin Brockovich led one of the first class action lawsuits for consumer protection.

Traffic
Steven Soderbergh, 2000
This film exposes drug trafficking in Mexico and the United States from different angles: the consumer, the trafficker, and the antidrug units.

The Life of David Gale
Alan Parker, 2003
This film tells the story of a philosophy professor and activist against capital punishment who is sentenced to death in Texas for rape and murder.

10e chamber—instants d'audience [The 10th Judicial Court: Judicial Hearings]
Raymond Depardon, 2004
In this documentary, Raymond Depardon presents everyday proceedings in a Paris courtroom without commentary. It's a chronicle of ordinary justice in France.

Gran Torino
Clint Eastwood, 2008
In this movie about racism and tolerance, Clint Eastwood plays a war veteran who must confront his prejudices when a troubled teen tries to steal his prized car.

Un prophète [A Prophet]
Jacques Audiard, 2009
Malik, a young delinquent, is sent to jail for six years. There he discovers the laws ruling the prison, its violence, power relationships and intergroup battles. It's also a crime school. A descent behind bars.

West of Memphis
Amy Berg, 2012
This film follows the fight of three teenagers sentenced to life for a crime they did not commit.

A Touch of Sin
Jia Zhangke, 2013
This film presents four stories of Chinese men and women confronting injustice: corruption in the coal mines, sexual abuse, and exploitation in giant electronics factories. It is the story of a country that is changing quickly, too quickly, where those who cannot rely on the judicial system are plunged into situations where accounts are settled in blood.

Timbuktu
Abderrahmane Sissako, 2014
Islamists in Mali invade the city of Timbuktu in this nuanced and courageous film about the appalling mediocrity and hypocrisy of brutes.

VIDEO GAME

Papers, Please
Lucas Pope, Steam, 2013
The player becomes an immigration officer working for a fictitious Soviet country. Responsible for inspecting the passports of new arrivals, the player must decide whether to let the holders in. What if they beg? And will he be efficient enough to meet the needs of his family? Presented in simple graphics, this game questions our moral choices.

WEBSITES

International Court of Justice
This court was created to settle disputes between states and must not be confused with the International Criminal Court, which prosecutes individuals accused of genocide, crimes against humanity, and war crimes. www.icj-cij.org

European Court of Human Rights
The final recourse for citizens of the Council of Europe (47 countries). It allocated more than 56,000 applications to a judicial formation in 2014. www.echr.coe.int

Restorative Justice Online
An online source of information on restorative justice provided by the Prison Fellowship International Centre for Justice and Reconciliation. www.restorativejustice.org

Truth and Reconciliation Commission (South Africa)
A somewhat austere site but one that provides useful information. www.justice.gov.za

Equal Justice Initiative
Bryan Stevenson's NGO site. He tells his story on page 122. www.eji.org

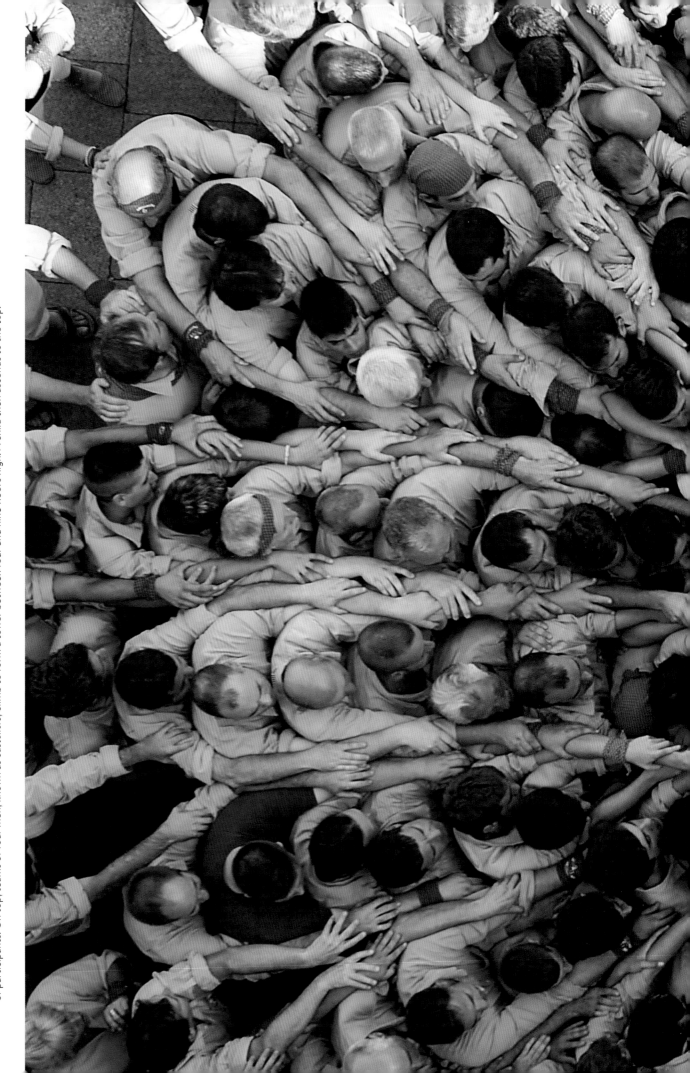

CASTELLERS, VILAFRANCA DEL PENEDÈS, CATALONIA, SPAIN 41° 20' 31" N – 1° 42' 25" E

The tradition of building human towers is thought to date to the Middle Ages. It lives on in Catalonia, where it is the focus of great festivals. The *castells*, meaning "castles," are formed by a compact base of participants. On top, teams of four men, known as *castellers*, climb to form a tower between four and nine floors high. A child then ascends to the top.

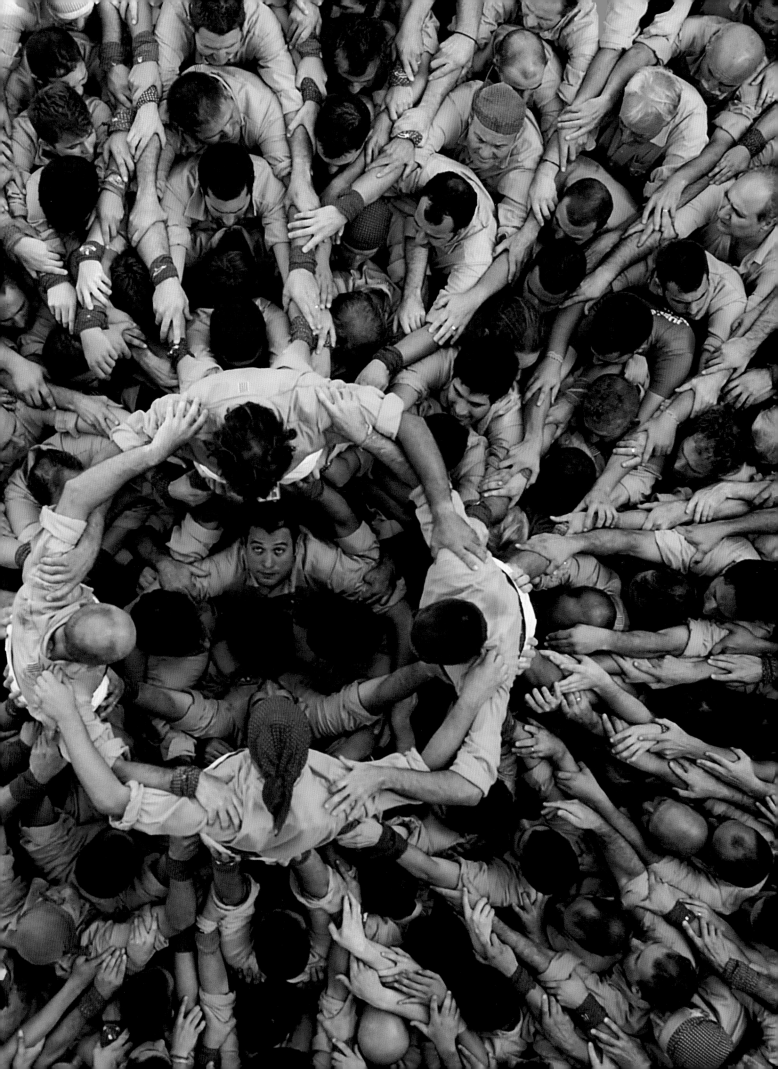

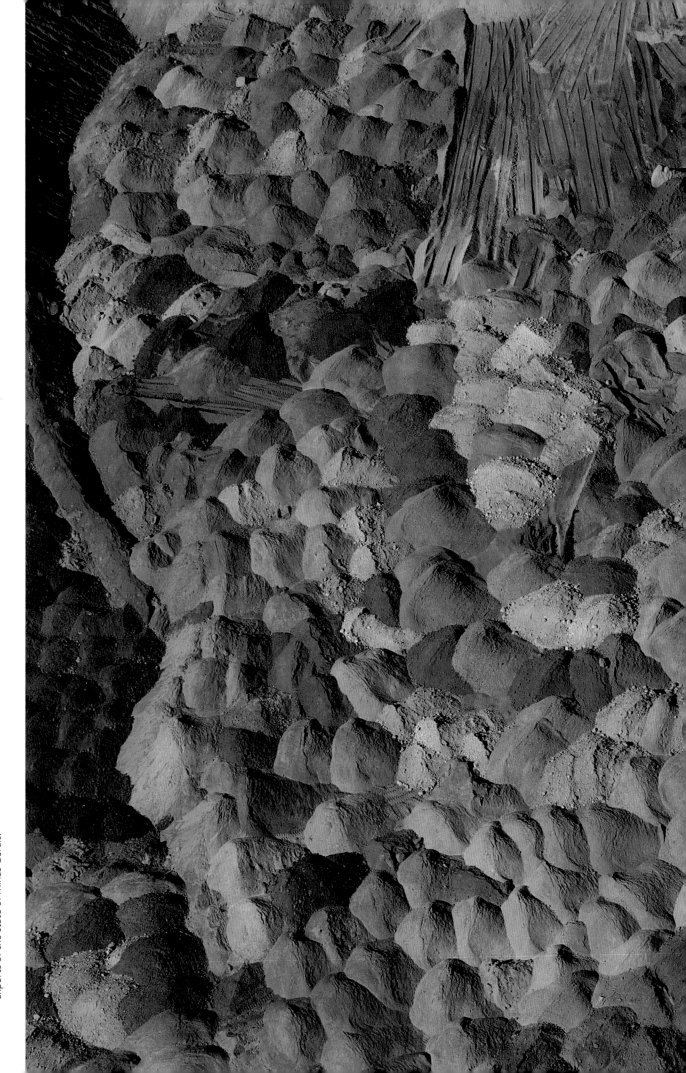

PICO DO ITABIRITO MINE, MINAS GERAIS, BRAZIL 20°13' S – 43°51' W

The Itabirito mines are considered the third largest iron-ore mining operation in the world. In 2012, over 31 million tons of iron-ore mining operation were extracted. Ore and metal make up half of the exports of the state of Minas Gerais.

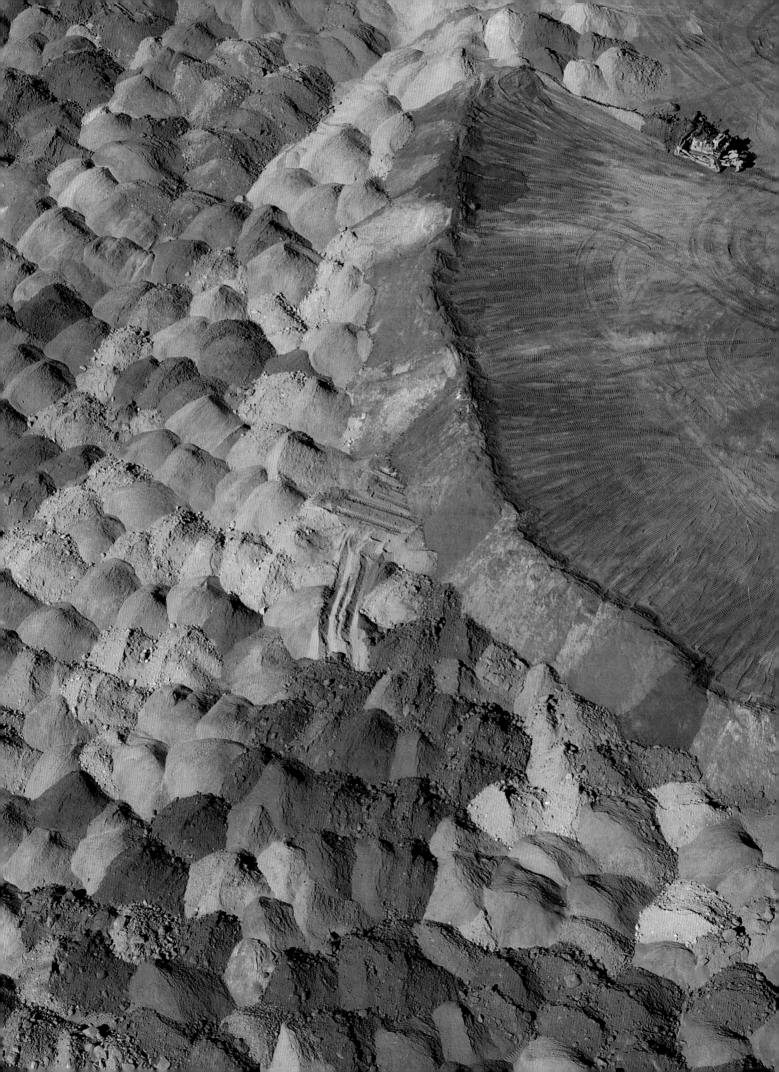

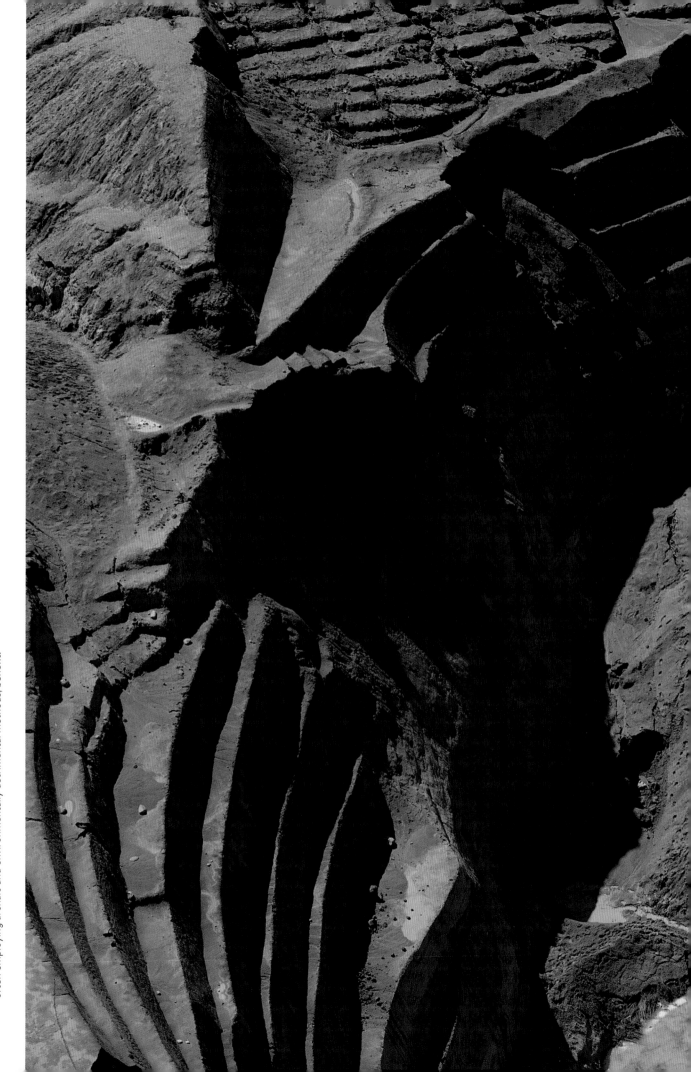

OPEN-PIT SAPPHIRE MINE, IHOROMBE, MADAGASCAR 22° 41' S – 45° 13' E

Madagascar's land is rich in diamonds and sapphires. But political instability and corruption complicate the legal extraction of these resources by large-scale, formalized organizations. Artisanal miners, often employing archaic and environmentally detrimental methods, benefit.

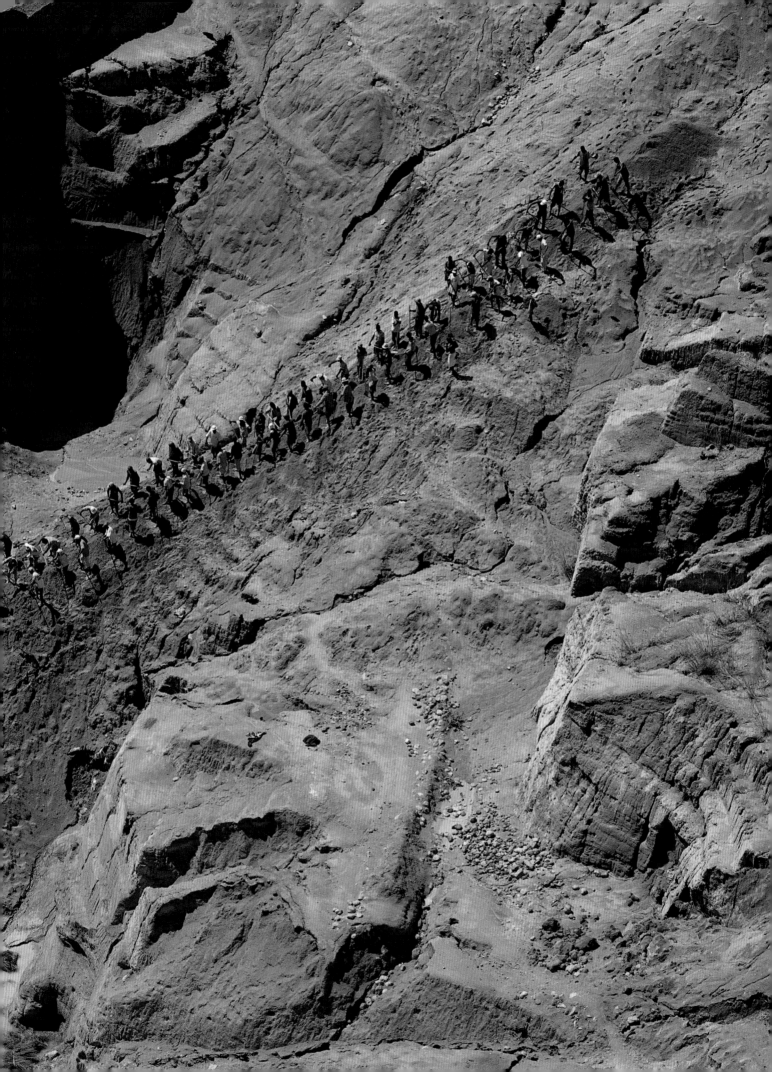

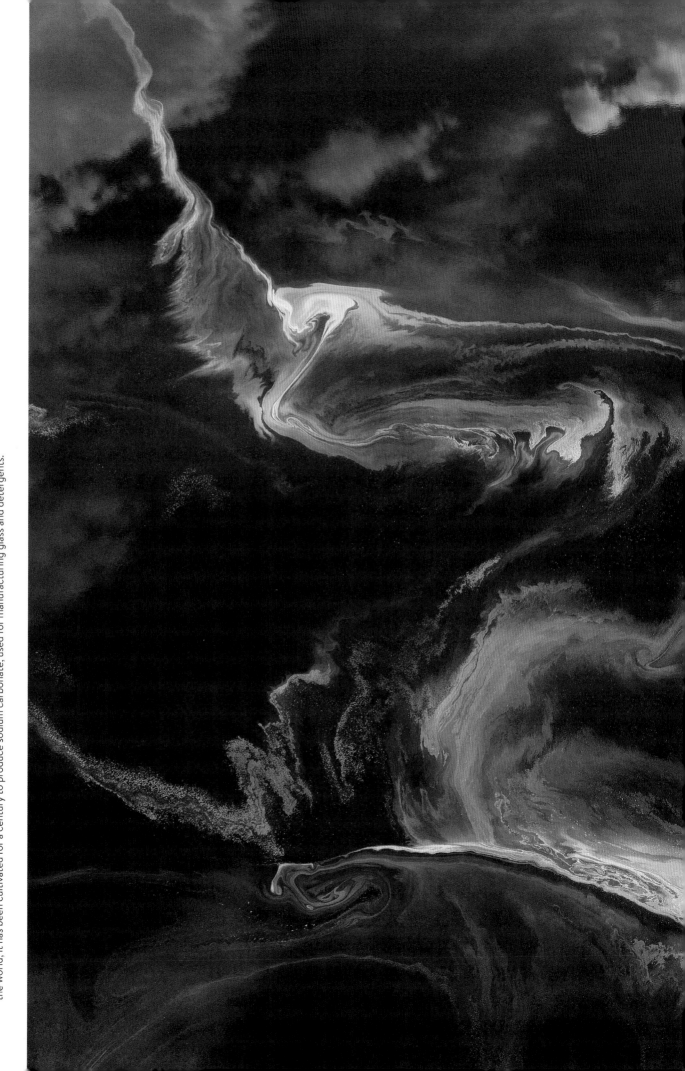

PINK FLAMINGOS IN FLIGHT ABOVE LAKE MAGADI, KENYA 1° 52′ S – 36° 17′ E

Thousands of pink flamingos come together at Lake Magadi to feed on the microalgae, shrimp, and shellfish that proliferate there. Sodium sesquicarbonate in the lake's water is considered to be the purest in the world; it has been cultivated for a century to produce sodium carbonate, used for manufacturing glass and detergents.

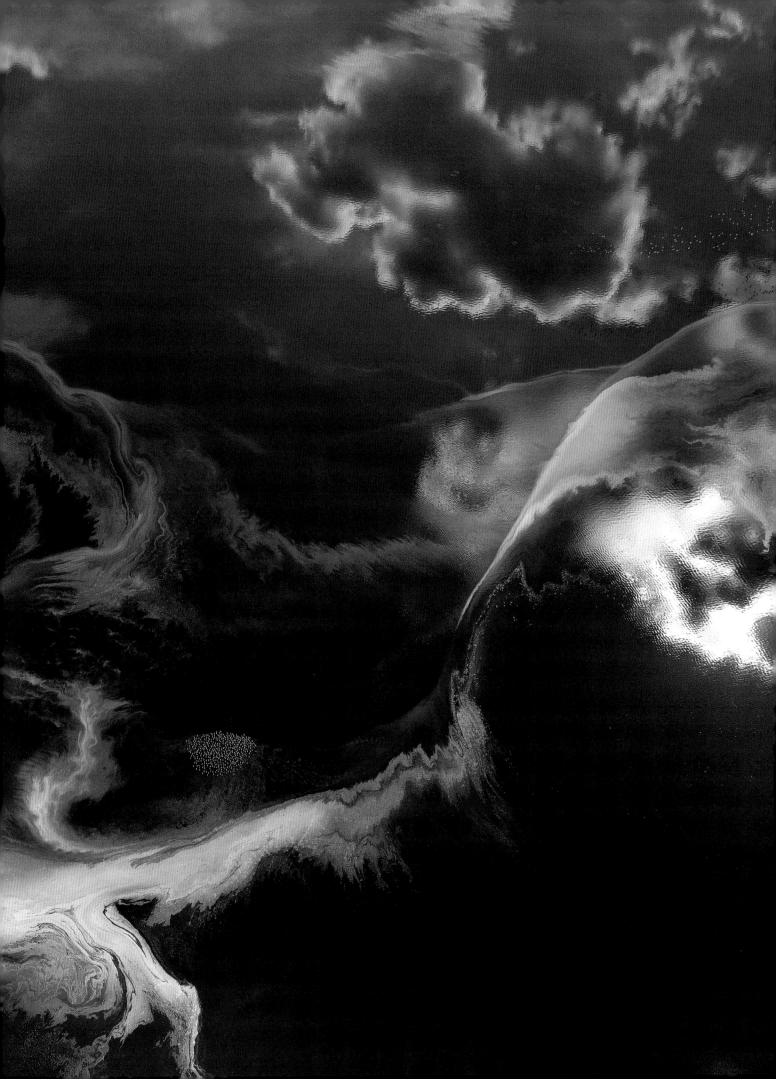

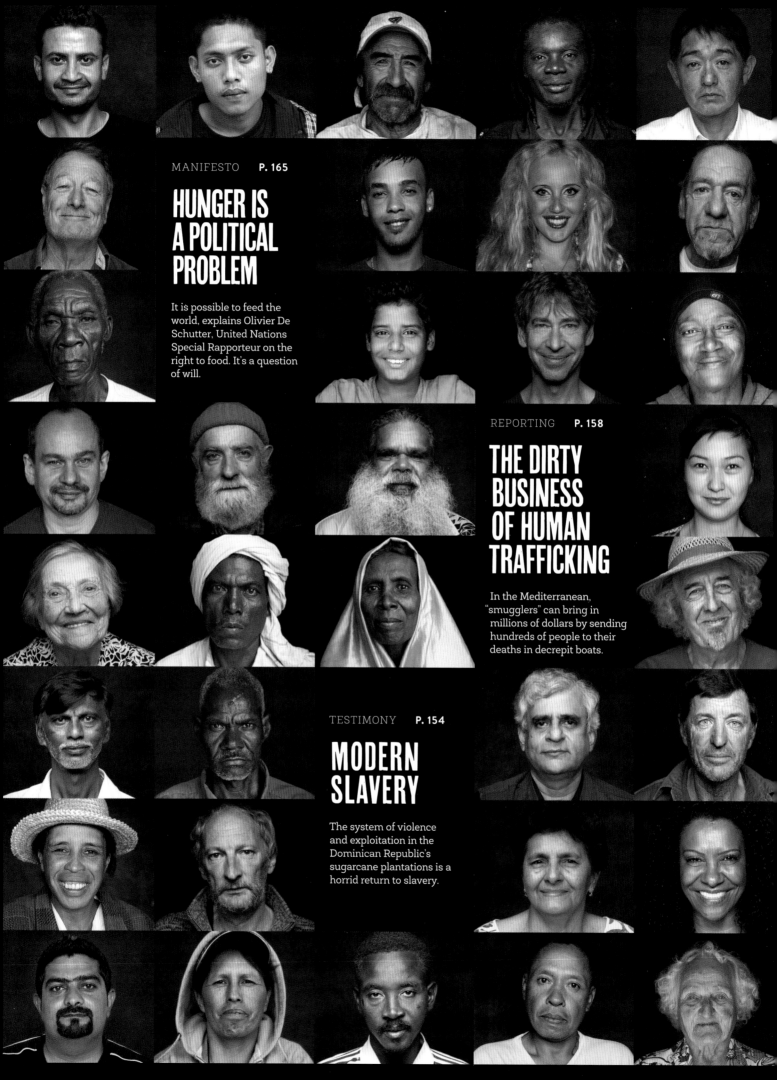

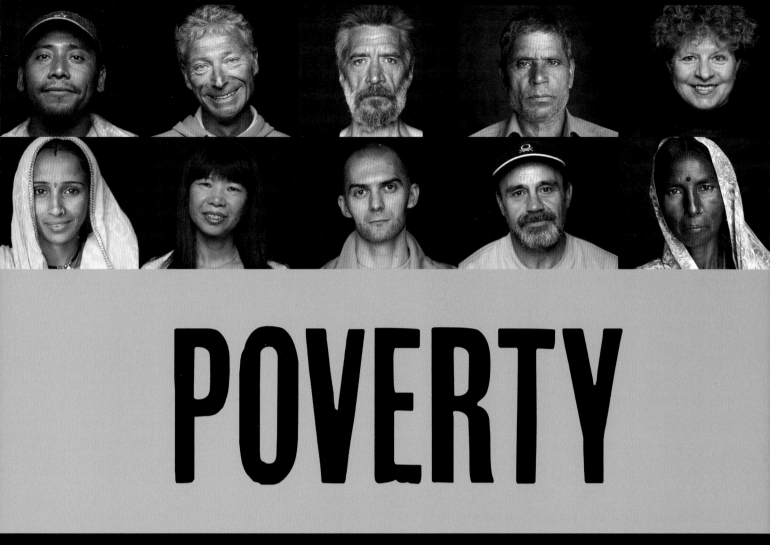

POVERTY

Poverty is in decline in the world—the number of people living on less than $1.25
per day has gone down by more than 900 million in a few decades—
but it is still too prevalent and continues to affect more than 1 billion people.
Poverty has multiple faces, including those of the men and women who
reject the idea of fate and have decided to take their destiny into their
own hands, leaving their home countries for opportunities abroad.

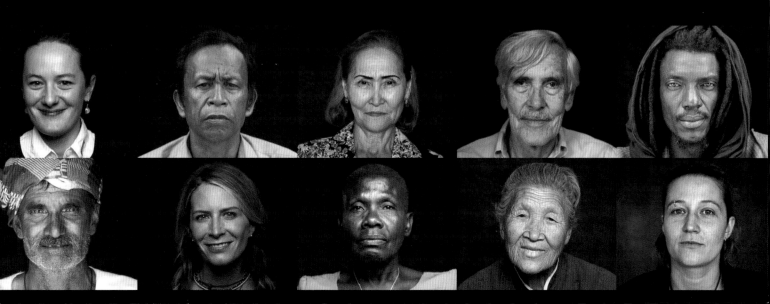

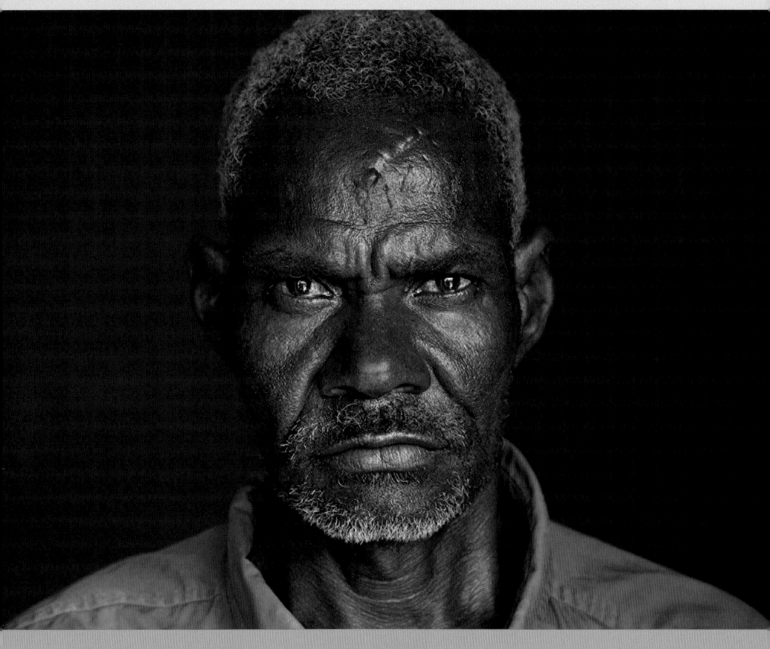

MODERN SLAVERY

HUNGER IS HITTING HAITI AND SOME HAITIANS ARE CHOOSING TO WORK IN THE SUGARCANE PLANTATIONS OF THE DOMINICAN REPUBLIC. THERE, LIFE IS LIKE PRISON.

Slavery: It's an amazing word, almost surreal in 2015. You tell yourself it should be long gone. But no, it's alive and well. Absolutely real. And I saw it. Many Haitians cross the border to the Dominican Republic to go work in the sugarcane fields. Their hope is to earn enough money to have a more comfortable life, to support their family back home, and to prepare for retirement when they return.

But the Dominicans pay their Haitian workers so little that it's impossible to save up, impossible to have housing outside what's offered in the *bateyes* (camps near the sugarcane fields where the men have no privacy, and sometimes no drinking water or electricity), impossible even to go back home since they don't have the means anymore. Once they arrive at their work site, these men are condemned to stay and serve the rich landowners. And if they attempt to protest their situation, their demands are met with violence.

It's dangerous to come into contact with this slave system in the Dominican Republic. That's why we're at Fond Parisien, about six miles (ten kilometers) from the border, on the Haitian side. Here, almost nothing happens; it's a city where everyone is waiting: You meet men and women who hope to one day work in the Dominican Republic, or people who were chased out by their boss, or escaped from him, and can't go any farther because they have no money.

We arrive in the city on a Sunday. Almost all the residents are in church. When it lets out, Fred, from the organization Groupe d'Appui aux Rapatriés et Réfugiés (GARR), introduces us to some people willing to talk to us in front of our camera. They show a lot of kindness, but their eyes are dim. They're both there and not there.

For *Human*, I've already interviewed people who live below the poverty line—in other words, who live on less than $1.50 per day. It's hard, it's not a life either, but year in, year out, they're able to eat. That's not the case here. Johnny Laguerre explains, "I was twenty when I began cutting sugarcane. You worked from six in the morning to six at night. You spent the whole day there without anyone bringing you anything to eat or drink. You spent the day starving and only ate at night. That's what poverty is. When it came time to make dinner, your body hurt so much that you almost would rather go straight to bed without eating and go right to sleep. That's what poverty is."

The atmosphere grows even heavier when we begin talking with Joseph Estima. His face is marked by exhaustion, lost illusions, a life that isn't a life. He didn't go to school; he worked in the fields and was exploited. He has always been poor and today, at age fifty-six, he's even poorer. He ultimately returned to Haiti because he'd rather live badly in his own country than live badly in the one next door. Joseph says, "When you wake up in the morning and see that you don't have a single *gourde* [Haitian currency] at home to feed your children and you're scared you'll find them pleading at your feet, you go back to bed…You're waiting to die, because what they call life is over."

I'm someone who has everything I want. My throat tight, I continue, asking him questions about his anger, about protesting. But he doesn't respond to what I'm saying. He answers, "I'm waiting my turn because I know the Good Lord. He has a plan for each one of us. Today for you, tomorrow for me. You're lucky; it's your turn first. I'm behind you."

I always thought challenges made you stronger. It's true; you learn a lot from difficulty. But what can not eating teach? No, what Joseph is living is an endless, unjust, and useless ordeal!

I do understand that faith in God allows Joseph to accept his poverty and be fatalistic. I would want to fight, to do something to convict and punish his exploiters. But I also know I have the energy of someone who has eaten.

—Hervé Kern

> WHEN IT CAME TIME TO MAKE DINNER, YOUR BODY HURT SO MUCH THAT YOU ALMOST WOULD RATHER GO STRAIGHT TO BED WITHOUT EATING AND GO RIGHT TO SLEEP. THAT'S WHAT POVERTY IS

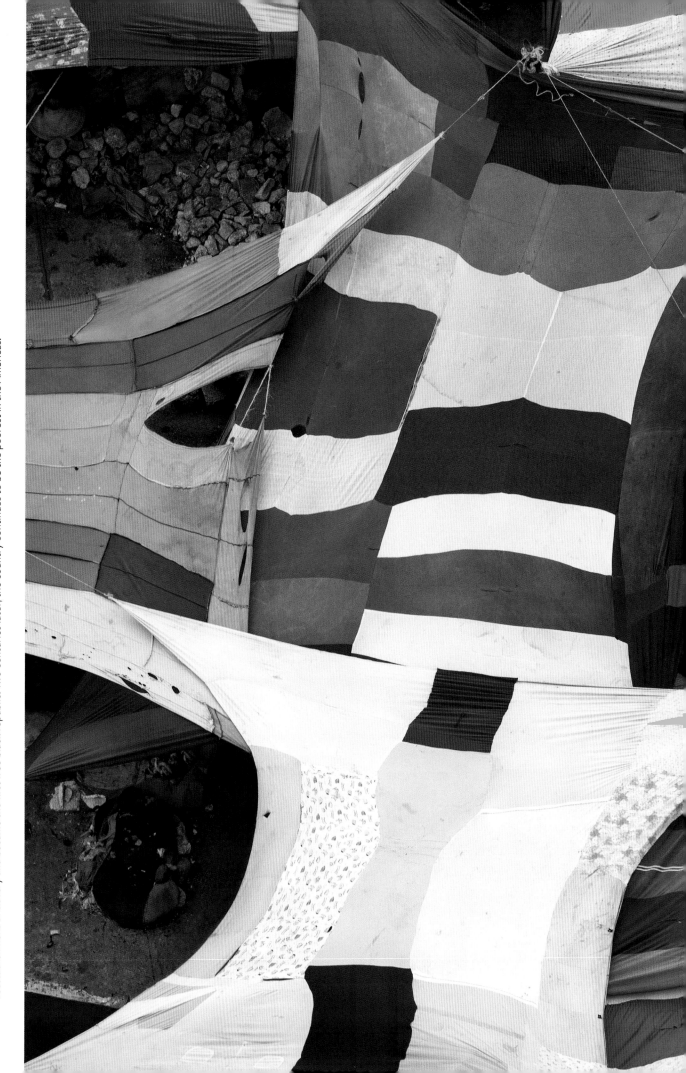

"COVERED" MARKET, CITÉ SOLEIL, PORT-AU-PRINCE, HAITI 18° 34' 26.31" N – 72° 19' 56.47" W

The history of Haiti is one of drama, instability, violence, and catastrophe. Upon defeating the French, it became independent in 1803. The Republic of Haiti was founded after a revolt against the reestablishment of slavery and became the first free black republic. Two centuries later, the country continues to be the poorest in the Americas.

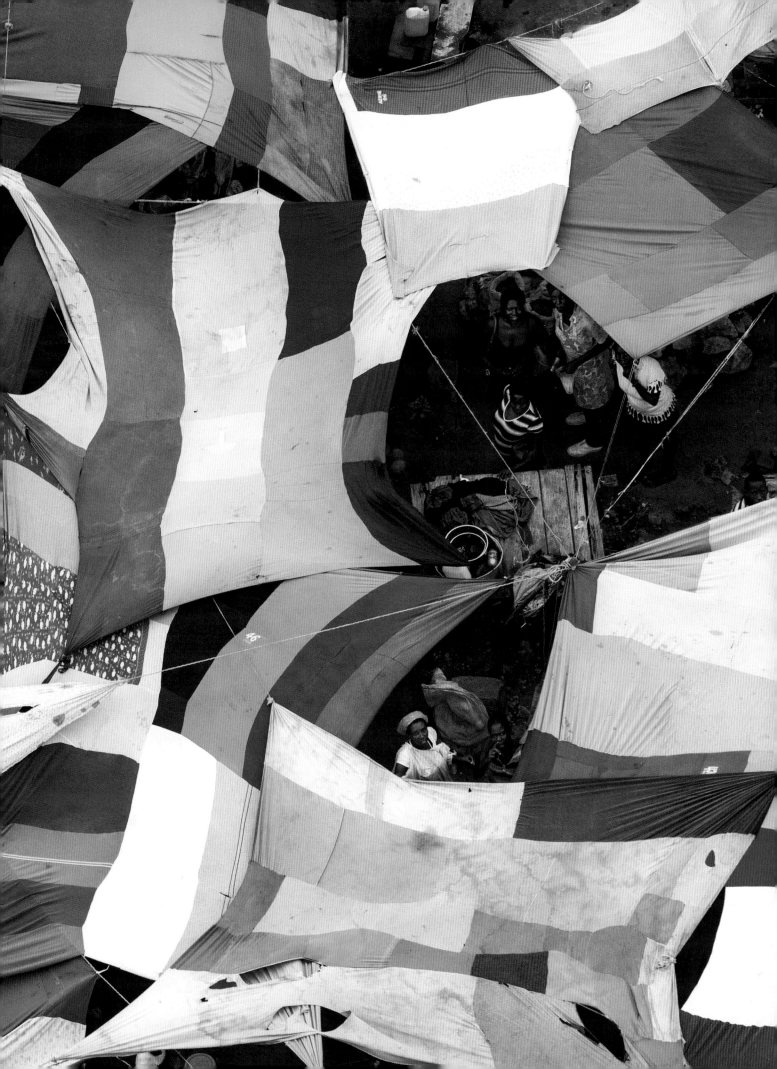

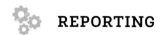

THE DIRTY BUSINESS OF HUMAN TRAFFICKING

By Fabrizio Gatti
First published in *L'Espresso*, October 16, 2013

The smugglers, who bring refugees on makeshift boats across the Mediterranean, are one link in the vast and lucrative network of human trafficking. In this excerpt from his investigative report published in *L'Espresso*, the Italian writer and journalist Fabrizio Gatti discusses the tragedy of October 3, 2013, when more than 360 refugees died at sea off Lampedusa, in what was then the greatest Mediterranean maritime disaster of the twenty-first century.

I met my first smuggler some ten years ago in Chaffar, near Sfax in Tunisia. He was sitting on the beach in the shade of a large wooden boat....Commandant Khaled was twenty-seven years old and had the scarred forearms of a former long-term inmate, a red T-shirt, Bermuda shorts, and big sneakers.

He began to trust me when he learned that I had been locked up in the detention center for foreigners in Via Corelli in Milan, just as he had been. In my case, as an embedded journalist; in his, as an undocumented criminal. That's how I became his personal driver for a few days. Khaled loaded passengers onto stolen trawlers: unemployed Arabs, exiled Eritreans, or Libyans and Somalis fleeing civil war. After making three sea voyages as far as Sicily, he had become a "commandant," the one who stayed on land to organize the departures. But, he didn't know how to drive. From behind the wheel, I was able to observe the typical day of a human trafficker.

Later on, in temporary detention in Lampedusa, I got to know other smugglers in the barbed wire enclosure (since disappeared) where we were confined alongside the airport. A man whose first name was Cherriere spoke five languages. He claimed to be Tunisian but looked Turkish. His long career began back in the days when the Turkish Kurds first arrived in Italy. Sherif the Syrian, tall, slender, a blond mustache, only responded to questions in Arabic....Nothing was happening with him. He was released—who knows why—within twenty-four hours. He was flown to Crotona before disappearing with his sack full of money, €5,000 in cash. His payment for shipping a cargo of souls to heaven.

Years have passed since my investigation [traveling undercover as a refugee from Africa to Europe] for *L'Espresso.* The Africa on the other side of the Mediterranean is no longer the same. But between the smugglers back then and the arrest of Khaled Ben Salem,

thirty-five years old, also a Tunisian from Sfax and the captain involved in the disaster of October 3, 2013, at Lampedusa, nothing has changed. They hold the fate of refugees, exiles, emigrants in their hands. No one else....They're the only ones who can offer an escape to those whose lives have been devastated by war, by a tyrannical regime, or simply by poverty—provided that their clients or relatives in Europe or America are in a position to pay. The trafficking mafia spreads its tentacles even into the camps of Turkish or Lebanese refugees. It manages to operate deplorable detention centers in Libya. Through a network of autonomous organizations they control the routes that lead through the Sahara Desert and now control routes from Syria as well. This mafia profits from the complete absence of humanitarian corridors and relief efforts that are equal to the ongoing crisis. It has become the sole cure for what ails hundreds of thousands....

In the meantime, prices and traffickers' profits have remained more or less the same: US$1,500 per Liberian in 2003, US$1,600 for each refugee who boarded Khaled Ben Salem's trawler. One ship, the ship involved in the tragedy, was packed to the gunwales. When the lights of Italy appeared on the night of Thursday, October 3, there were on board: the smuggler (survived), his young Tunisian first mate (deceased), 7 Ethiopians (deceased), 2 Sudanese (1 survived, 1 deceased), and 507 Eritreans (153 survived, 354 deceased). Among the Eritreans there were sixteen children, aged three to six (deceased), some dozen pregnant women (deceased), and approximately one hundred other women (only four survived). Tally: of 518 passengers, 363 drowned and 155 survived. It represented the greatest tragedy ever in Lampedusa but hardly the worst along the Mediterranean frontiers.

Libyan traffickers collected more than €500,000, levied from the passengers on this trawler alone. All that money for a single night, for a single trip. The figures are easy to calculate. In their interviews with Alganesh Fisseha, whose organization named Gandhi has come to the aid of the Eritrean diaspora for years, the survivors confirmed that the price was US$1,600 per person. The price of liberty. That amounts to US$825,000 in total.

The leaky old tub of a ship could not have cost more than US$20,000 on the second-hand market, assuming it wasn't stolen in the first place. Expenses could have reached a maximum of US$35,000, including reserve fuel, truck transport for the passengers, a few bribes here and there, and payment for Khaled Ben Salem and his first mate. This massacre has to have brought in US$790,000 tax-free, minus expenses, for the traffickers....

Smugglers like Khaled Ben Salem occupy the lowest rank of the organization. "The traffickers, the ones who really count, don't ever get on board," explains Leonardo Marino, a lawyer from Agrigento. Marino succeeded in obtaining acquittals for two Tunisian trawler captains and their five crew members, who had been accused of complicity in illegal immigration. They had been indicted in 2007 for having brought forty-four foreigners to Lampedusa, the nearest port, after having picked them up at sea. This was an incident that had an effect on sea conduct. There have since been multiple cases of boatloads of migrants floating adrift being ignored by passing ships, even though an article of Italian immigration law exempts such rescue from any prosecution. Mariners have not been notified that at the end of the trial, Italy had to pay the Tunisian sailors €9,000 each for the fifty days of wrongful detention, on account of a misapplication of the law.

As in this case, prosecutors have often carelessly applied the article that punishes the offence of criminal association for purposes of illegal immigration. This is so even when it is a case of refugees being forced to pilot their own vessel because no smuggler came on board at the moment of departure in Libya or Egypt. Thus the Italian Court of Appeals has established that in such circumstances the indicted may not be placed in custody. This is a legal battle that has been sustained and explained on the blog meltingpot. org by Fulvio Vassallo Paleologo, lawyer and professor of law (asylum law and foreign national status) at the University of Palermo.

The halt declared by the Italian Court of Appeals is presently keeping dozens of exiles from being thrown into prison like common mafiosi. It has, however, inevitably facilitated the flight of

DEATH IN THE MEDITERRANEAN

Crossing the Mediterranean Sea is often the most perilous stage for migrants from Africa and the East. Since early 2000, almost twenty-four thousand people have died attempting to cross the sea, according to the International Organization for Migration (IOM). The Strait of Gibraltar, the island of Lampedusa, and the coasts of southern Italy are the stages for numerous tragedies. Often these deaths are ignored even though their numbers are on the rise.

In 2014, some 219,000 people attempted to cross the Mediterranean, up from 70,000 in 2011. Almost 90 percent of the time, their destination is, first, Italy, then Greece and Spain. In the last few years, almost half of these migrants hae been coming from Syria and Eritrea, but the numbers also include Sub-Saharans, Afghans, Malians, Nigerians, Gambians, Somalis, Palestinians, Bangledeshis, and more.

More than 3,400 migrants perished at sea in 2014. Eighty-five thousand were saved by the Italian marines as part of the Operation Mare Nostrum; more than 35,000 were saved by the Italian coast guard and more than 40,000 by a total of 237 commercial ships contacted by the Italian authorities to provide aid in these emergency situations, according to the IOM.

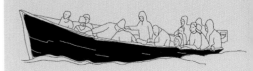

SOUTH-SOUTH MIGRATIONS

In Europe and North America, much attention is paid to a particular type of migration, North-South Migration—migration from developing countries (sometimes called the "Global South") to developed countries (the "Global North"). However, there is much more to the migration story. Of the 232 million migrants in the world, which constitute 3 percent of the population worldwide, only 40 percent migrate south to north. According to the International Organization for Migration (IOM), approximately 33 percent migrate south to south, 22 percent north to north, and only 5 percent north to south.

South-south migrants have diverse profiles. They generally are migrating to bordering or relatively nearby countries. They are the Pakistani worker leaving for Dubai or the Philippine maid leaving for Singapore, for example. They don't bring their families; they leave them in their countries of origin. They don't plan on migrating permanently, and they generally return to their country after a few years. Their life conditions are precarious, and they are often at the mercy of their employers, who could fire them at any moment; they rarely benefit from true social protections, even when they are in legal situations, and are highly monitored.

That said, these migrants play a very important role in the worldwide economy: They constitute an inexpensive labor force in the receiving country, and they send money back to their native country. In 2013, migrants from developing countries sent home $414 billion.

several smugglers and their return to the African shore. Among the returned, according to the mobile patrol of Agrigento, was the infamous Khaled Ben Salem who had already disembarked 250 passengers in April of that year. He had been identified, registered, and simply repatriated. In any case, his arrest had had no impact on the trafficking business. The more blood flows around the world, the more refugees there are to ship. As the commandant in Chaffar said to me: "We are still working. As long as there are Moroccans, Tunisians and Africans paying to leave, we'll be there waiting for them."

Even on the first night of sailing, still completely unaware of the carnage to come, Khaled Ben Salem must have known that the crossing would be complicated. After two hours at sea he was still in coastal waters.... The prow couldn't even break the waves because the ship had too heavy a load. A smuggler is just a smuggler. He can't complain about too many passengers to those who've organized the voyage. It was Libyans who came to his aid. They sent an inflatable dinghy, one of those used a few hours earlier to transport the refugees from the beach out to

the trawler waiting for them in deep water. They took twenty-five Eritreans back to land, having no idea they had probably just saved their lives.

Their destination was Sicily, according to the testimony of survivors. That was what the traffickers had promised the Eritreans in any case. Perhaps Khaled Ben Salem thought that he couldn't reach Sicily. He sailed toward Lampedusa. He must have been an experienced sailor. It's not easy to reach this speck in the middle of the sea. Still, he didn't stray from the course. That's when the trouble began. A smuggler is a criminal, not a tour guide. In order to gain some time and be able to hide after the events, Khaled Ben Salem ordered all cell phones thrown overboard. He wanted to avoid anyone calling from the boat. The passengers had to trust him. They had no other choice.

The lights of Lampedusa were in sight. They had arrived, or almost. Everyone had complied with Khaled Ben Salem's order and thrown their only contact with the rest of the world into the sea—their last way to call for help. Khaled Ben Salem had also demanded that some young boys come

232,000,000

232,000,000 PEOPLE ARE CLASSIFIED AS MIGRANTS BY THE UNITED NATIONS. THEY REPRESENT 3% OF THE WORLD'S POPULATION.

THE MORE BLOOD FLOWS AROUND THE WORLD, THE MORE REFUGEES THERE ARE TO SHIP

and stand at his side so as to pass them off as smugglers. He seems to have mastered all the tricks for extricating himself. The rest of it—the engine shut off, their cover on fire to indicate their position, the fuel on fire, panic, the capsizing—yet another example of a world gone mad, a world that turns a blind eye to refugees.

Muhamed Arafat, thirty-three, and Muhmed Fakhri, twenty-eight, both Egyptian, also ended up in prison. They were the smugglers involved in a disembarkation that had taken place a few days earlier at Sicily in the province of Ragusa: 13 Eritreans died, 161 fellow countrymen survived, 1 or 2 fled as fugitives, 5 Syrians were taken for traffickers, arrested, and then freed by the judge. And this testimony from an onlooker: the sight of a man whipping his travel companions in order to drive them into the water. The man who did this was not the smuggler, as the prosecutor of Ragusa (Sicily) confirmed. He was one of the Eritreans, who could not be identified.

Muhamed Arafat and Muhmed Fakhri's story is, nevertheless, very different than Khaled Ben Salem's. They told the chief prosecutor, Serena Meniculli, and lawyer Giorgio Terranova that they had piloted the ship in return for a discount in the price for the trip: US$500, instead of the usual 1,600. They left Egypt after the chaos, the coup d'état, and the riots. Muhamed Arafat knew about engines somewhat and proposed that he act as mechanic on board, but Fakhri hadn't the least experience at the helm. One night the Libyans took them aside and explained to them how to use a portable GPS. They just had to follow the bright line on the little screen.

As if it were a road, they were told, and at the end, you'll see Sicily. They were overloaded as well. It took three trips from the shore in an inflatable dinghy to fill the boat. The motor was overheated. The Libyans advised them to let it cool off. They had to stop three times during the course of the trip. The waves surged over the boat in deathly silence.

Every time someone threw a bag into the sea, the plastic was sucked into the cooling circuit. Fakhri plunged into the sea, knife in hand, to clear the obstruction that would have set them adrift. He climbed back into the boat, cursing. He asked the others to be careful. There was enough water and food for everyone. Things in the ship calmed down—until the middle of the day, at the Scicli sand bar, 165 feet (50 meters) from the beach at Sampieri. The old tub ran aground. Fakhri dove in. He found footing. The water came up only to his waist. Then the others dove in. The waves were high. It was only a sand bar. The sea all around was deep.

Some of them were able to reach the beach by themselves. They ran away. One of them was struck by a hit-and-run car driver....Alberto Proietto, a lifeguard, and Carmelo Floridia, a law enforcement officer, rushed to their aid, but they were not able to save everyone. Thirteen young Eritreans drowned in front of their eyes. Right at the shore. As journalist Tiziano Terzani wrote, coming face-to-face with the tragedy in Cambodia: While saving them, they decided who would live and who would die.

THE TRAIN OF DEATH

Another focal point of international migrations is the border between Mexico and the United States. Every year, hundreds of thousands of people from Latin America are apprehended attempting to cross it illegally. More than 1,900 miles (3,000 km) long, this border is closely monitored and even has a noncontinuous fence spanning approximately 650 miles (1,046 km) of the border. To cross this border, migrants often have to use smugglers, called "coyotes" by the locals. These services can sometimes cost between three and four thousand dollars.

In 2012, there were an estimated 700,000 clandestine crossings, but U.S. police authorities arrested more than 350,000 people. Since 2009, this migratory flux has decreased slightly. And it's also changing; Mexicans aren't the only ones crossing north. There are also more people from Central America, mainly El Salvador, Guatemala, and Honduras. Often, they take two freight train lines called the *Bestia* (Beast) and the *Tren de la Muerte* (Train of Death). And every stage of their journey is difficult: Accidents are frequent and violence provoked by the local mafia—the *maras*—is manifold.

In 2013, approximately 11.6 million Mexican immigrants resided in the United States, more than 6 million of them illegally.

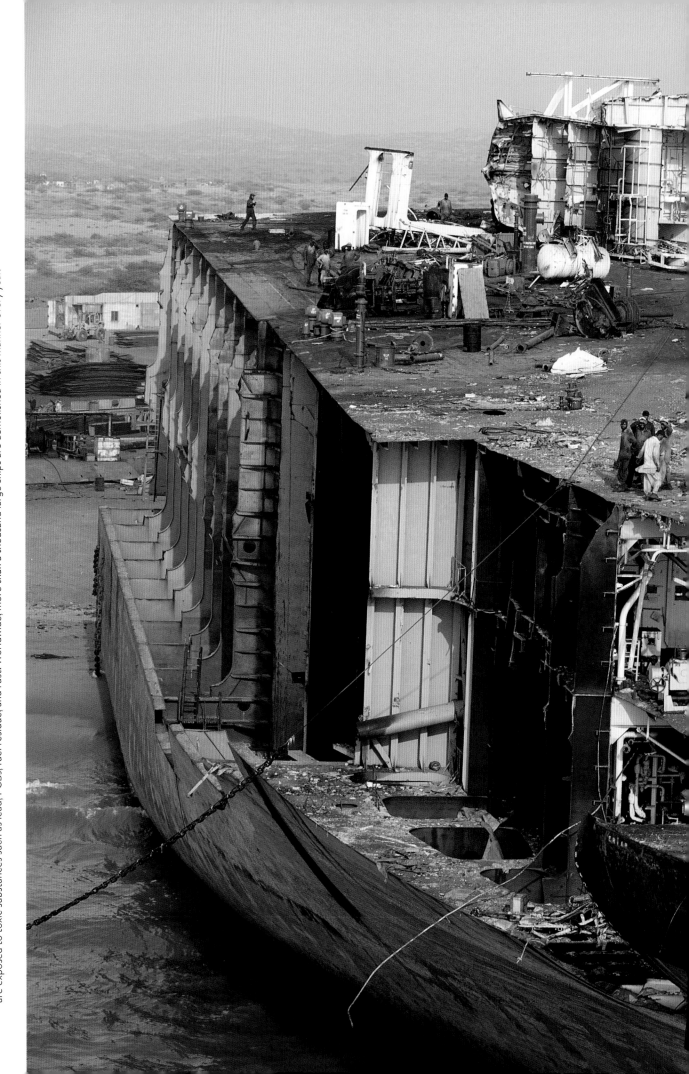

SHIP-BREAKING YARD, GADANI, BALOCHISTAN, PAKISTAN 25° 05' N – 66° 42' E

Located some thirty miles (fifty km) to the northeast of Karachi, the Gadani ship-breaking yard can accommodate about one hundred boats and employs as many as nine thousand people. The workers are exposed to toxic substances such as lead, PCBs, fuel residue, and rust. Worldwide, more than a thousand large ships are demolished in this manner every year.

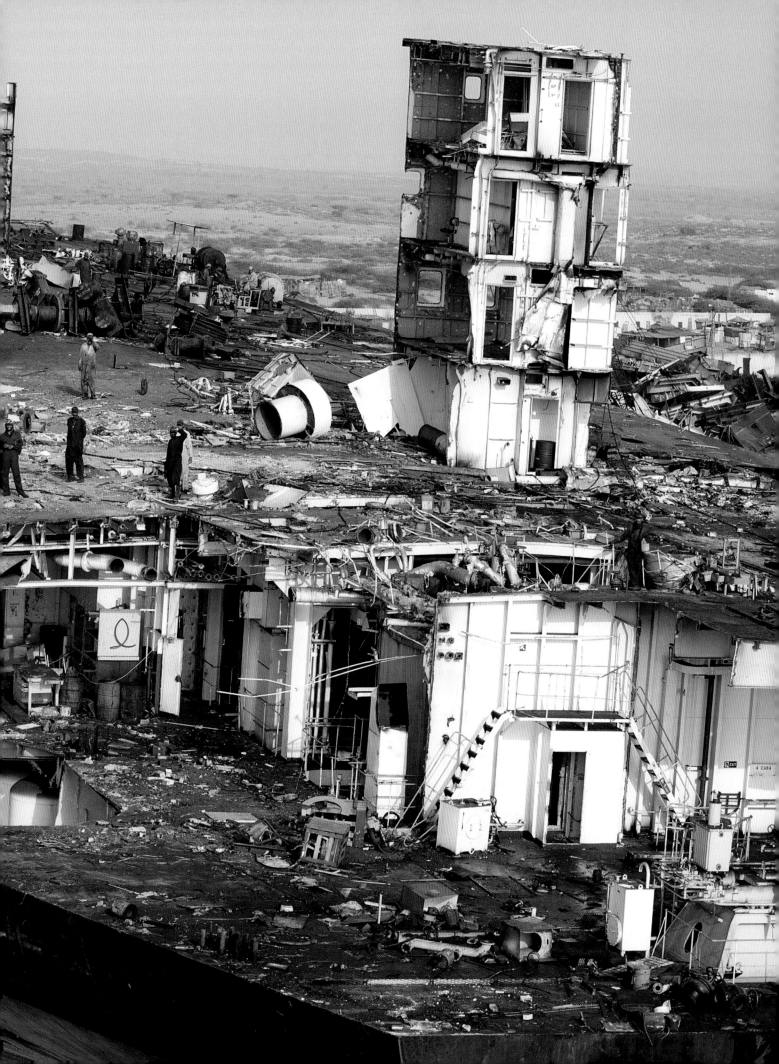

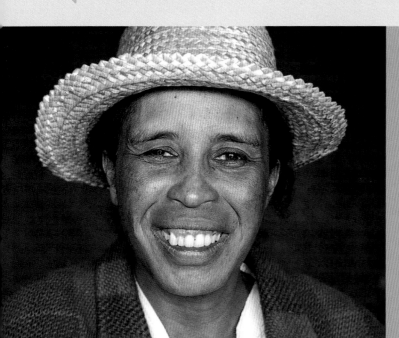

WORKING THE EARTH

AIMÉE HAS ONLY HER HANDS TO WORK HER FIELDS.

We farmers have no respite. As soon as you are able to work, you do, and you do so until you die. It's the sweat from your forehead that feeds you. As long as you're standing, you have to find the strength to hold a spade in your hands. Even if you're old. That's the life of a peasant. Because there is no retirement for us.

What do you expect from the future? Nothing. Nothing at all. You expect nothing from nobody. To survive, you depend on what you grow. And that's the way it is until you die.

Working the land is really very, very hard, especially where we're from, in Ambohibary [in central Madagascar]. There's nothing else to do, unless you own zebus and harrows. For everyone else, you have only your hands. You have to force yourself to like this kind of work, even if your hands are full of blisters—and mine, for example, are full of them!

You also have to communicate to your children the importance of working the land. Any activity they are able to do has to be connected to agriculture; everything you earn isn't worth a thing if you don't farm. On top of all your small jobs, you have to continue farming. So, as a parent, you have to make your children understand. You can't let the land go; you have to farm it.

When you wake up in the morning, you make breakfast, which will give you strength, and then you go into the fields. Then, at midday, when the time comes to eat, you rest a bit and you sing, "Help me, take my hand with love, Jesus. If I count only on my strength, I'll lose heart along the way. Fulfilling your mission is my goal, yesterday, today and always, you'll be there, Jesus." Then, when the break is over, you go back to work. Around two o'clock you go home, because you're tired. The work is never done but you have to go home and take care of things there: feed the chickens and pigs, cook dinner. When the sun sets, you haven't finished it all. But it's dark, so you go to bed. And that's your only moment to relax.

But I want to say something: You don't respect us. Don't forget that without me—the farmer—you'd have nothing to put on your plate; you wouldn't eat, you wouldn't drink, you'd have no life if I, the peasant, stopped working.

> YOU DON'T RESPECT US. DON'T FORGET THAT WITHOUT ME—THE FARMER— YOU'D HAVE NOTHING TO PUT ON YOUR PLATE

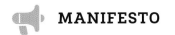

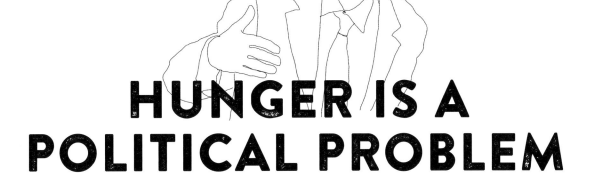

HUNGER IS A POLITICAL PROBLEM

OLIVIER DE SCHUTTER

Olivier de Schutter was the United Nations Special Rapporteur on the right to food from 2008 to 2014. He is also a professor of international human rights law at the Université Catholique de Louvain and the College of Europe.

OVER THE PAST TWENTY YEARS, HOW HAS THE FIGHT AGAINST HUNGER EVOLVED?

In 1992, 840 million people in the world could not feed themselves with dignity. Today there are approximately 925 million, 98 percent of which live in developing countries. These figures have to be considered in relation to population growth, which remains vigorous—every year, the planet gains seventy-five million people. Nevertheless, 16 percent of the population in developing countries experienced hunger in 2012, a slight reduction only, compared to the 20 percent in 1990, and very far from the top United Nations Millennium Development Goal, which was set in 2000. What's more, in one region at least—Sub-Saharan Africa—the proportion of people affected by hunger is growing rather than shrinking: 30 percent of the population today does not have access to sufficient caloric intake.

IN YOUR OPINION, WHY HAS THE PROBLEM OF HUNGER NOT YET BEEN RESOLVED?

The causes of hunger are essentially political. In most developing countries, not enough has been invested in small family farms, the purpose of which is to feed local communities. Rural poverty has grown. Small peasants have migrated toward cities by the millions, but the industrial and service sectors have not undergone sufficient development to absorb this workforce: Today, 1.3 billion people live in slum areas, on the edge of big cities in developing countries. The response of governments, counseled by international institutions, has often been to import foodstuffs, which has further accelerated the ruin of local options. It is a vicious circle, difficult to break out of.

WHAT CHANGES NEED TO HAPPEN OVER THE NEXT TWENTY YEARS?

There needs to be a massive overhaul of our efforts to eliminate hunger in two directions. The first is the reconstruction of local food-processing systems, which is the only way to break away from the current competition between export culture and subsistence agricultural culture, which plays against the most marginalized farmers. The second is the dissemination of agro-ecological practices so as to free agricultural production from fossil fuels and reduce agriculture's ecological footprint. These transitions can be made only on the condition that our governmental mechanisms be improved. We are hostages of shortsightedness, which affects both political and market decision-making. We have to escape this shortsightedness by prioritizing the long term in political decision-making. We don't have the luxury of waiting: Now is when we need to act, because tomorrow, it'll be too late.

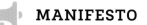
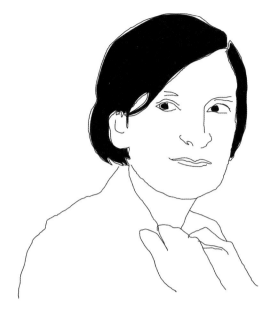

POOR ECONOMICS

ESTHER DUFLO

From her February 2010 TED Talk

Esther Duflo is a professor at the Massachusetts Institute of Technology (MIT). She is part of the team advising President Obama on global development policy and was named one of *Time* magazine's most influential people in the world. Here is a summary of her TED (Technology, Entertainment, and Design) talk.

...Imagine you have a few million dollars that you've raised—maybe you're a politician in a developing country and you have a budget to spend. You want to spend it on the poor: How do you go about it? Do you believe the people who tell you that all we need to do is to spend money? That we know how to eradicate poverty, we just need to do more? Or do you believe the people who tell you that aid is not going to help; on the contrary, it might hurt, it might exacerbate corruption, dependence, etc.?...

Sadly, we don't know. And worst of all, we will never know....Take Africa, for example. Africans have already got a lot of aid....And the GDP in Africa is not making much progress. Okay, fine. How do you know what would have happened without the aid? Maybe it would have been much worse, or maybe it would have been better. We have no idea. We don't know what the counterfactual is. There's only one Africa.

So what do you do? [Do you] give the aid, and hope and pray that something comes out of it? Or do you focus on your everyday life and let the earthquake every eight days continue to happen? The thing is, if we don't know whether we are doing any good, we are not any better than the medieval doctors and their leeches. Sometimes the patient gets better; sometimes the patient dies. Is it the leeches? Is it something else? We don't know.

So here are some other questions. They're smaller questions, but they are not that small. Immunization: That's the cheapest way to save a child's life. And the world has spent a lot of money on it: The GAVI and the Gates Foundations are each pledging a lot of money towards it, and developing countries themselves have been [making] a lot of effort. And yet, every year at least twenty-five million children do not get the immunizations they should get. So this is what you call a "last mile problem." The technology is there, the infrastructure is there, and yet it doesn't happen. So you have your million [dollars]. How do you use your million to solve this last mile problem?...

And [another] question: Education. Maybe that's the solution; maybe we should send kids to school. But how do you do that? Do you hire teachers? Do you build more schools? Do you provide school lunches? How do you know?…

I cannot answer the big question, whether aid [does] any good or not. But these [smaller] questions, I can answer them. It's not the Middle Ages anymore; it's the twenty-first century. And in the twentieth century, randomized, controlled trials have revolutionized medicine by allowing us to distinguish between drugs that work and drugs that don't work. And you can do the same randomized, controlled trial for social policy. You can put social innovation to the same rigorous, scientific tests that we use for drugs. And in this way, you can take the guesswork out of policy-making by knowing what works, what doesn't work, and why.…

So I start with immunization. Here's Udaipur District, Rajasthan. Beautiful. Well, when I started working there, about 1 percent of children were fully immunized. That's bad, but there are places like that. Now, it's not because the vaccines are not there—they are there and they are free—and it's not because parents do not care about their kids.…So what is the problem? Well, part of the problem, surely, is people do not fully understand. After all, in this country [the United States], as well, all sorts of myths and misconceptions [surround] immunization. So if that's the case, that's difficult, because persuasion is really difficult. But maybe there is another problem, as well. [That is moving] from intention to action. Imagine you are a mother in Udaipur District, Rajasthan. You have to walk a few kilometers to get your kids immunized. And maybe when you get there, what you find is this: The subcenter is closed. [So] you have to come back, and you are so busy and you have so many other things to do. You will always tend to postpone and postpone, and eventually it gets too late.…

So what we did is we did a randomized, controlled trial in 134 villages in Udaipur District.…In the red dots [referring to a map of the area], we made it easy and gave people a reason to act now. The white dots are comparisons; nothing changed. So we make it easy by organizing this monthly camp where people can get their kids immunized. And then you…give them a reason to act now by adding a kilo of lentils for each immunization. Now, a kilo of lentils is tiny. It's never going to convince anybody to do something that they don't want to do. On the other hand, if your problem is [that]

you tend to postpone, then it might give you a reason to act today rather than later.

So what do we find?…Just having the camp, immunization increases from 6 percent to 17 percent.…That's not bad; that's a good improvement. Add the lentils…[and] multiply [the] immunization rate by six. Now, you might say, "Well, but it's not sustainable. We cannot keep giving lentils to people." Well, it turns out [that's] wrong economics, because it is cheaper to give lentils than not to give them. Since you have to pay for the nurse anyway, the cost per immunization ends up being cheaper if you give incentives than if you don't.…

So suppose your goal is to get kids into school. There are so many things you could do. You could pay for uniforms, you could eliminate fees, you could build latrines, you could give girls sanitary pads, etc., etc. So, what's the best [approach]? Well, at some level, we think all of these things should work. So, is that sufficient? If we think they should work intuitively, should we go for them? Well, in business, that's certainly not the way we would go about it.…

Suppose you have one hundred dollars to spend on various interventions. How many extra years of education do you get for your hundred dollars? Now I'm going to show you what we get with various education interventions. So the first ones are…the usual suspects: hire teachers, school meals, school uniforms, scholarships […these get you] between one and three extra years of education.…And here are the most surprising results…in places where there are worms, intestinal worms, cure the kids of their worms. And for every hundred dollars, you get almost thirty extra years of education. So this is not your intuition, this is not what people would have gone for, and yet, these are the programs that work. We need that kind of information, we need more of it, and then we need [it] to guide policy.…

You have to keep experimenting, and sometimes ideology has to be trumped by practicality. And sometimes what works [in one place] doesn't work [in another]. So it's a slow process, but there is no other way. These economics I'm proposing, [they're] like twentieth-century medicine. It's a slow, deliberative process of discovery. There is no miracle cure, but modern medicine is saving millions of lives every year, and we can do the same thing.

> YOU HAVE TO KEEP EXPERIMENTING, AND SOMETIMES IDEOLOGY HAS TO BE TRUMPED BY PRACTICALITY

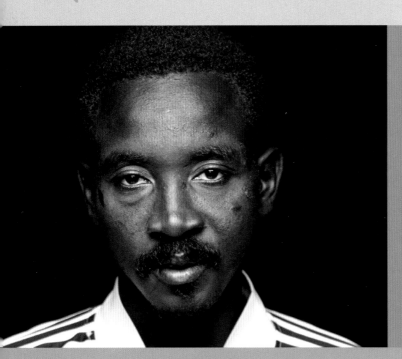

WAITING FOR ELSEWHERE

CALAIS MIGRANTS TELL OF THE DANGERS OF THEIR JOURNEY.

Calais, in northern France, has for some ten years been a point of passage for migrants wishing to go to England, hoping to find work or to join family members there. We were able to set up our camera in one of the camp's mobile offices. We found ourselves among more than four hundred people of twenty different nationalities at a crucial time in their lives. But this moment mostly consists of waiting, for several weeks or several months, until the hypothetical day when they'll be able to cling to the top of a truck and brave the police to cross the border.

By speaking in English and with help from Hedy, our Arabic interpreter, we were able to get discussions under way. We introduced the movie; we listened to their stories. And we started the interviews.

For everyone there, the journey to Calais took months. Each person had stopped in Libya to work and save enough money to pay the smugglers. Their road was riddled with pitfalls: hunger, violence, anxiety, doubt, and thoughts about family. Some died along the way, but these people made it to Calais alive.

We felt their exhaustion, of course, their sadness. Tears streamed down, but they hadn't given up their generosity along the way and smiles appeared on their lips. From where did they draw their life force? Yousif comes from Sudan; he gives us an answer: "In all the migrating I did, none of it was easy. Some periods are harder than others, but you always smile. Because you have hope, and hope makes you stronger."

The next day, we prepared for a new day of interviews. We arrived near the camp, but the neighborhood was surrounded by French police and we couldn't get through. We waited, powerless, trying to get information. We heard that some of the migrants were able to escape the police by hiding in the city, but many others were now locked in buses. The newly elected mayor of Calais had promised her residents that she would solve "this migrant problem." A few moments later, the buses passed in front of us. From inside, all eyes were on us.

For those migrants, a year—sometimes two—of effort and sacrifice was undone by the police action. It would all end with a flight back to their countries of origin.

Our filming came to an abrupt stop as well. That was the much lesser evil. But a team would leave for Lampedusa and another would return to Calais. Our work for the film was not complete and would continue—much like their migration.

> ## YOU HAVE HOPE, AND HOPE MAKES YOU STRONGER

MAKE SMALL LOANS TO THE IMPOVERISHED

KIVA AND BABYLOAN

Microcredit, a simple idea based on trust and responsibility, allows the poorest to borrow small sums of money in order to launch profit-making endeavors. With a few hundred dollars, borrowers are able to acquire cattle or poultry to breed, a sewing machine to make clothes to sell, or a telephone or computer to develop a business. The idea comes from Bangladesh, where, since 1976, Grameen Bank has granted microcredits that have helped numerous people climb out of poverty. As a result, Grameen Bank and its founder were awarded the Nobel Peace Prize in 2006. The microcredit system has spread to numerous countries through philanthropic lending organizations such as Kiva and Babyloan.
www.kiva.org
www.babyloan.org

BUY AT A FAIR PRICE

FAIRTRADE INTERNATIONAL

It makes good sense to pay a fair price for a product, one that allows its producer to live decently. This principle has guided fair trade, which aims to better compensate small producers and workers. Among its beneficiaries are small coffee growers. Generally, a label—for example, those of well-known Max Havelaar or Fairtrade International—ensures the origin of these products. Fairtrade International works with more than 1.4 million small producers across the globe. These organizations guarantee that the products distributed respect certain standards, for example, no child labor, and especially guarantee better pay for small producers.
www.fairtrade.net

FIGHT POVERTY

OXFAM

The international confederation Oxfam is unquestionably the largest nongovernmental organization (NGO) devoted to fighting poverty in the world. The Oxford Committee for Famine Relief (Oxfam) was founded in 1942 by students who had chartered a ship filled with provisions to help Greece, at the time in the grips of famine due to war. Since 1995, Oxfam has grown to represent seventeen national NGOs committed to fighting poverty and injustice, offering citizens the possibility of influencing political decisions—one of its most recent campaigns focuses on fighting fiscal fraud—and intervening in crisis situations, for example, helping African farmers deal with catastrophes.
www.oxfam.org

SPONSOR A CHILD

UNICEF

You can sponsor a child and follow his or her development. Multiple organizations such as Save the Children and World Vision offer options. UNICEF directs funds to the needs of 150 countries. Your regular donations can help a child get fed and go to school, and you'll receive regular updates on his or her progress.
www.unicef.org

MEALS FOR CHILDREN IN SCHOOL

AKSHAYA PATRA FOUNDATION

The Akshaya Patra Foundation distributes meals to children in more than ten thousand schools in India every day. It delivers hot meals to the country's schools in its blue vans. This effort ensures that children are not hungry while taking classes, and it liberates women from the traditional job of preparing lunch. It is furthermore a way to fight malnutrition.
www.akshayapatra.org

POVERTY IN NUMBERS

WHERE IS POVERTY THE MOST PREVALENT?

Nearly two-thirds of the poor live in just five countries.

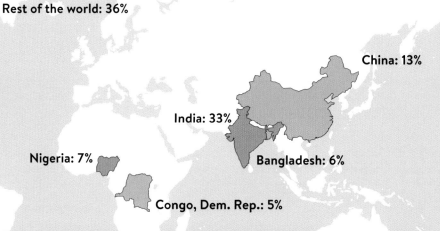

Rest of the world: 36%

China: 13%

India: 33%

Nigeria: 7%

Bangladesh: 6%

Congo, Dem. Rep.: 5%

There are, however, smaller countries with high extreme-poverty headcounts.

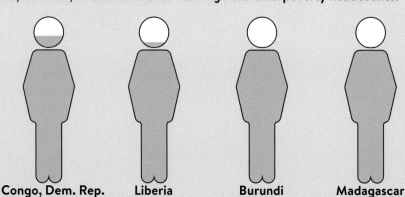

Congo, Dem. Rep.   Liberia   Burundi   Madagascar   Zambia

Thus the need to fight extreme poverty in every country.

EXTREME POVERTY IS ON THE DECLINE GLOBALLY

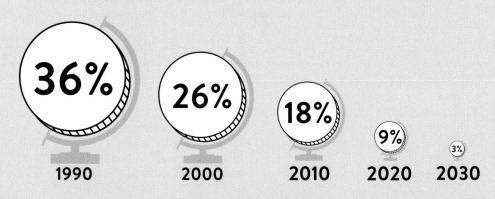

1990 36%
2000 26%
2010 18%
2020 9%
2030 3%

Proportion of world population living on less than $1.25 a day.

The challenge ahead: Reduce extreme poverty from 36% in 1990 to 3% by 2030.

POVERTY REDUCTION PROGRESS BY REGION

	1990	2010	
East Asia and Pacific	51.0%	11.4%	
Europe and Central Asia	1.1%	0.3%	
Latin America and the Caribbean	12%	5.4%	
Middle East and North Africa	5.1%	2.1%	
South Asia	54.4%	31.5%	
Sub-Saharan Africa	57.9%	47.9%	

KEY FIGURES

Approximately one billion people, or 14.5% of the world's population, live on less than $1.25 per day.

In 2012–2103, an estimated 842 million people, or about one in eight people in the world, suffered from chronic hunger. The vast majority of these people (827 million) reside in developing regions.

Between 2000 and 2012, the population of people in developing regions living in slums declined, from 40% to 33% of urban residents. The absolute number, however, increased by more than 100 million, due in part to the fast pace of urbanization.

In 2012, 748 million people relied on unsafe drinking water; 173 million obtain their drinking water straight from rivers, streams, or ponds.

Between 1990 and 2012, almost 2 billion people obtained access to improved sanitation. However, 1 billion people still resort to open defecation.

One in four children under age five in the world—an estimated 99 million—has inadequate height for his or her age. This number represents 15% of all children under five.

Almost 300,000 women died globally in 2013 from causes related to childbirth and pregnancy.

781 million adults and 126 million youth worldwide lack basic literacy skills, and more than 60% of them are women.

Half of the 58 million out-of-school children of primary school age live in conflict-affected areas. And more than one in four children in developing regions entering primary school is likely to drop out.

TIMELINE

1315
Louis X, King of France, abolishes slavery and declares that anyone setting foot in France is immediately free.

1450–1850s
The slave trade furnishes labor for colonies in the New World. Approximately twelve million Africans are deported to the Americas.

1883
German chancellor Otto von Bismarck introduces the first social laws for health care, accident and disability insurance, and retirement pensions. Costs are divided between employers and employees.

1894
New Zealand is the first country to establish a legal hourly minimum wage.

1948
The Universal Declaration of Human Rights, adopted by the United Nations General Assembly, recognizes the right to social security.

2000
The United Nations General Assembly adopts the Millennium Development Goals (MDGs), the first of which is to eradicate extreme poverty and malnutrition.

2015
The first MDG regarding reducing extreme poverty by half has been attained: Fewer than one billion people live on less than $1.25 per day.

BOOKS

Les Misérables
Victor Hugo, 1862
The characters in this vast novel have become icons of popular culture worldwide.

The Rebellion of the Hanged
B. Traven, 1936
The terrible story about a revolt waged by agricultural workers enduring inhuman work conditions in Mexico in the 1920s. A book by one of the most important and most mysterious novelists of the twentieth century. A parallel to the report on modern-day slavery, p. 154.

The Grapes of Wrath
John Steinbeck, 1939
This important social novel has retained all of its power.

Open Veins of Latin America
Eduardo Galeano, 1971
A great classic of leftist political literature, and a descent into the terrible history of inequalities in Latin America, and why centuries of colonization continue to make their mark on the social structure of the continent.

La Cité de la joie [City of Joy]
Dominique Lapierre, 1985
This novel, which was also adapted into film, looks at daily life in an impoverished section of Calcutta, India. A Polish priest shares the life of the neighborhood residents. In particular, he meets a rural family that has just moved there. Its members face destitution, sickness, hunger, and a lack of education, but they continue to believe that life is precious and call this area "Anand Nagar," which means the city of joy.

A Fine Balance
Rohinton Mistry, 1997
This novel focuses on the untouchables in India and their plight. They are said to number almost two hundred million.

The Wealth and Poverty of Nations
David S. Landes, 1998
This book looks into the origins of the industrial revolution, which allowed Western countries to amass wealth. The subject is debated and has fed numerous historical theories. Even though at the end of the Middle Ages the world's regions were mostly at the same level of economic development, Europe would gradually pull away and establish its control over a large part of the globe. A professor of economics and history, David S. Landes deems Europe, because of the competition that reigned between nations at the time, to have been more open to innovations than elsewhere.

Dream of Ding Village
Yan Lianke, 2006 (Chinese), 2011 (English)
This novel takes place in China in the 1990s. Enticed by easy money, a Chinese village sells its blood. Some do it just to buy a bottle of shampoo or a jacket. But the dream of easy money turns to nightmare when AIDS comes onto to the scene, dividing the community and causing many deaths.

Poor People
William Tanner Vollmann, 2007
Varied, striking, and at times unexpected, these stories—collected from Yemen, Thailand, and the United States, from the slums of Calcutta, Japan, and Mexico—upend our understanding of poverty.

Poor Economics
Abhijit V. Banerjee and Esther Duflo, 2012
This critical analysis of theories regarding how to fight poverty takes an empirical approach that is decidedly new.

Le Capital au XXIe siècle [Capital in the Twenty-First Century]
Thomas Piketty, 2013
French economist Piketty theorizes that the rate of return on capital is greater than the rate of economic output during crisis periods, and in combination these realities encourage inequality.

FILMS

The Lower Depths
Akira Kurosawa, 1957
This movie, based on a play by Maxim Gorki, looks at the lives of people at the bottom of the social heap in a tenement, divided between good and evil.

Midnight Cowboy
John Schlesinger, 1969
The life of two men struggling to survive in 1970s New York. One is a former cowboy who attempts to become a male prostitute.

Moonlighting
Jerzy Skolimowski, 1982
Polish laborers working illegally in London learn that the Soviets have declared marshal law in their country.

Rosetta
Luc and Jean-Pierre Dardenne, 1999
A young woman refuses to sink into poverty and attempts against all odds to find a job and confront life's hardships. An exceptional movie that was awarded the Palme d'Or in Cannes in 1999.

City of God
Fernando Meirelles and Kátia Lund, 2002
In Brazil, a *favela* is overrun by crime and violence. A young boy attempts to escape from the vicious cycle of poverty and violence through photography. It tells of the growth of gang violence in the 1960s and 1970s.

Sweet Sixteen
Ken Loach, 2002
This film is one of many the renowned filmmaker has made that shows the underbelly of British society.

Tokyo Godfathers
Satoshi Kon and Shôgo Furuya, 2003
A wonderful anime film about three homeless people who find an abandoned baby on Christmas Eve and try to locate the child's parents.

The End of Poverty?
Philippe Diaz, 2008
This documentary aims to turn back to the historic origins of poverty and worldwide inequality and talks with economists and populations fighting against poverty. Its origins are found in colonialism and its consequences: land appropriation, exploitation of natural resources, debt, etc.

Let's Make Money
Erwin Wagenhofer, 2008
This documentary denounces neo-liberal economics, which is presented as one of the causes of inequality.

Slumdog Millionaire
Danny Boyle, 2008
This is a modern-day fairytale with Bollywood flair.

8
Jan Kounen, Gaspar Noé, Jane Campion, Wim Wenders, Gus Van Sant, Abderrahmane Sissako, Gael García Bernal, and Mira Nair, 2009
These eight short films each focus on the United Nations Millennium Development Goals (MDGs).

Nero's Guests
Palagummi Sainath, 2009
This documentary addresses farmer suicide in India.

Sin Nombre
Cary Fukunaga, 2009
This film traces the journey of a young boy and girl through Central America as they attempt to reach the U.S. border in Mexico.

Champ of the Camp
Mahmoud Kaabour, 2013
This documentary focuses on the plight of laborers in work camps in the United Arab Emirates.

WEBSITES

Millennium Development Goals
www.un.org/millenniumgoals

Oxfam
www.oxfam.org

The Abdul Latif Jameel Poverty Action Lab
www.povertyactionlab.org

World Food Programme
www.wfp.org

UNDP – United Nations Development Programme
www.undp.org

Poverty Matters, a film by 7 Billion Others
www.ledeveloppementenquestions.org/?q=en/the-films/poverty-matters

One
www.one.org

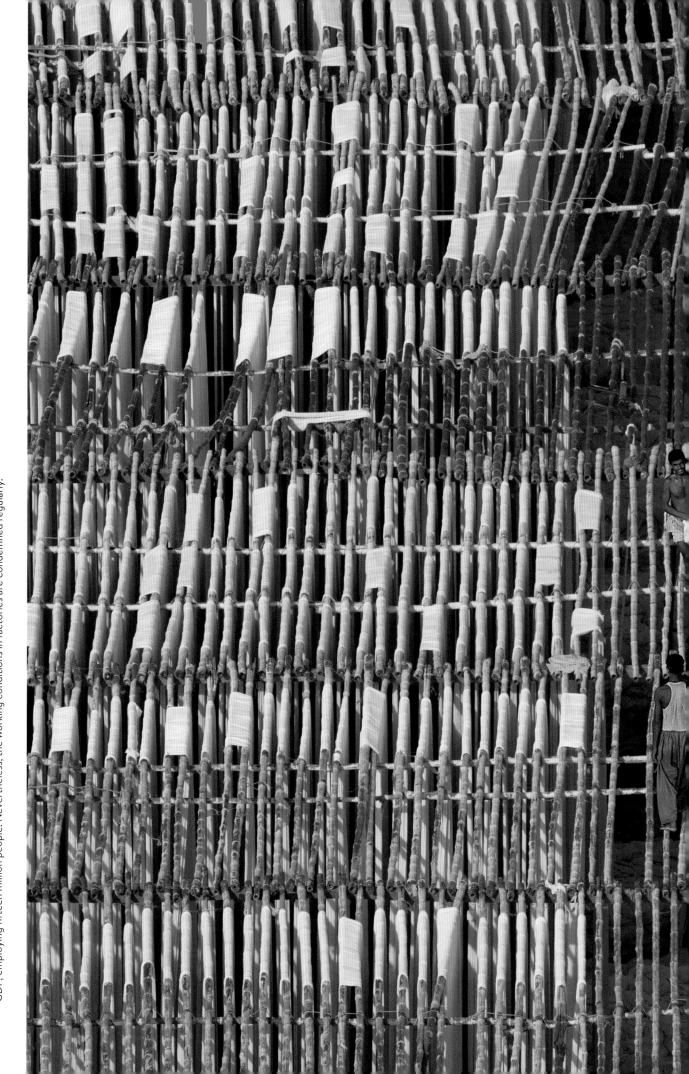

DYEING FACTORY, NEAR KARACHI, SINDH, PAKISTAN 24° 52' 44" N – 67° 16' 09" E

Several yards up, workers in this dyeing factory install beams for recently dyed fabric. Pakistan is the fourth largest producer of cotton in Asia, and the textile industry represents almost 10 percent of its GDP, employing fifteen million people. Nevertheless, the working conditions in factories are condemned regularly.

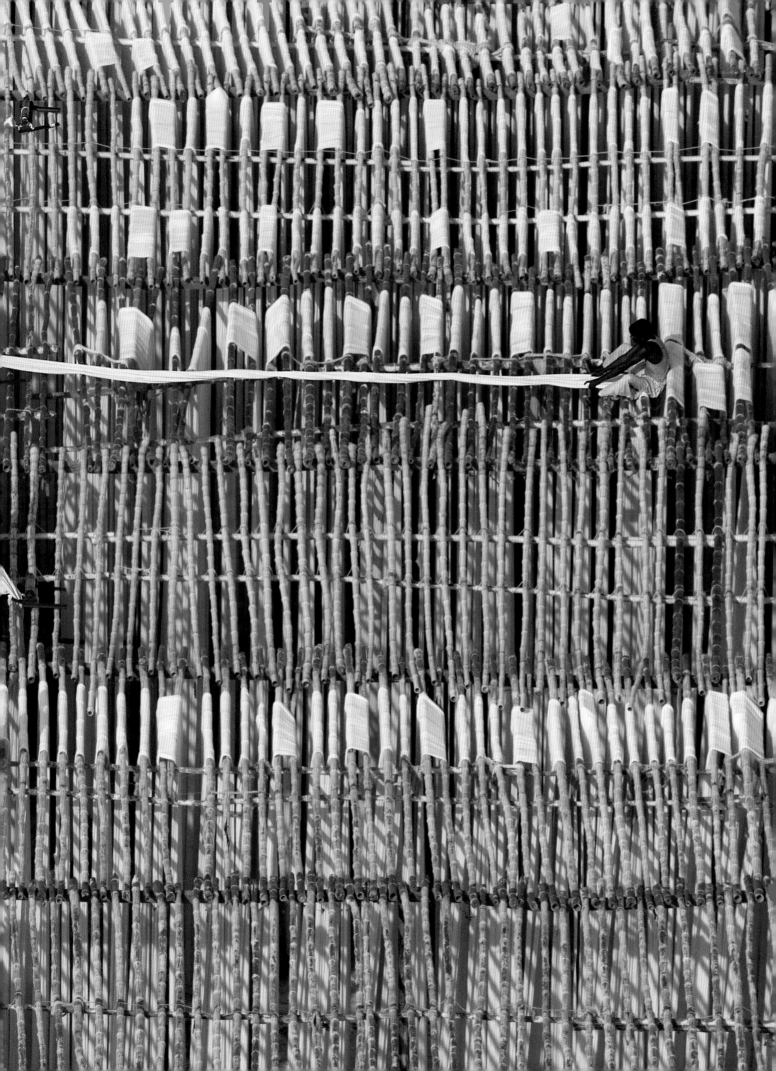

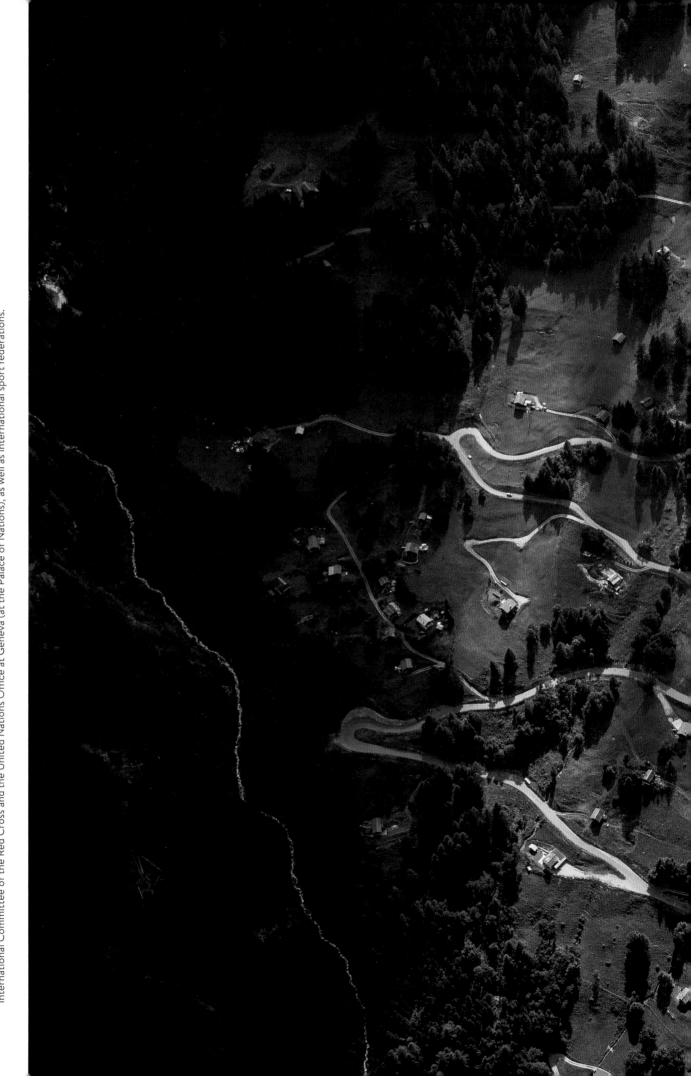

BAGNES, VALAIS, SWITZERLAND 46° 04' 47" N – 7° 12' 46" E

Situated in the heart of the Alps, Switzerland has been able to maintain its independence and neutrality in Europe. The Swiss Confederation consists of twenty-six cantons with wide-ranging resources and brings together populations that speak four different languages. Its policy of neutrality and its tax laws have made it the headquarters of numerous international organizations, for example, the International Committee of the Red Cross and the United Nations Office at Geneva (at the Palace of Nations), as well as international sport federations.

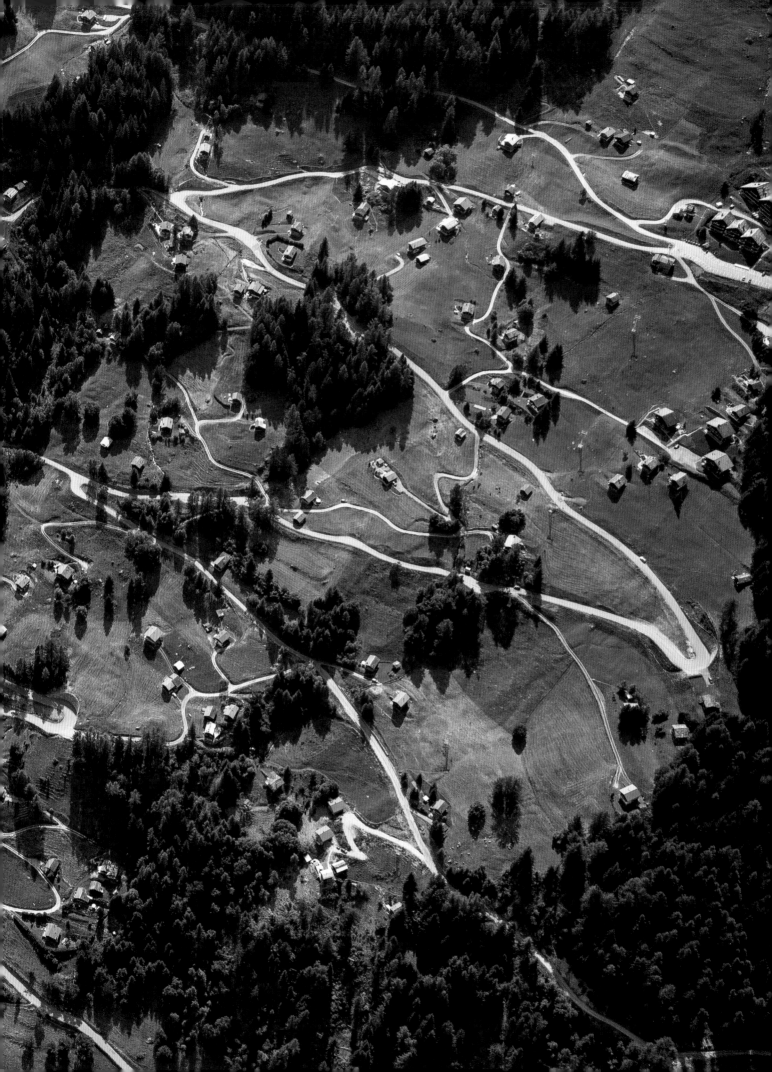

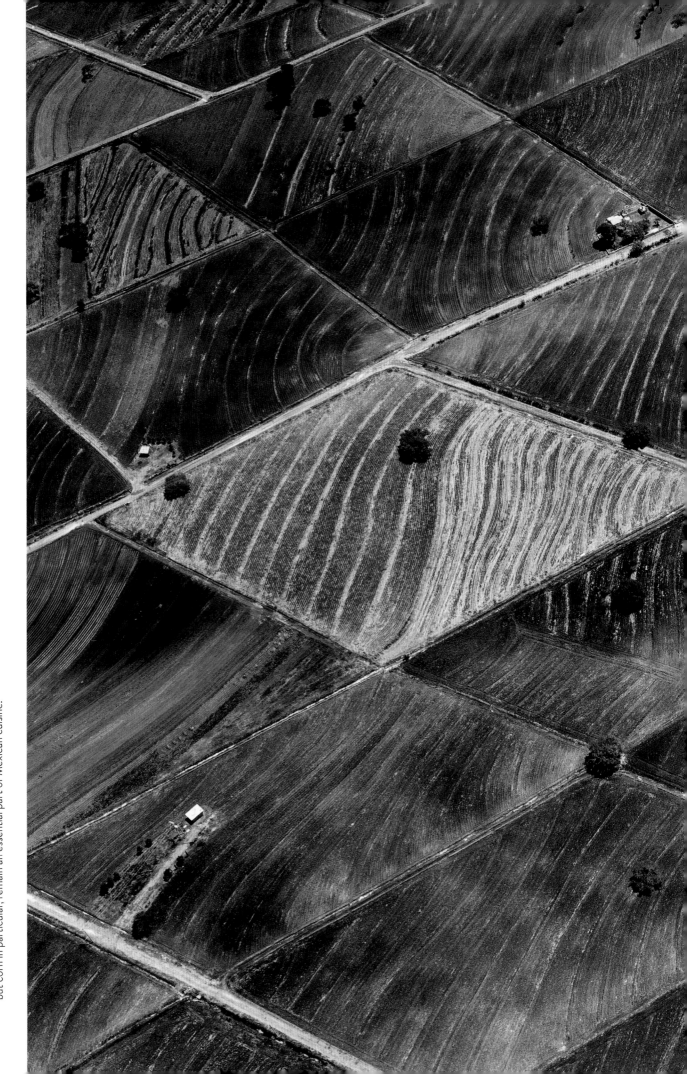

FARMED FIELDS, BETWEEN ATLIXCO AND TEHUACÁN, PUEBLA, MEXICO 19° 01' N – 98° 38' W

In Mexico, the agricultural sector hires 13 percent of workers but represents less than 3.5 percent of the GDP. Corn, tomatoes, and chilies are traditional products of the region, and today, all of these, but corn in particular, remain an essential part of Mexican cuisine.

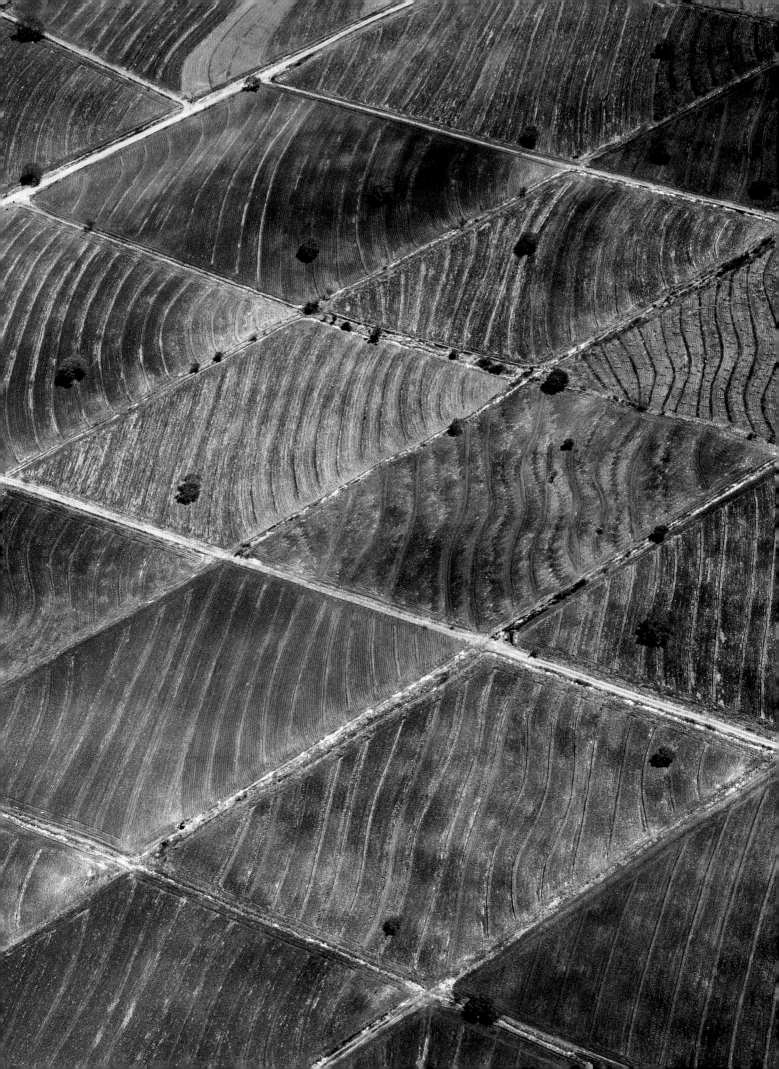

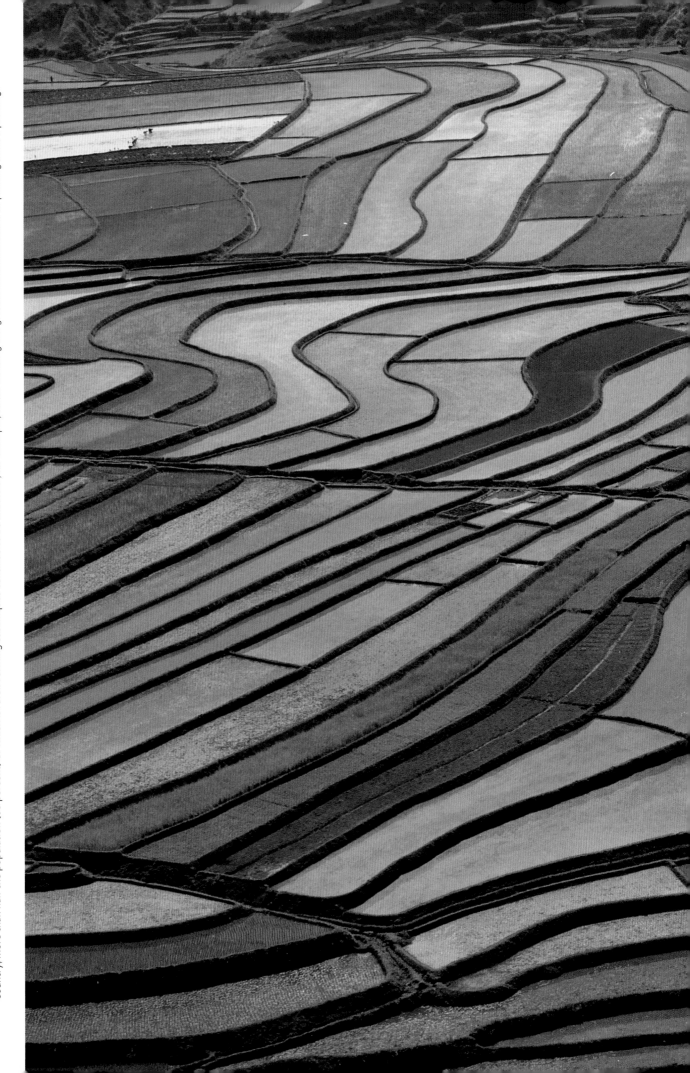

PADDY FIELDS NEAR BETAFO, VAKINANKARATRA, MADAGASCAR 19° 48' 57" S – 46° 52' 12" E

The introduction of rice in Madagascar coincided with the arrival of populations from Southeast Asia starting in the tenth century. Paddy fields from that point on became part of the landscape of this country, more than half the population (65 percent) of which is rural. Farming techniques continue to be ancestral; for example, cattle treading the ground remains a means of plowing before planting.

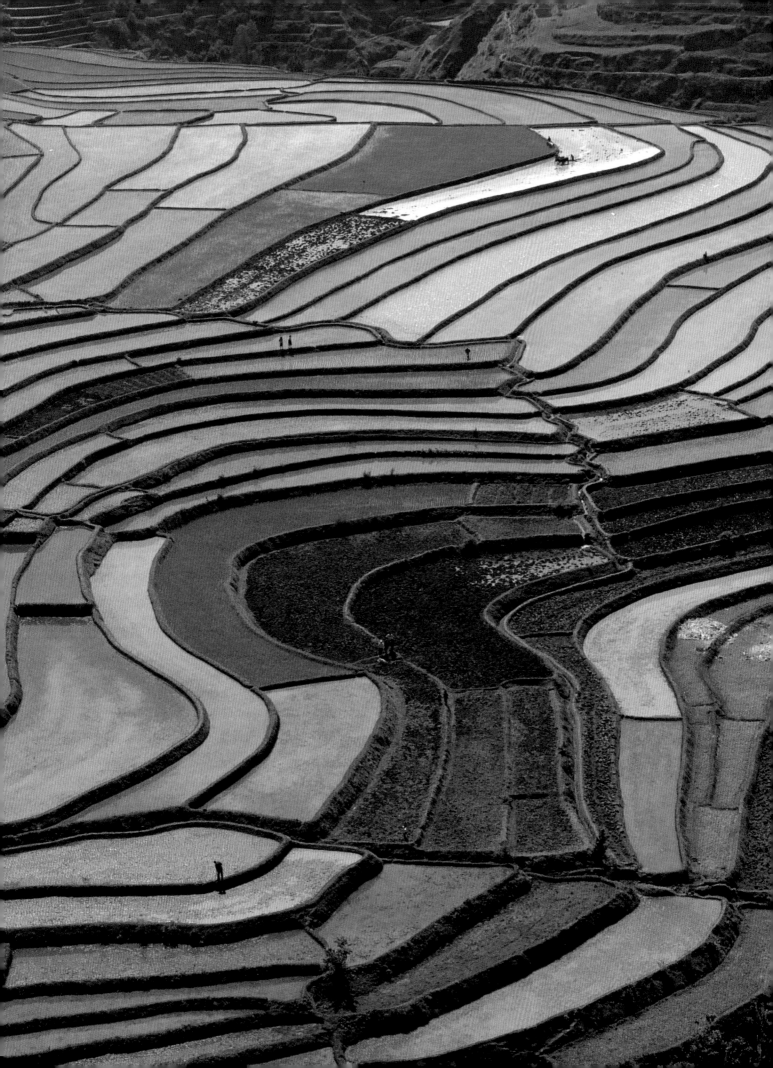

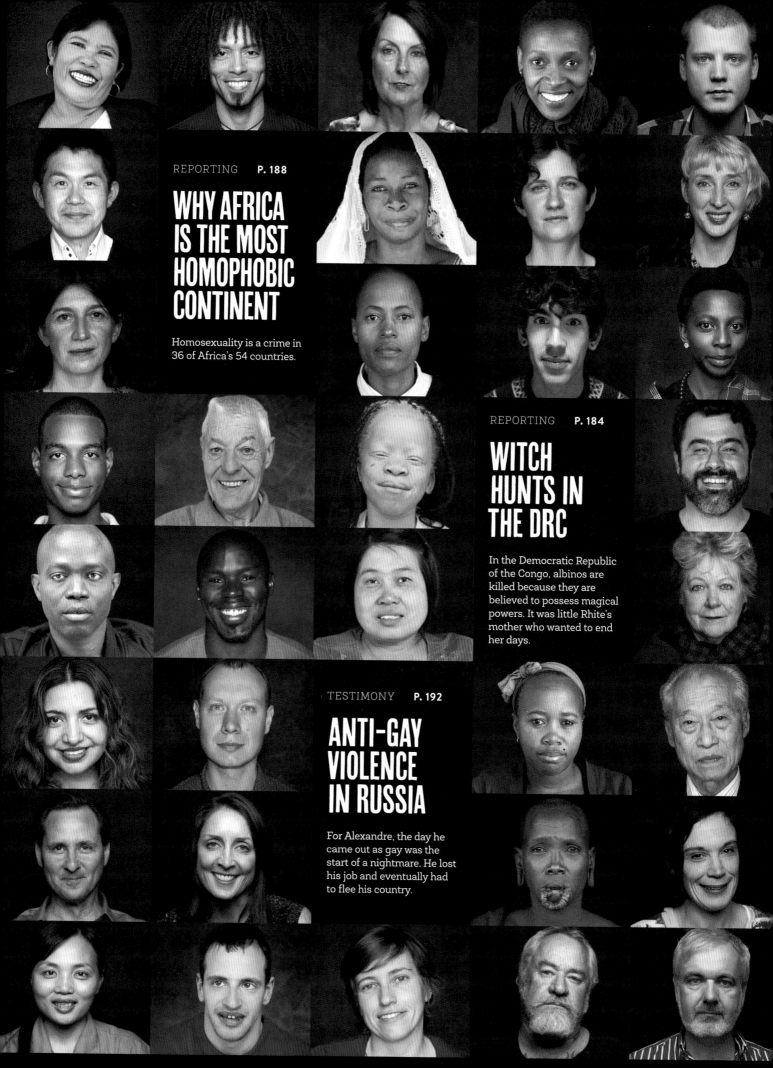

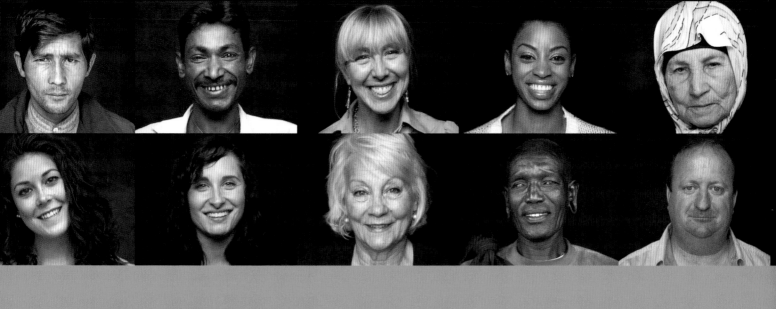

TOLERANCE

Prejudice needlessly impacts the quality of life of countless people, and sometimes even leads to death. Xenophobia affects gays, albinos, the disabled, people with HIV, and many others. But in our connected and changing world, everyone needs to live together and respect one another.

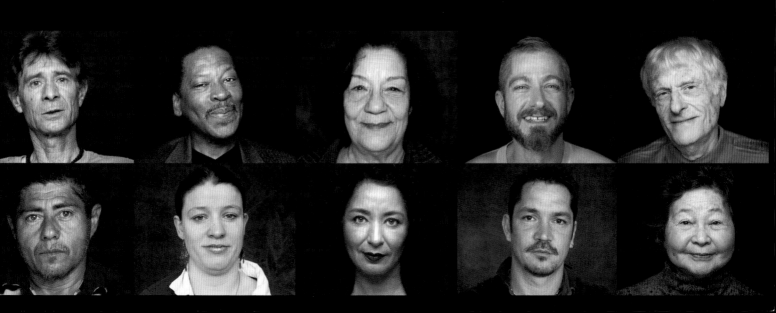

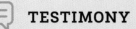
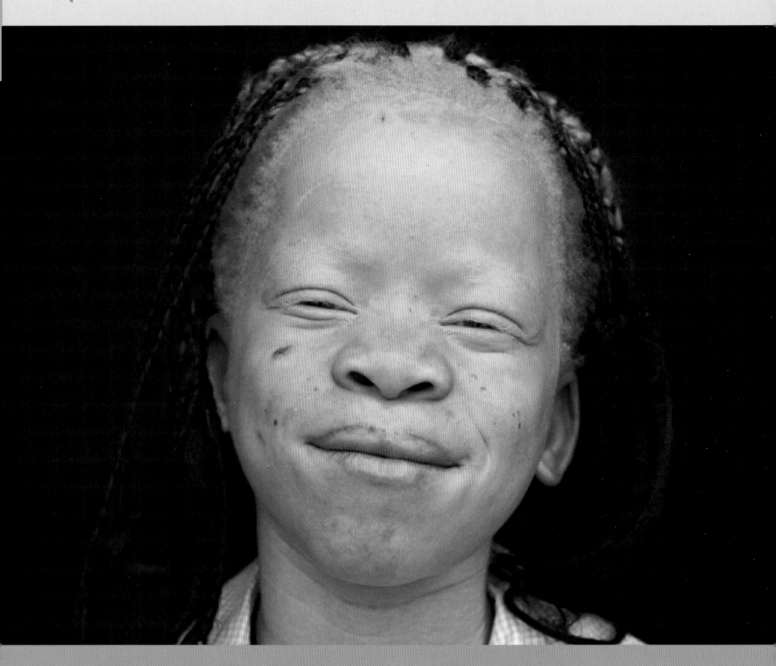

WITCH HUNTS IN THE DRC

IN THE DEMOCRATIC REPUBLIC OF THE CONGO, ALBINOS ARE KILLED OR ABUSED BECAUSE THEY ARE SUSPECTED OF POSSESSING MAGICAL POWERS. FOR YOUNG RHITE IT WAS HER OWN MOTHER WHO WANTED TO END HER LIFE.

She's a young girl from Kinshasa, the capital of the Democratic Republic of the Congo. Her name is Rhite. She walks quickly and comes toward us. Cowboy, our fixer, went looking for her at the Catholic mission of Kinshasa, near the port, where we've set up our studio.

Rhite approaches, head held high, her chin jutting forward. She has pretty extensions in her hair, fine braids and little beads. She's wearing a little pink plastic necklace and a bracelet that she fiddles with incessantly. Strangely, for someone who lives on the street, her yellow shirt looks impeccably ironed. Like many here, Rhite doesn't know her own age—probably ten or eleven.

She gives me a firm handshake and an assured smile. She says to me, "Bonjour, Monsieur," and to Jim, "Bonjour, Madame." It's at that moment that I understand she can't really see us. She's not blind, though. Not yet.

Her mother walks a bit behind. Rhite vaguely introduces her to us with, "She's not well." This woman of uncertain age with troubled features goes to sit down, a sagging shadow, behind our camera.

The interview begins. Rhite wants to reply in French. She has learned it in the street. One can imagine her loneliness, her isolation, the rejection by the other children. But her responses are too short, her sentences choppy, and to better understand her and for the sake of documentary, we ask her to continue in her mother tongue. She isn't too happy, because she's proud of her French and she finds Kikongo to be "vulgar."

We gently insist.

The interview resumes. We ask her about her childhood and her answer is a shock. Her first memory? When her mother wanted to drown her in the river.

> NO CHILD EVER WANTS TO PLAY WITH HER BECAUSE SHE BRINGS BAD LUCK, BECAUSE SHE'S A CURSED WHITE

She held her head underwater a very long time. She struggled. She was scared. And here she is, alive.

The sagging shadow that stays behind us reveals nothing. We don't know if she has heard, if she remembers. Even less, if she feels guilty for having tried to kill her only daughter…an albino.

Because here, in the Democratic Republic of the Congo, they kill albinos. Because here, their difference terrifies and it is believed that their white hair holds supernatural powers or that one of their body parts can be rendered into a potion. As a result of ignorance here, they end up on the street, at best. And so they can't do anything to prevent the blindness that afflicts them, the skin cancers that eat away at them.

Rhite no longer proceeds haltingly; she spits out her words, and Cowboy translates for us, at length, sometimes with tears in his eyes.

He tells us without looking at me about Rhite's daily life as an albino: She sleeps on top of a thin pile of cardboard on the very violent streets of Kin, she protects her mother with iron bars that she reddens in the fire to hurt attackers, she begs in the markets, and no child ever wants to play with her because she brings bad luck, because she's a cursed White whose mother couldn't or didn't know how to kill her as she had planned.

We'll never know if her mother's madness stems from this failed infanticide.

Rhite has the lively, flexible, joyous, and rare intelligence of someone who's hanging on to a dream, one that a little girl like her doesn't have access to: to go to school one day.

"Is it true," she asks when leaving, "that in Europe albinos have bank accounts?" And Rhite goes as she came, her head held high.

—Anne Poiret

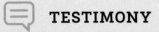
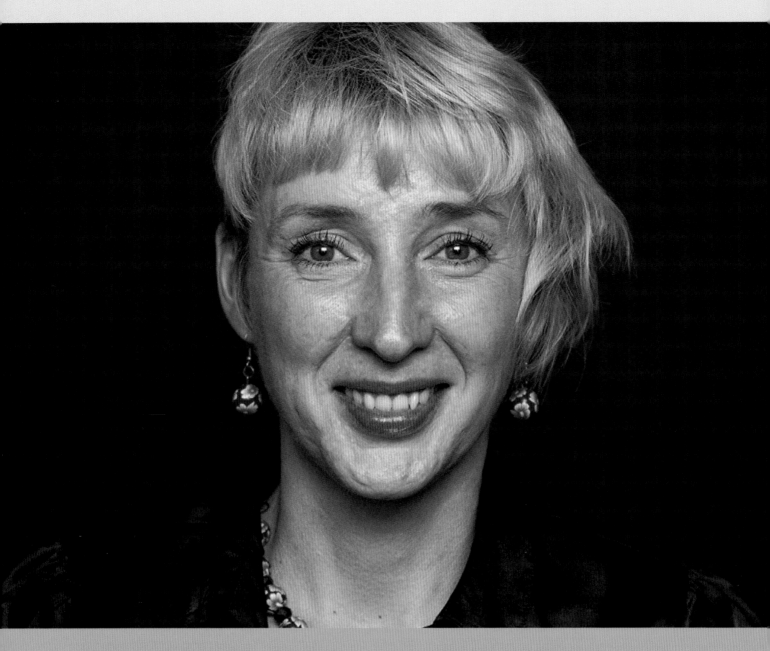

NO LEGS, BUT LOTS OF HAPPINESS

FOR YULIA, LIVING WITH PEOPLE WITH DISABILITIES IS A SOURCE OF CONSTANT JOY.

Every year, I navigate down the rivers of Siberia with my disabled friends. There are twenty-two of us on a catamaran and we boat for eight days. Some don't have legs, others don't have arms, and others don't see. But it has its advantages, because they can call out, "Come on! Faster!" and no one will hold it against them. As for me, I'm a river guide and lifeguard.

One day, we were boating together and we arrived at some traffic. Yes, there can be traffic on the water! There was a kind of barrier of tree trunks and the catamaran capsized. I was with my son, who has been volunteering for a long time; there was a friend with cerebral palsy who didn't know how to swim well—but that day, he understood that he could!

I don't know what happened; I couldn't swim anymore even though I'm a lifeguard. It was as if I were in a washing machine. I felt like everyone was drowning and I couldn't help them. They were in wheelchairs, they were blind, and I couldn't save anyone. I had just enough time to tell my son to help the others. That day, they were the ones who saved me from drowning—a very strong but blind friend and another whose legs were paralyzed but who had strong arms. And when I felt their arms under the water lifting me to the surface, I understood that I was going to survive. It wasn't God who saved me on that day; it was those men, my friends!

Some people I know, well, not the people I'm closest to, say to me, "You live with a disabled person!!!

YOU DON'T SEE THE SKY LIKE THEY DO; YOU DON'T HEAR THE WAY THEY DO

Oh wow! So, how does that work? That must be really hard?" I answer, "You won't believe me! Even though he doesn't have legs, you don't notice it. When I was pregnant, he would take me bike riding in the fields. He's a chess and ping-pong champion. He has a doctorate, well almost. He's very strong. He meets the needs of the family. He's very handsome. You can't find a better man. And when it comes to sex, well, he doesn't take up a lot of room in the bed, but that gives me more room. It's enriching to live with a deep man. So that's how it works."

People tell me, "You don't have a family; you have a bunch of handicapped people! That must be painful. They die sooner, and then there are the periods in the hospital. It must be hard having sick people around and having to help them." But that's not how it is at all! The people who don't know my disabled friends tell me, "How do you do it? You're a saint! It's a calling! We couldn't do it," and I answer, "Not at all! Get to know them and you'll see that they give you great strength. You can't feel life the way they feel it. You don't see the sky like they do; you don't hear the way they do. They're joyful. Maybe I got lucky.... But the people around me are like batteries: They fill me with energy. They're lawyers, PhD students, very athletic. We've become even stronger all together. We've grown up together in a certain way. How many stairs we've climbed when there was no elevator! And now look at my biceps! We recharge each other's batteries!

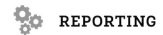

WHY AFRICA IS THE MOST HOMOPHOBIC CONTINENT

By David Smith
Originally published in the *Guardian* in February 2014

In February 2014, Uganda passed the Anti-Homosexuality Act. Although declared unconstitutional in August of the same year, the law underscored that for many political and religious leaders in Africa, homosexuality is an abomination, moreover one imposed by the West. In this article for the *Guardian*, David Smith shows that in reality the legacy of colonialism is not homosexuality, but rather homophobia.

Simon Lokodo cannot imagine kissing a man. "I think I shall die," he said last week. "I would not exist. It is inhuman. I would be mad. Just imagine eating your feces."

Lokodo is "ethics and integrity" minister in Uganda and a champion of the country's swingeing antihomosexuality bill, which looked set to become law on Sunday [February 16, 2014] until President Yoweri Museveni halted it, pending scientific advice. The delay was a small victory for activists dismayed [the week before] when Museveni insisted that he would approve the legislation. That news prompted Kenneth Roth, executive director of Human Rights Watch, to tweet: "In name of Africa culture Uganda Pres will sign anti-gay law pushed by U.S. evangelists toughening British colonial ban."

In 140 characters, Roth encapsulated a broad sweep of history and geography and one of the central paradoxes of Africa's new war on gay and lesbian people. It is a war marked by political opportunism, biblical fundamentalism, and a clash between cultural relativism and universal human rights. But it is also a measure of conservatives' anxiety that every day more and more African homosexuals are coming out and losing their fear. Western liberals eager to see the best in Africa must face an inconvenient truth: This is the most homophobic continent on Earth. Same-sex relations are illegal in thirty-six of Africa's fifty-four countries, according to Amnesty International, and punishable by death in some states. Now a fresh crackdown is under way.

In January, Nigerian president Goodluck Jonathan signed into law a bill criminalizing same-sex "amorous relationships" and membership of LGBT rights groups. Last week Gambian president Yahya Jammeh declared: "We will fight these vermins [sic] called homosexuals or gays the same way we are fighting malaria-causing mosquitoes, if not more aggressively."

This is not, however, merely the hate-filled bile of politicians. They make such statements because they know they will strike a popular chord in swaths of Africa. Anyone who has spent a fair amount of time on the continent is likely to encounter a warm, friendly, decent human being who will stop them short with an outburst of homophobic prejudice. Newspapers, TV, and radio often fan the flames.

So it is in Uganda, where a tabloid once published photographs of dozens of gay people under the words: "Hang them." Homosexuality was already a crime there, but the new legislation, rushed through parliament in December, broadens the scope of life imprisonment for a range of "offenses" including suggestive touching in public. Museveni has until Sunday to sign, veto, or amend the bill, and at first he indicated that he would knock it back.

SAME-SEX RELATIONS ARE ILLEGAL IN THIRTY-SIX OF AFRICA'S FIFTY-FOUR COUNTRIES, AND PUNISHABLE BY DEATH IN SOME STATES

On January 18, the Associated Press (AP) reported, he held a meeting with U.S.-based rights activists and, on the phone, South African retired archbishop Desmond Tutu, who drew a comparison between the legislation and racist laws under apartheid. Museveni "specifically said this bill is a fascist bill," Santiago Canton of the Robert F. Kennedy Center for Justice and Human Rights told the AP. "Those were the first words that came out of his mouth."

Something changed his mind. A month later the president, under domestic pressure, announced that he *would* sign the bill after receiving a report on homosexuality from a team of "medical experts." But the *Observer* has obtained the report, entitled "Scientific statement from the ministry of health on homosexuality"; it is far from the bigots' charter that might be expected. "Homosexuality existed in Africa way before the coming of the white man," it states. "There are a spectrum of sexual behaviours. Some people are less fixed in one form of sexuality than others. Thus sexuality is a far more flexible human quality than

used to be assumed in the past. Homosexuality has no clear cut cause; several factors are involved which differ from individual to individual. *It is not a disease that has a treatment.*"

But Simon Lokodo argues that the most important conclusion is that there is no definitive gene for homosexuality. "It is a social style of life that is acquired," he said by phone from Uganda. "They chose to be homosexual and are trying to recruit others. The commercialization of homosexuality is unacceptable. If they were doing it in their own rooms we wouldn't mind, but when they go for children, that's not fair. They are beasts of the forest."

With chilling conviction, Lokodo, a former Catholic priest, set out why he believes the state should interfere in the choices of consenting adults in private. "Homosexuality is unnatural, abnormal and strange to our cultures," he said. "It has no output whatsoever; it only does damage and destruction. You cannot have a right to be a sick human being. There is no right in homosexuality. It must be cured."

The minister has also considered the anatomical implications. "Excretion is through the anus, like the exhaust of an engine. The human body receives what it takes from the mouth. They're twisting nature the wrong way. Homosexuality will destroy humanity because there is no procreation; it will destroy health because the backsides will not hold."

After the bill drew criticism from Barack Obama, Lokodo accused the West of trying to "blackmail" Uganda. "When I heard the U.S. saying they will cut aid, we said fine. Will they be comfortable if we come to America and started practicing polygamy? Homosexuality is strange to us and polygamy is strange to you. We have divergent views."

Promoters of the bill in Uganda, which gained independence from

GAY PRIDE

On June 28, 1969, the New York police raided the Stonewall Inn, a bar in Greenwich Village run by the mafia but where its gay clientele had been accepted for a long time. Until then, it was enough to slip a bribe to police to buy their leniency. But that night, the situation degenerated. Bottles were thrown at the police, who arrested and beat people passing by. Nearly two thousand people assembled. What followed was six days of clashes.

A year later, the city's gay activists organized a march to commemorate the event. This was the first Gay Pride parade.

Since then, many Gay Pride parades have taken place around the world: At first unlawful and clandestine, they soon grew exponentially in the West and became open celebrations for one and all.

But in certain countries, these kinds of demonstrations are forbidden, and expose those participating to violence and repression.

Gay Pride has now been expanded to include lesbian, gay, bisexual, and transgender people—generally abbreviated as LGBT. What's more, the concept of pride has now been adopted by other movements (e.g., Veggie Pride).

HOMOPHOBIA IN THE UK

Close to 49,000 men were convicted in Great Britain by the law forbidding homosexuality. Among them, Oscar Wilde was sentenced to two years hard labor, a term that inspired his astounding *De Profundis*. Alan Turing was also affected, and his story is told in the Oscar-nominated film *The Imitation Game*. Perhaps the greatest mathematician of the twentieth century and a pioneering logician, during the Second World War, Turing broke the secret codes for the Enigma machine used by the German army. It has been said that Winston Churchill claimed Turing had made the single biggest contribution to Allied victory. Yet, this same Turing was prosecuted in 1952 for homosexual acts and accepted chemical castration. He committed suicide shortly thereafter.

It was only in 2009 that the British government expressed its "regrets" over this prosecution, all while refusing to overturn the law. It would not be until December 24, 2013, that the Queen of England granted an exceptional and posthumous pardon to Alan Turing. A petition was circulated demanding the pardon of others prosecuted by this law, 15,000 of whom are still alive.

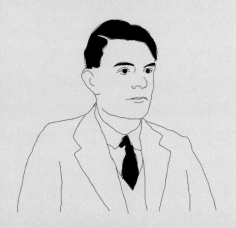

Britain in 1962, appealed to populist notions of culture that frame homosexuality as an "un-African," alien behavior foisted on the continent by Western imperialists. Seen through this prism, a strike against gay and lesbian people is a strike against colonialism and in favor of African nationalism and self-worth.

Yet as the scientists' report noted, homosexuality has existed throughout human history. Anthropologists found an ethnic group in central Africa where it was customary for a male warrior to marry a teenage boy and celebrate victory in battle by having sexual intercourse. In many cases, the very laws being imposed so zealously were introduced by the European empires that carved up and plundered Africa.

"Prior to Western colonization, there are no records of any African laws against homosexuality," said Peter Tatchell, the veteran human rights and gay rights campaigner. "The real import into Africa was not homosexuality but homophobia."

It was enforced legally by colonial administrators and ideologically by Christian missionaries. Tatchell, who twice tried to arrest Zimbabwean president Robert Mugabe over human rights abuses, added: "The colonial narratives of racism and homophobia are very closely intertwined. It's one of the great tragedies of Africa that so many people have internalized the homophobia of that colonial oppression and now proclaim it as their own authentic African tradition."

Defense of "tradition" can be a sleight of hand to trade on cultural relativism and exploit postcolonial guilt. Some in the West may be reluctant to criticize African attitudes, lest they be accused of racism. But activists counter that they are appealing to human rights, such as the right not to be tortured, that apply everywhere at all times. A minority has an absolute right to be protected from violations by a majority, they argue.

This counts for little at the altar of political expediency, however, according to Kapya Kaoma, an Episcopal priest from Zambia, and religion and sexuality researcher at the U.S.-based think tank Political Research Associates. Politicians tend to "blame the gays" to distract attention from their own failings, he says, casting them as the enemy within. Mugabe peppered his speeches with praise of Adam and Eve and denunciations of homosexuals as animals while electioneering last year.

The share of the sub-Saharan Africa population that is Christian climbed from 9 percent in 1910 to 63 percent

36 COUNTRIES

36 OF THE 54 COUNTRIES IN AFRICA HAVE ADOPTED LAWS AGAINST HOMOSEXUALITY. THERE ARE MORE THAN 76 COUNTRIES WORLDWIDE WITH THESE KINDS OF LAWS.

GAYS AND LESBIANS ARE COMING TO CONSCIOUSNESS, ORGANIZING THEMSELVES AND SPEAKING OUT

in 2010, says the Pew Research Center. Kaoma said: "Religious fundamentalism is strong in these countries. That provides the militant reaction to LGBT rights. One of the fears for fundamentalists is losing grip of the country; they are told they have lost grip because of the gays. They say, 'We don't want to lose Nigeria or Uganda just as our brothers lost America to the gays. If it means killing, we will kill.'" He said homosexuality is a rare point of convergence for Christian and Islamic hardliners.

U.S. evangelicals have been accused of turning their attention to Africa and whipping up homophobia with lurid stories about child molestation, bestiality, rape, and deadly diseases. Kaoma reflected: "In America the conservatives are losing. In Africa they are winning and the progressives are on the retreat. People are not paying attention to how world religions are taking advantage of globalization. Those opposed to gay rights can connect very easily with African groups opposed to gay rights. In the past they had to travel; now they send an email and share tactics. Conservatives argue that gays are out to destroy 'traditional family values'; as Africans encounter fast-changing values, this language sounds very attractive."

There is, however, a paradox in the wave of oppression: The harsh laws being enacted may be a measure not of failure but of success, a reaction to gays and lesbians asserting their political identity and rights as never before. Graeme Reid, director of the Lesbian, Gay, Bisexual, and Transgender Rights Program at Human Rights Watch, said: "I do see it as a backlash against the increasing visibility. Over the last 25 years there's been an unprecedented growth of LGBT movements across sub-Saharan Africa. Clearly, this is an indigenous African phenomenon. There are various reasons: one is the HIV/AIDS epidemic and the funding that became available for men who have sex with men. There was a more open discussion around sexuality."

Anyone who attended the recent opening of the Queer and Trans Art-iculations: Collaborative Art for Social Change, an exhibition at the Wits Art Museum in Johannesburg, could not help but feel hopeful. Many among the spectacular first-night crowd were confidently gay, lesbian, transgender, and, in the word of one guest, "performative." Despite the works' reminder of the deadly hate crimes that persist in South Africa, the event's celebratory, out-and-proud atmosphere offered a glimpse of another possible future.

Last week, Edwin Cameron, a South African constitutional court judge and one of the first public figures in Africa to come out as gay and HIV-positive, reflected: "The most interesting thing going on here is what I call an 'unstable transition.' It explains the force of the backlash just as African gays and lesbians are starting to come out. It releases hatred and rage, but what is happening is irreversible. Gays and lesbians are coming to consciousness, organizing themselves and speaking out."

SURVIVAL

Racism is not the prerogative of whites alone. Most civilizations and cultures have known or know this ignominy. One of the most ferocious forms of "ordinary" racism is the kind conceived of by the citizens of one country or region of the world against indigenous populations: white Australians against Aboriginal Australians, South Americans against Amerindians, southern Africans against Bushmen, for example. It is to defend these native peoples that the international organization Survival was founded.

As an example, the Bushmen hunter-gatherers are among the oldest inhabitants of southern Africa. They settled there more than 20,000 years ago but are held in contempt by their fellow citizens who see them as "primitives living in the stone age." At the head of the Botswani government, the president of the Republic even made multiple racist declarations against them. Gradually forced into the Kalahari Desert, many Bushmen lived in the Central Kalahari Game Reserve until the discovery of diamonds incited the government to drive them out, starting in 1997, forcing them into exile in resettlement camps.

Following a trial led by the Bushmen against the government, made possible by financial support from Survival, Botswana's Supreme Court issued a historic verdict in 2006, deeming the expulsion of Bushmen "unlawful and unconstitutional." However, more progress still needs to be made, as they continue to be persecuted nevertheless.

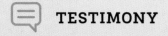
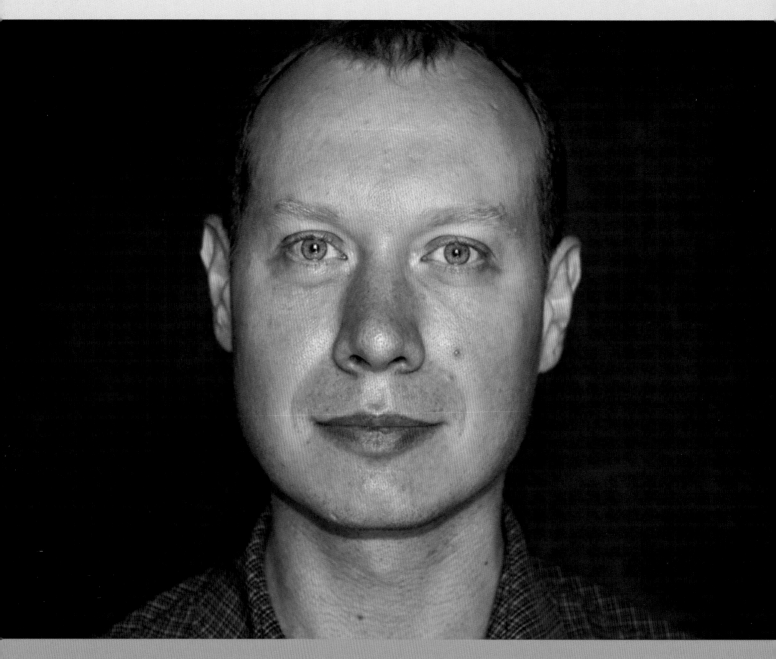

ANTI-GAY VIOLENCE IN RUSSIA

FOR ALEXANDRE, COMING OUT AS GAY WAS THE BEGINNING OF A NIGHTMARE THAT DROVE HIM INTO EXILE.

Before going to film in Russia, we corresponded for several weeks via email. Alexandre was suspicious and hesitant; he wanted to know everything about the project and about how his story would be used in *Human*. Never had I been asked so many questions before mine were answered. As soon as I asked him anything, he stopped answering, and then when he finally did, it was very vague. But I knew he had already spoken about it. He was even fired after publishing an interview with a Moscow newspaper. Why? Because Alexandre is the first Russian civil servant to have come out publicly.

What's more, he did it at a time when Russia was hardening its line against homosexual "propaganda." It's difficult to know what might constitute "propaganda." Is it saying it loud and clear that you're gay, or is it holding your partner's hand in the street? The law is very vague...But most gays in the country are now scared. Everyone who had initially said yes later changed their minds. I understand. Who wants to risk going to jail? So I didn't push anyone to reconsider, even if it seemed essential to me to cover the subject.

In the end, Alexandre did show up for the appointment. He called me from downstairs at the building where we were filming, asking me to come get him alone. He wanted to make sure this wasn't a trap. I showed him the brochure for the movie and a few other testimonies we had collected elsewhere in the world. He felt reassured. He admitted that since he came out, he has received so many threats by phone and email that he doesn't trust anyone anymore. I attempt in vain to imagine what his life is like when, every time he goes somewhere, he has to wonder what could happen to him.

The interview begins. Alexandre explains that two days after his famous coming out, when he was still a press attaché at the Moscow city hall, his boss came into his office and told him nicely, "You're going to have to resign." They had been working together for more than seven years. She was well aware that he was gay, but now she didn't want to have anything to do with him. "You made your decision; you have to live with it."

A few weeks later, Alexandre met a man on the Internet, saw him several times in a café; he was attracted to the man, trusted him. Alexandre invited him home. The day of the date, while he was preparing dinner, his new "boyfriend" went to open the door and let in another man. When Alexandre turned around, he understood what was about to happen. Too late: He was hit on the head with a bottle and ended up on the floor. When he came to, he heard the two men next to him discussing how they were going to kill "this dirty fag."

Alexandre tells me his story calmly, as if it had happened to someone else, as if it were a movie. But this was real. "You know," Alexandre says to me, "I understood at that moment what life meant to me, so I stayed on my knees for more than an hour, begging them not to kill me." Finally, the two men left, after beating him up and robbing him. He can't even file a report because he knows perfectly well that when they find out he's gay, the police will have their turn at beating him. Or they'll prosecute him under the famous homosexual propaganda law, because he's not hiding the fact that he's gay.

Since this meeting, we've become friends. Alexandre isn't dead. Living in exile in the United States, he has started a new life in New York where he's learning English. But how many other men and women like him are prosecuted, humiliated, beaten, or killed around the world every day?

> WHEN ALEXANDRE TURNED AROUND, HE UNDERSTOOD WHAT WAS ABOUT TO HAPPEN. TOO LATE: HE WAS HIT ON THE HEAD WITH A BOTTLE AND ENDED UP ON THE FLOOR

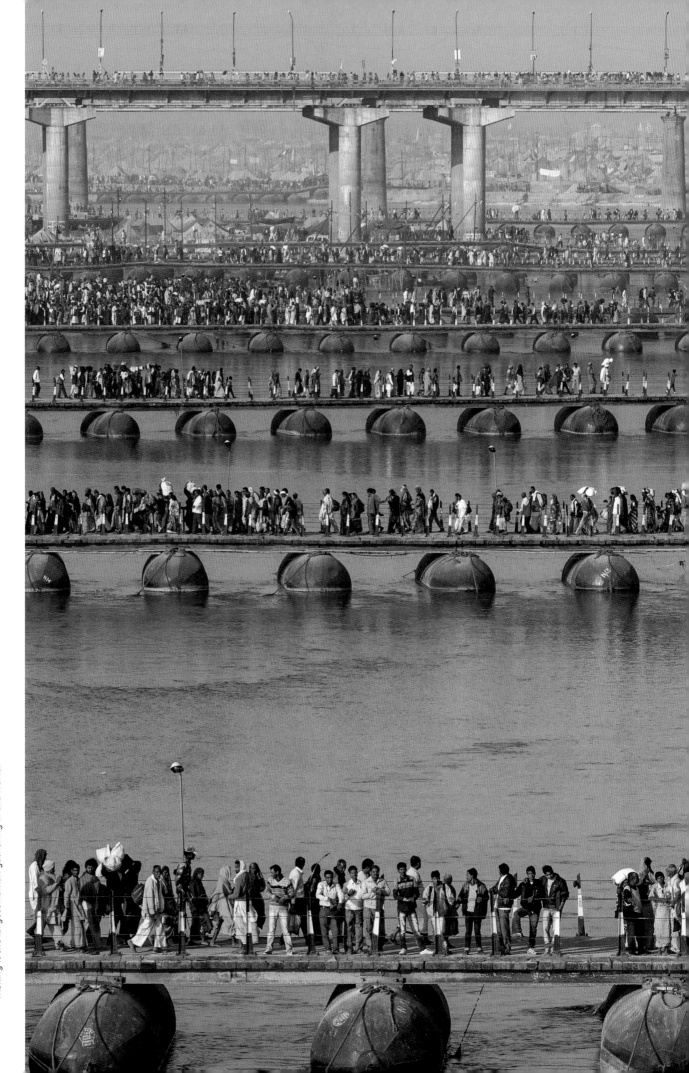

KUMBH MELA HINDU PILGRIMAGE, ON THE GANGES, ALLAHABAD, UTTAR PRADESH, INDIA 25° 26' 13.10" N – 81° 53' 25.62" E

The Kumbh Mela pilgrimage draws many faithful Hindus to the Ganges River once every twelve years—its date is set according to an astrological calendar. It attracts up to one hundred million people, making it the largest human gathering in the world.

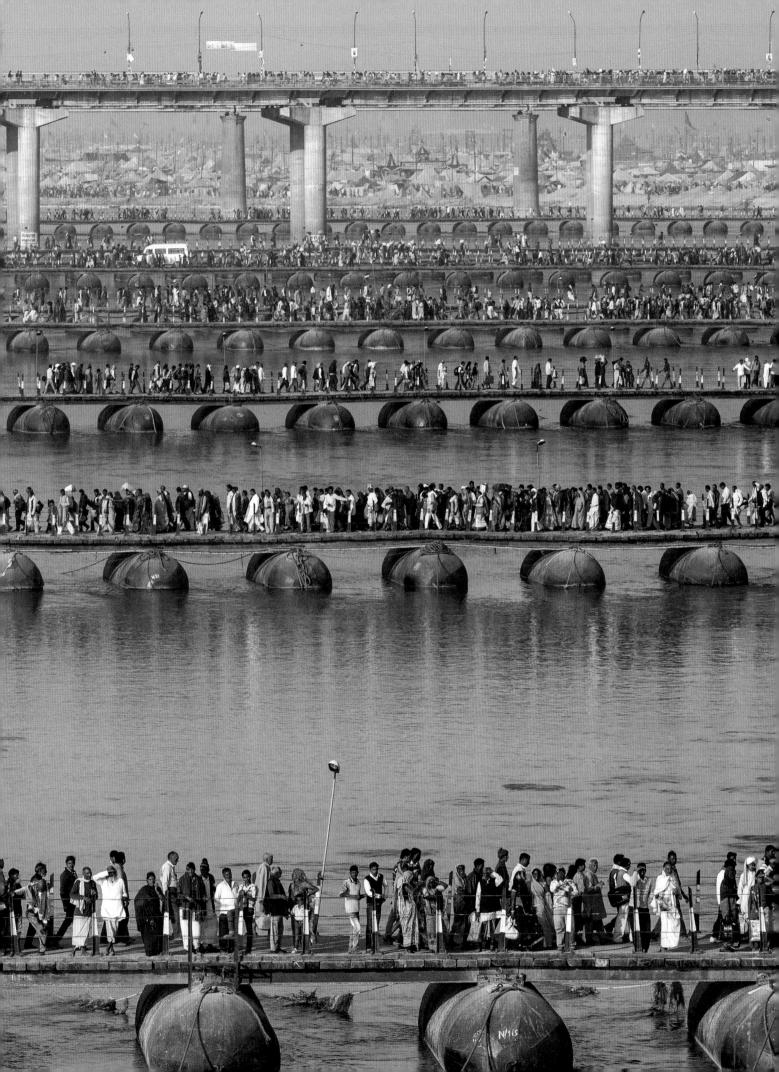

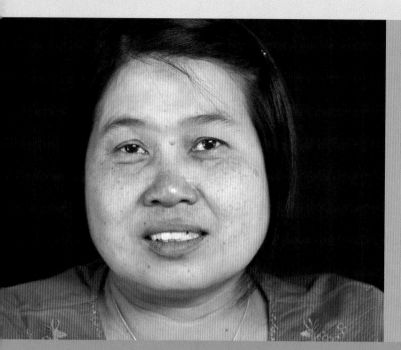

LIVING WITH AIDS

KASEMARI HAS BEEN HIV-POSITIVE FOR TEN YEARS. SHE FIGHTS DISCRIMINATION AGAINST THE SICK.

When I learned, in 1996, that my husband had been infected with HIV by another woman, I was very angry. It was the first time someone had become infected in the village. I couldn't accept it, and people in the village didn't accept it either. Even the head of the village said that we shouldn't help my husband because it was his fault and that we should let him die.

I was doing really badly....They didn't accept us in the village....So we all moved to Khon Kaen, three hundred miles to the southwest. We stayed there about a year. My husband was always sick; he wasn't working. I spent all of my time taking care of him.

I was so sad during that period that we even thought about committing suicide with the whole family. And then I thought about my child who had just been born; he hadn't done anything wrong, so why should we kill him? I had to be there for him, so that he wasn't subjected to the same life I am.

> I HAVE TO HELP OTHERS, SO I HAVE NO RIGHT TO DIE

I learned how to live with the disease. I began to volunteer, and I was able to pass on what I knew to others. I explained to them that you can live with the disease, that you can manage it, that while the disease never goes away, you can be in good health. I share this with my friends so that they can have an easier life, and that makes me happy. I have to help others, so I have no right to die. And when I'm unhappy, I go to the temple, I pray, and I feel better.

It has been more than ten years since I was infected by the virus that causes AIDS. I would like to send a message of encouragement to all of my friends throughout the world infected with the virus: Don't forget that you're worth something, contrary to what people think and say about you. We're human beings like everyone else; we're worth something and we're useful to society.

ENDING THE DISCRIMINATORY CASTE SYSTEM

INTERNATIONAL DALIT SOLIDARITY NETWORK

Although officially repealed with Independence in 1947, the caste system persists in India. About two hundred million people are still considered untouchables, pariahs, or Dalits. They're still victims of discrimination, of forced labor, of sexual violence, and of rejection, because they carry out jobs, such as garbage collection or burials, that are considered degrading. Numerous NGOs offer support. The International Dalit Solidarity Network, for example, fights to stop discrimination based on caste, familial origin, or work.
www.idsn.org

I SAY NO TO RACISM

LET'S FIGHT RACISM!

The United Nations acknowledges that racism, xenophobia, and intolerance are major problems in every society. It has launched the "Let's Fight Racism!" campaign to raise awareness about our shared humanity. Each and every one of us plays a role in feeding or fighting racial prejudice and intolerance.
www.un.org/en/letsfightracism

EQUAL RIGHTS FOR ALL

ILGA

The International Lesbian, Gay, Bisexual, Trans and Intersex Association (ILGA) unites more than a thousand organizations in defending the rights of gay, lesbian, bisexual, transgender, and intersex people throughout the world. Founded in 1978, the ILGA has been fighting for equal rights and against discrimination based on sexual orientation and disease and maintains a map of the locations of anti-gay laws.
www.ilga.org

MAKING INFORMATION ACCESSIBLE TO THE DEAF

I DEAF NEWS

For the visual and hearing impaired, access to news and other information can prove complicated. The nonprofit organization i DEAF NEWS makes the news accessible to those who are deaf and hard of hearing.
www.ideafnews.com

EVERYONE IS DIFFERENT

KEY FIGURES

The Universal Declaration of Human Rights, adopted by the United Nations on December 10, 1948, stipulates: "Everyone is entitled to all the rights and freedoms set forth in this Declaration, without distinction of any kind, such as race, color, sex, language, religion, political or other opinion, national or social origin, property, birth or other status."

In a survey of the United States carried out in 2015, women receive salaries 18% lower on average than those of men. Black men receive salaries 24% lower on average than those of white men, Hispanics 33% lower, and Asians 19% higher.

One person in seven—that is, more than one billion people across the world—has a disability.

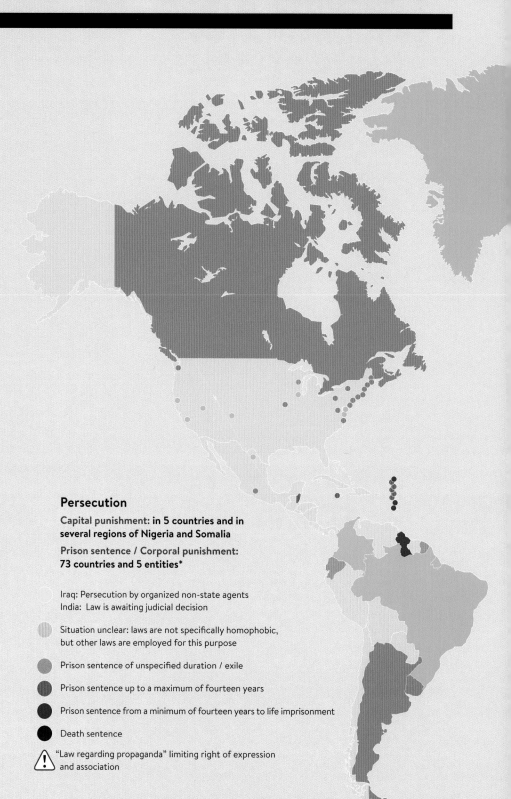

Persecution

Capital punishment: **in 5 countries and in several regions of Nigeria and Somalia**

Prison sentence / Corporal punishment: **73 countries and 5 entities***

Iraq: Persecution by organized non-state agents
India: Law is awaiting judicial decision

Situation unclear: laws are not specifically homophobic, but other laws are employed for this purpose

Prison sentence of unspecified duration / exile

Prison sentence up to a maximum of fourteen years

Prison sentence from a minimum of fourteen years to life imprisonment

Death sentence

"Law regarding propaganda" limiting right of expression and association

GAY AND LESBIAN RIGHTS ACROSS THE WORLD

Recognition

Recognition and registration of unions between same-sex partners:
30 countries and 44 entities*

Joint adoption by a couple: **14 countries and 37 enities***

- ● Marriage
- ● Similar measure (substitute for marriage)
- ● Alternative measure with inferior value to marriage
- ○ Absence of specific legislation

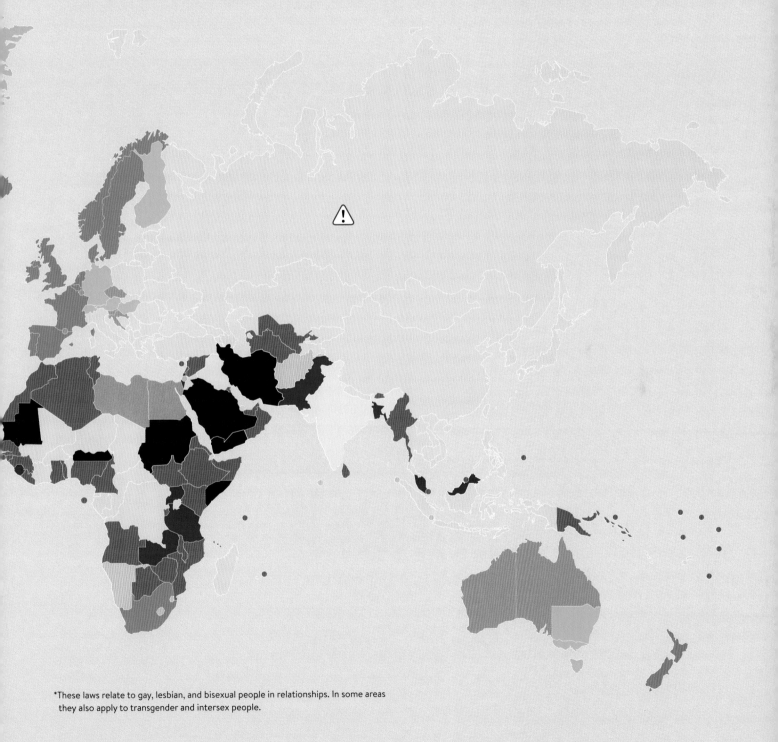

*These laws relate to gay, lesbian, and bisexual people in relationships. In some areas they also apply to transgender and intersex people.

TIMELINE

1550–1551
The Valladolid debate is held. Bartolomé de Las Casas, a Dominican friar and the Bishop of Chiapas, becomes an avid defender of the rights of the indigenous peoples in South America.

1789
The Declaration of the Rights of Man and of the Citizen is passed by France's National Constituent Assembly. It asserts, "Men are born and remain free and equal in rights."

1794
Slavery is prohibited in France by the Convention. It would be reestablished in 1802 by Napoleon Bonaparte.

1933–1945
More than six million Jews are exterminated in Europe by the Nazis. Tens of thousands of gay people, gypsies, and black people are also deported and murdered.

1946
The Indochina War begins, triggering several decades of conflict over decolonization.

1948
The Universal Declaration of Human Rights is adopted by the General Assembly of the United Nations.

1963
Martin Luther King Jr. gives his famous I Have a Dream speech. He would be assassinated in 1968.

June 28, 1970
The first Gay Pride parade is held, in New York.

BOOKS

De Profundis
Oscar Wilde, 1905, complete version 1962
Wilde wrote this moving letter to his lover from prison in 1897. The author had been sentenced to two years' hard labor for homosexuality.

The Forty Days of Musa Dagh
Franz Werfel, 1933
This Austrian novel is based on the little-known Armenian genocide: the self-defense of a few thousand Armenian refugees on a mountain, the Musa Dagh, and their rescue by a French fleet.

If This Is a Man
Primo Levi, 1947
In one of the most important books of the twentieth century, the author offers an account of dehumanization at the Auschwitz concentration camp.

La Question [The Question]
Henri Alleg, 1958
This book was banned upon its release, but 150,000 copies were distributed illegally and helped reveal torture practices in Algeria by the French army.

Black Like Me
John Howard Griffin, 1961
In this nuanced nonfiction portrait of racial discrimination in the United States, an American white journalist passes as a black man through the South.

The Autobiography of Malcolm X
As told to Alex Haley by Malcolm X, 1965
This text chronicles the American black radical movement and one of its principal leaders, Malcolm X, who was assassinated in 1965.

A Dry White Season
André Brink, 1979
This is one of many novels that denounce apartheid, which was still in effect in South Africa at the time it was published.

The God of Small Things
Arundhati Roy, 1997
This largely autobiographical book is also a denunciation of the caste system, which, although officially repealed, remains in effect in India.

Grâce et dénuement [Angelina's Children]
Alice Ferney, 1997
In this moving story, a librarian introduces reading to the children of a gypsy community.

Le racisme expliqué à ma fille [Racism Explained to My Daughter]
Tahar Ben Jelloun, 1998
This introduction to antiracism is addressed to children through the celebrated author's daughter.

The Human Stain
Philip Roth, 2000
This is one of the most powerful novels about contemporary prejudice in America.

Dans le nu de la vie; récits des marais rwandais [Life Laid Bare: The Survivors in Rwanda Speak]
Jean Hatzfeld, 2000
In this chilling book, the author, a French journalist and witness to the Tutsi genocide, gives voice to its survivors.

I, Rigoberta Menchú: An Indian Woman in Guatemala
Elisabeth Burgos-Debray, 1983
Rigoberta Menchú received the Nobel Peace Prize for defending Indian communities in Latin America. She became one of the voices of the populations whose lifestyle had been upturned with the arrival of Europeans. She has fought for many years for human rights in Guatemala.

FILMS

Shadows
John Cassavetes, 1959
This film follows two African American brothers and a sister and their interracial relationships in New York in the 1950s.

Ali: Fear Eats the Soul
Rainer Werner Fassbinder, 1974
This film is about everyday racism and interracial marriage.

Querelle
Rainer Werner Fassbinder, 1982
This provocative film about homosexuality is adapted from Jean Genet's novel.

My Beautiful Laundrette
Stephen Frears, 1985
This is the story of a young Pakistani who runs a launderette in England.

Shoah
Claude Lanzmann, 1985
This documentary is the ultimate source on the Holocaust.

Hairspray
John Waters, 1988
This light comedy is about segregation in the United States.

Mississippi Burning
Alan Parker, 1988
This film addresses the civil rights movement in the United States.

Le huitième jour [The Eighth Day]
Jaco Van Dormael, 1996
This film's starring role is played by Pascal Duquenne, a young man with Down syndrome. He would be awarded best actor at the Cannes Film Festival in 1996—a first for a disabled actor.

Boys Don't Cry
Kimberly Peirce, 1999
This film addresses the murder of a young transgender man in the United States, based on the real-life story of Brandon Teena.

Brokeback Mountain
Ang Lee, 2005
This award-winning movie tells the love story of two men in the American West, from 1963 to 1983.

Milk
Gus Van Sant, 2008
This film follows one of the first openly gay politicians in the United States.

Benda Bilili!
Renaud Barret and Florent de La Tullaye, 2010
This documentary follows a music group with disabled members, from the streets of Kinshasa to their triumphant international tour. It garnered much praise at the Cannes Film Festival in 2010.

La Vie d'Adèle [Blue is the Warmest Color]
Abdellatif Kechiche, 2013
In this winner of the Palme d'Or at the Cannes Film Festival in 2013, two young women discover their love for one another.

Charlie's Country
Rolf de Heer, 2013
This film addresses the status of Aboriginal Australians.

The Imitation Game
Morten Tyldum, 2014
This film is inspired by the biography of Alan Turing, perhaps the greatest mathematician of the twentieth century, who was prosecuted by British law and made to undergo chemical castration in 1952 for homosexuality. He committed suicide shortly thereafter.

MUSIC

"Strange Fruit"
Billie Holiday, 1939
This heart-wrenching tune is one of the first antiracist songs.

"We Shall Overcome"
1947
This protest song inspired by a gospel hymn is an emblem of the civil rights movement in the United States.

"Imagine"
John Lennon, 1971
This song offers a bit of hope in a cruel world.

"Asimbonanga"
Savuka and Johnny Clegg, 1986
This song was dedicated to Nelson Mandela, imprisoned at the time on Robben Island. For many years, its chorus would serve as an anthem against apartheid.

WEBSITES

The Universal Declaration of Human Rights
www.un.org/en/documents/udhr/

International Convention on the Elimination of All Forms of Racial Discrimination
www.ohchr.org/EN/ ProfessionalInterest/Pages/ CERD.aspx

International Lesbian, Gay, Bisexual, Trans, and Intersex Association (ILGA)
www.ilga.org

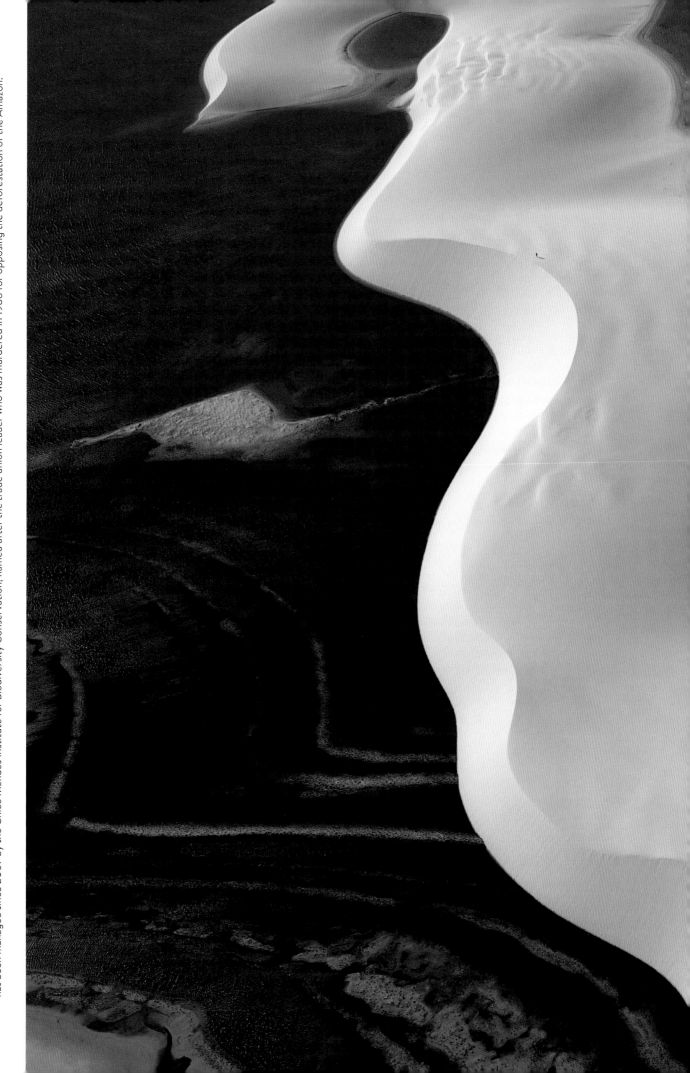

LENÇÓIS MARANHENSES NATIONAL PARK, MARANHÃO, BRAZIL 2° 32′ 00 S – 43° 07′ 00 W

Lençóis Maranhenses National Park, established in 1981, is a dune and laguna preserve that extends over an area of 600 square miles (1,500 km²). Like three hundred other natural reserves in Brazil, it has been managed since 2007 by the Chico Mendes Institute for Biodiversity Conservation, named after the trade union leader who was murdered in 1988 for opposing the deforestation of the Amazon.

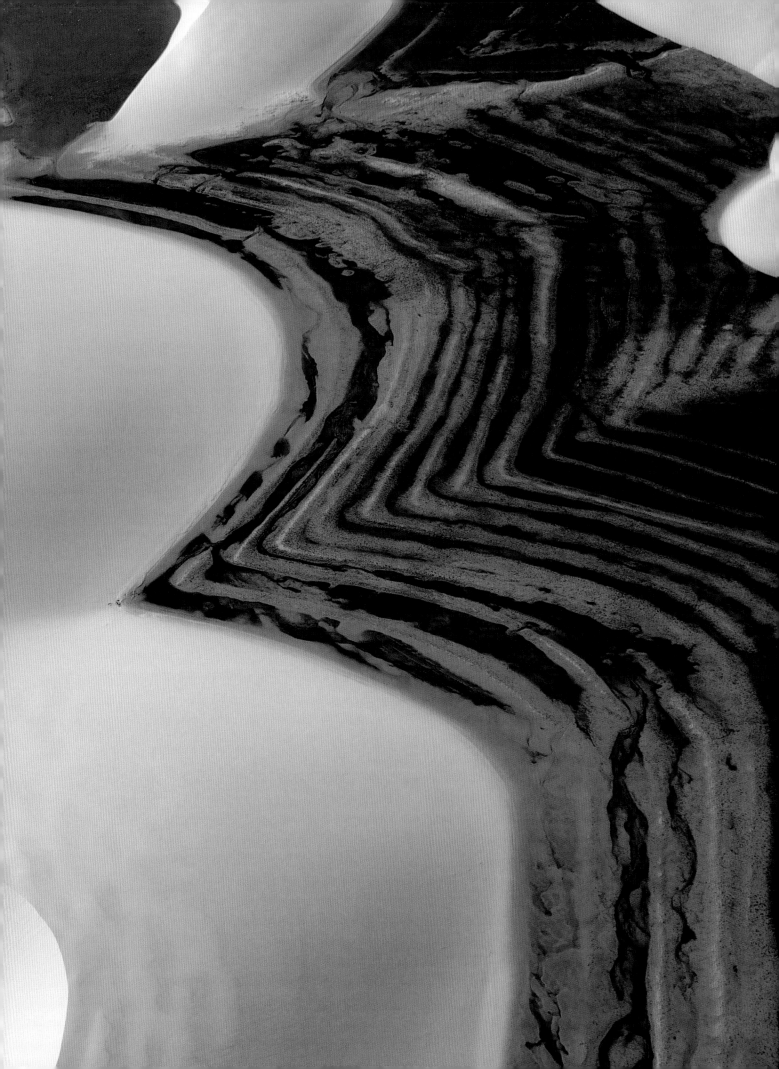

THE STATUE OF LIBERTY, A LIGHT FOR THE WORLD, LIBERTY ISLAND AND THE ISLAND OF MANHATTAN, NEW YORK, UNITED STATES 40° 41′ N – 74° 03′ W

New York is home to more than 8.5 million people. Numerous immigrants have moved there throughout its history in search of the American dream. The city is a mix of multiple communities—English, Irish, Italian, Jewish, Haitian, and Russian, to name a few.

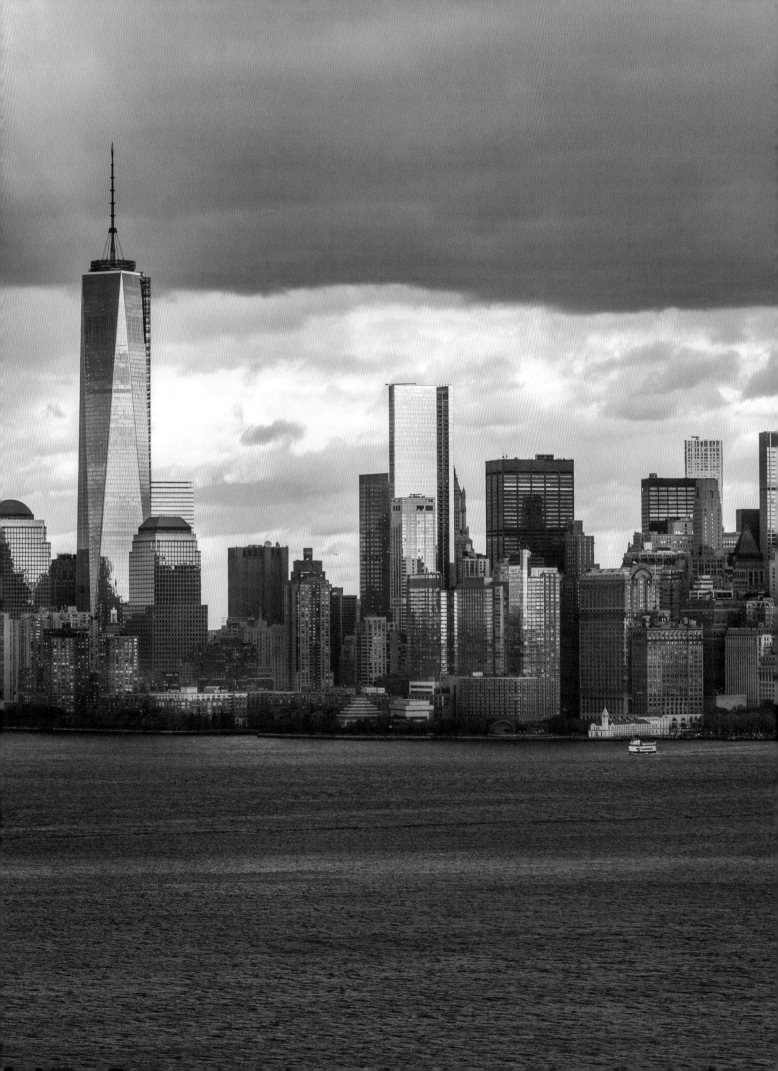

TRADITIONAL FISHERMAN NEAR PORT-AU-PRINCE, HAITI 18° 34' 50" N – 72° 20' 22" W

This fisherman is seeking his catch in an oil slick. Haitians consume almost 35 million tons of fish per year. One-fifth of these fish are brought to land by local fishermen.

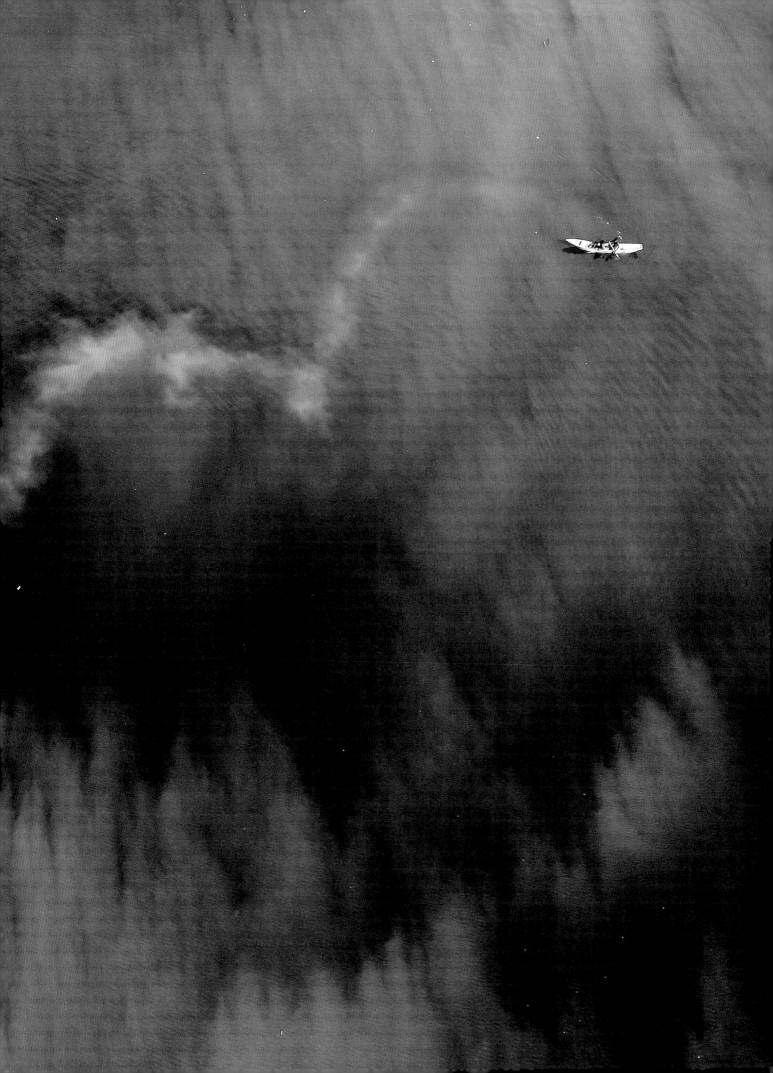

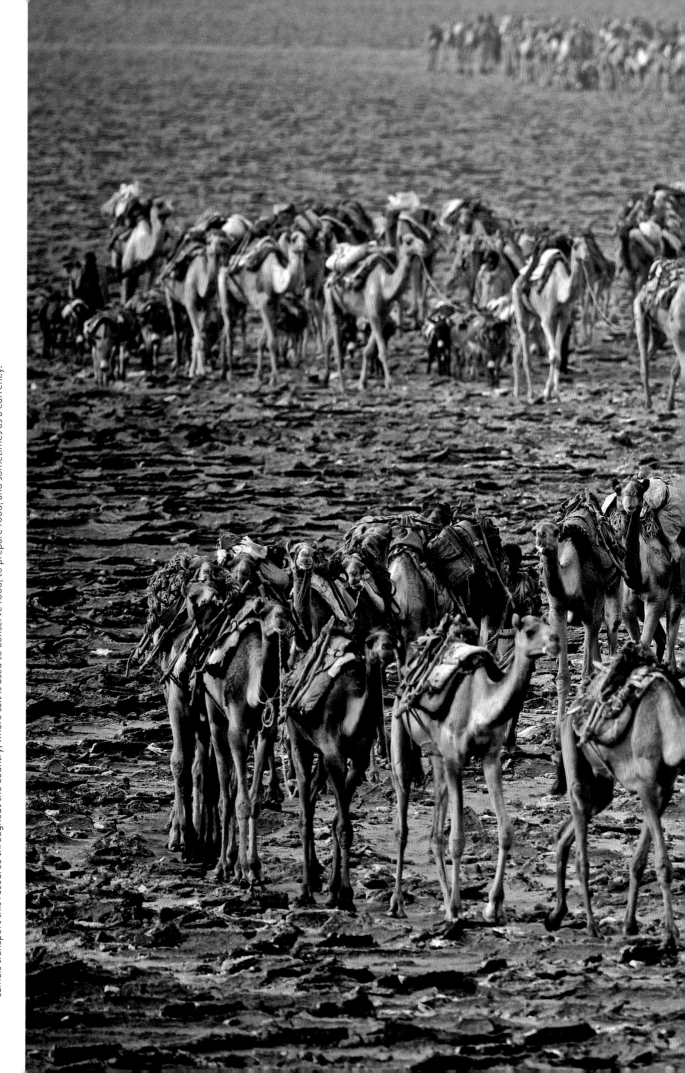

LAKE KARUM SALT CARAVAN, DANAKIL, ETHIOPIA 14° 06′ N – 40° 20′ E

The Danakil Depression, also known as the Afar Depression, is the lowest region in Africa in terms of altitude. This salt desert is also the hottest spot on Earth, with diurnal temperatures reaching 120 degrees Fahrenheit (50 degrees Celsius). The Danakil is therefore home to a resource that has been farmed for centuries: salt, extracted from open-air mines. Huge caravans of several hundred camels transport this resource throughout the country, where salt is used to conserve food, to prepare food, and sometimes as a currency.

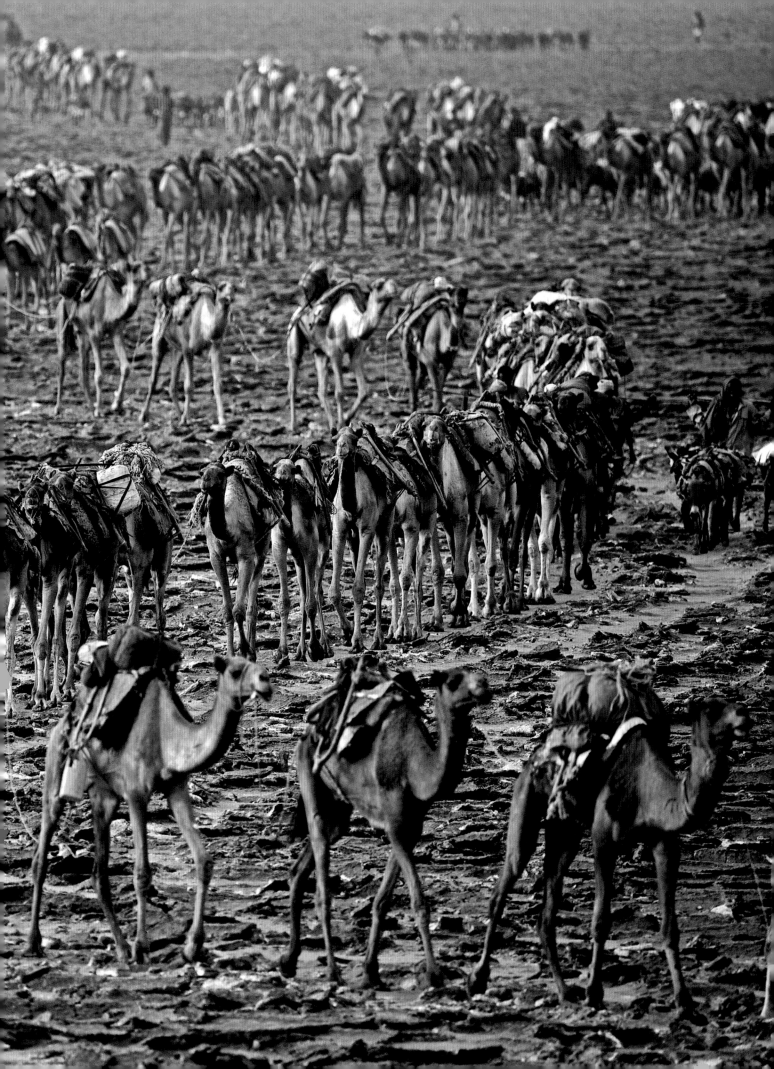

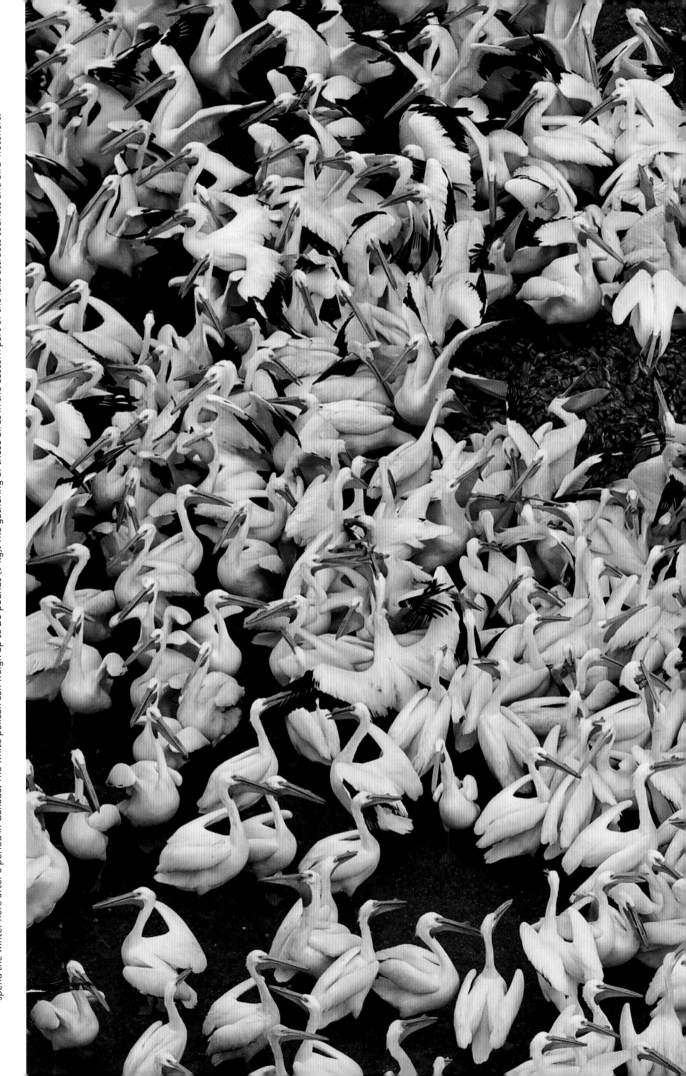

PELICANS, LAKE CHAPALA, JALISCO, MEXICO 20° 15' N – 103° 00' W

Lake Chapala is the largest lake in Mexico, with an area of over 400 square miles (1,080 km²). It is located 250 miles (400 km) to the west of Mexico City. Up to three thousand white pelicans come to spend the winter here after a period in Canada. The white pelican can weigh up to 20 pounds (9 kg). The gathering of these birds in the eastern part of the lake attracts tourists and bird-watchers.

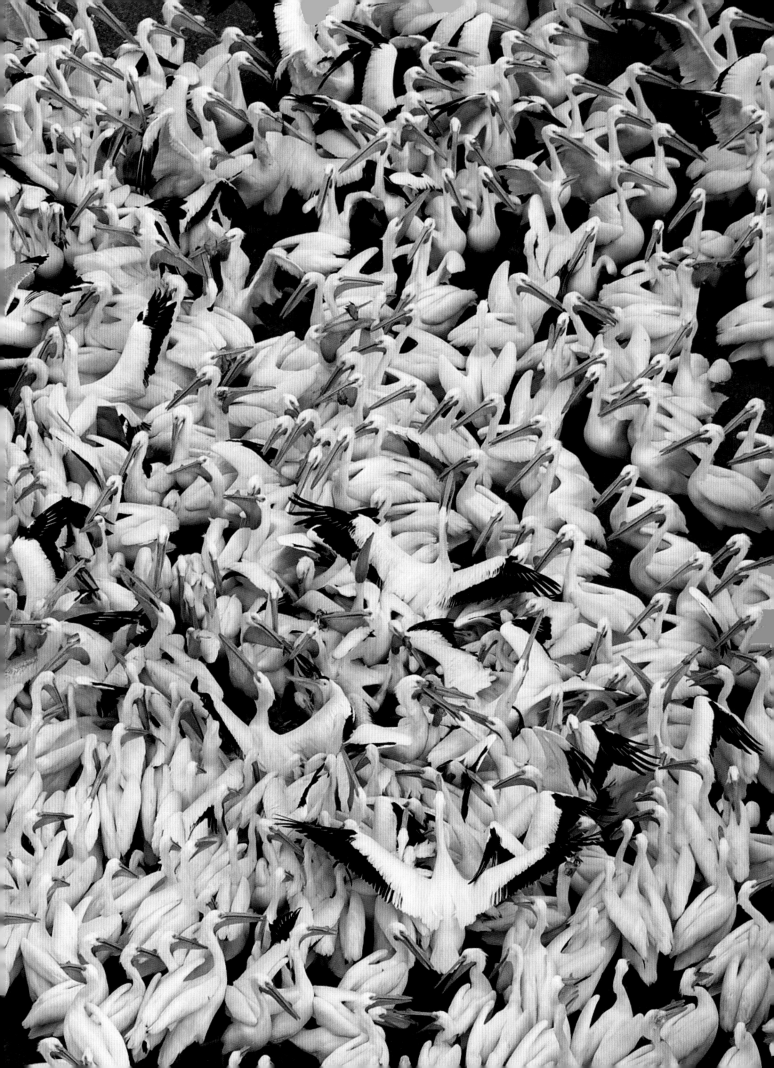

THE ANTHROPOCENE PERIOD

WORLD HUMAN POPULATION

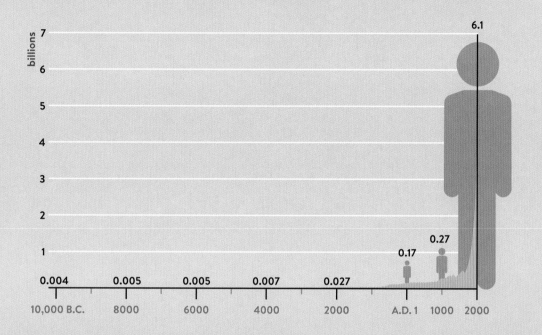

CONCENTRATION OF GREENHOUSE GASES UP TO 2005

Carbon Dioxide (CO_2)

Nitrous Oxide (N_2O)

Methane (CH_4)

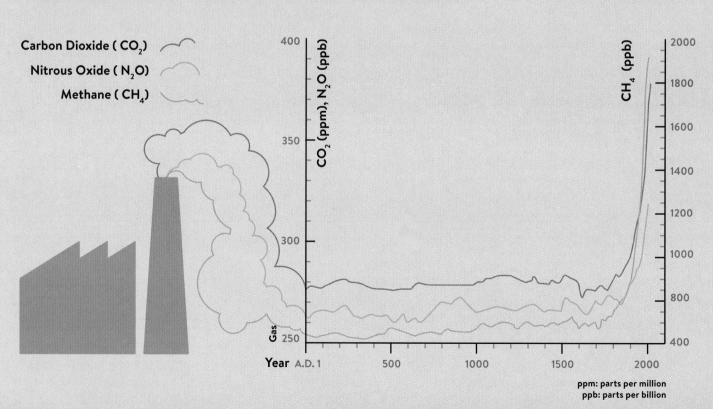

ppm: parts per million
ppb: parts per billion

GLOBAL TEMPERATURE ANOMALIES (°C)

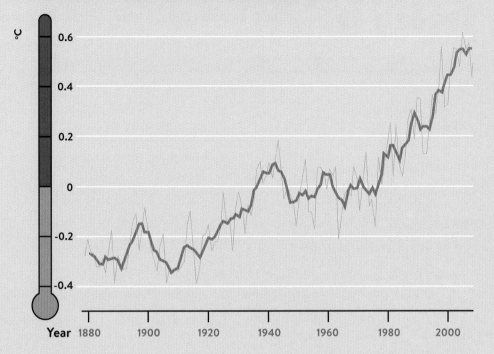

°C

Year

KEY FIGURES

The Anthropocene is the contemporary period in Earth's history. Humans now exert an influence over the planet that is comparable to the events of the great geological transformations of the past.

50,000 square miles (13 million hectares) are deforested every year. In the 1990s, 62,000 square miles (16 million hectares) of forest were disappearing annually.

Between 1990 and 2010, global emmissions of all major greenhouse gases increased. Net emissions of carbon dioxide increased 42%.

78% of greenhouse gas emissions are caused by the production or consumption of fossil fuel energies such as coal and petroleum.

Coal produces 40% of electricity worldwide. Worldwide consumption of coal increased more than 70% between 2000 and 2013. This can be explained by the economic growth of developing countries like China, India, and South Africa.

136 million tons of fish were caught or farmed worldwide in 2012.

4.8 to 12. 7 metric tons of waste are dumped into oceans every year.

Four planets would be required for humanity if the world's population had a mode of consumption like North America's.

In 2009, humanity extracted 68 billion tons of material from our planet's ground. In 1990: 42 billion.

FRESH WATER DIVERTED FOR HUMAN USE

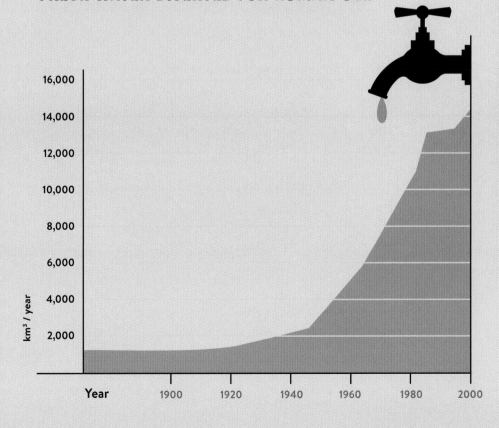

km³ / year

Year

HUNGER

PREVALENCE OF MALNUTRITION

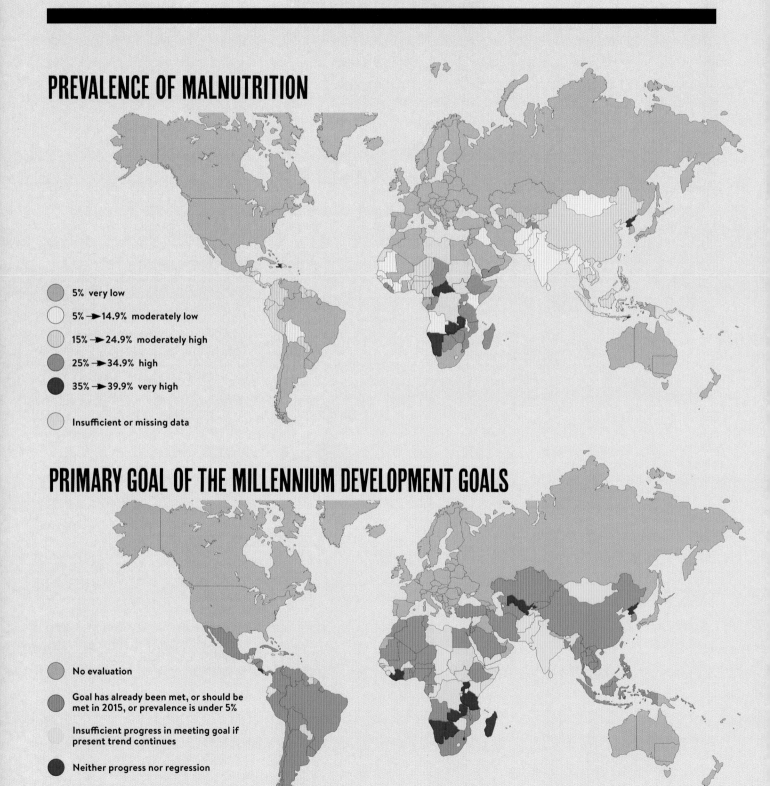

- 5% **very low**
- 5% → 14.9% **moderately low**
- 15% → 24.9% **moderately high**
- 25% → 34.9% **high**
- 35% → 39.9% **very high**
- Insufficient or missing data

PRIMARY GOAL OF THE MILLENNIUM DEVELOPMENT GOALS

- No evaluation
- Goal has already been met, or should be met in 2015, or prevalence is under 5%
- Insufficient progress in meeting goal if present trend continues
- Neither progress nor regression
- Insufficient or missing data

AGE-STANDARDIZED PREVALENCE OF OBESITY

KEY FIGURES

in **men** aged 18 years
and over (BMI ≥30 kg/m²), 2014

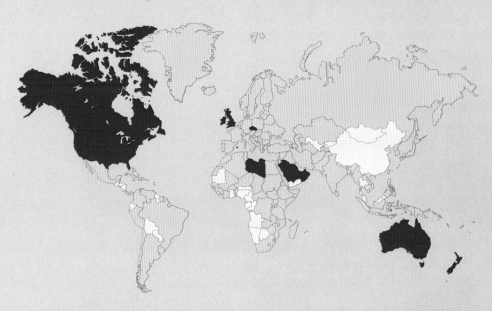

A person living in a developed country eats 210 pounds (95.7 kilograms) of meat per year, compared with only 70 pounds (31.6 kilograms) per inhabitant in a developing country.

"Mega-crops" (rice, wheat, maize) provide more than half the world's food. Three-quarters of the world's food depends on just twelve plant species.

Almost 1 billion people in the world do not have enough to feed themselves properly.

80% of the people suffering from hunger are farmers. More than 1 billion people are employed in agriculture, representing 1 in 3 workers.

Agriculture is responsible for 14% of greenhouse gas emissions.

There are more than 36,000 McDonald's restaurants in more than a hundred countries. They employ more than 1.9 million people.

Worldwide, the number of cases of obesity has more than doubled since 1980. In 2014, more than 1.9 billion adults—people aged 18 and over—were overweight, including more than 600 million who were obese.

in **women** aged 18 years
and over (BMI ≥30 kg/m²), 2014

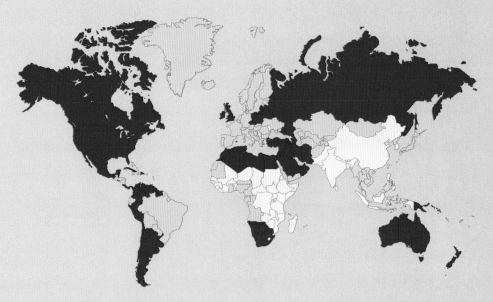

Prevalence of obesity (%)*

 <5%

15% → 24.9%   Data not available

5% → 14.9%   ≥25%   * BMI ≥ 30 kg/m²

INEQUALITY

INCOME INEQUALITY (2013)

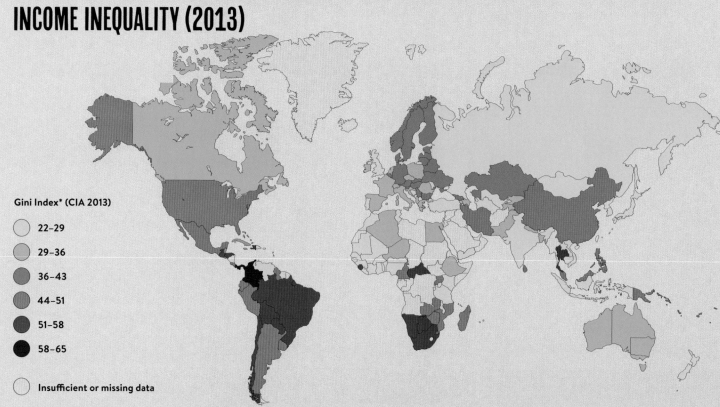

Gini Index* (CIA 2013)

- 22–29
- 29–36
- 36–43
- 44–51
- 51–58
- 58–65

Insufficient or missing data

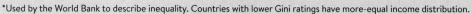

*Used by the World Bank to describe inequality. Countries with lower Gini ratings have more-equal income distribution.

INTERNATIONAL HUMAN DEVELOPMENT INDICATORS

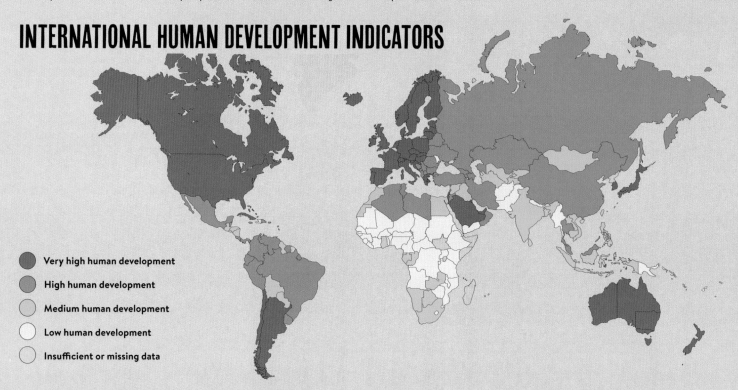

- Very high human development
- High human development
- Medium human development
- Low human development
- Insufficient or missing data

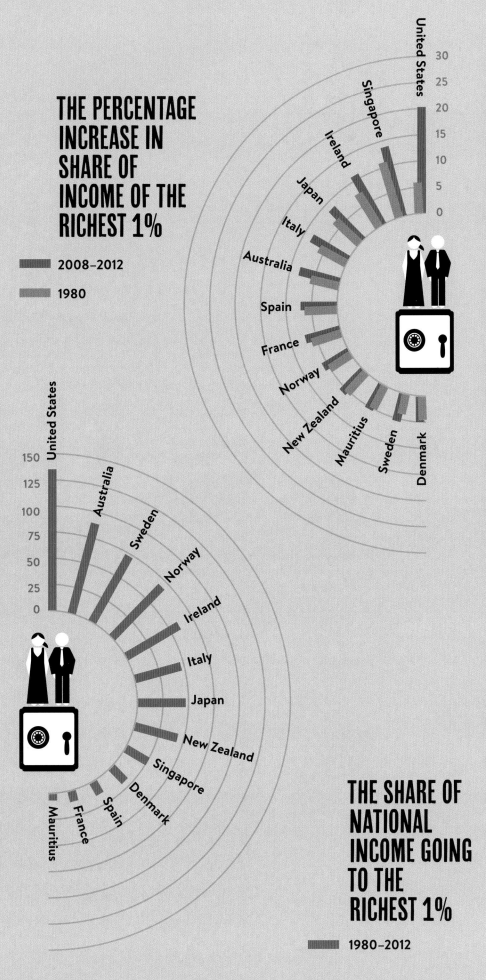

THE PERCENTAGE INCREASE IN SHARE OF INCOME OF THE RICHEST 1%

- 2008–2012
- 1980

THE SHARE OF NATIONAL INCOME GOING TO THE RICHEST 1%

- 1980–2012

KEY FIGURES

The world GDP increased by almost 70% between 1992 and 2010.

In 2016, the combined wealth of the richest 1% will be greater than that of the other 99% of people, according to a controversial study by Oxfam.

A boy born in 2012 in a high-income country can expect to live 75.8 years—that's fifteen years more than a boy in a low-income country (60.2 years). For girls, the difference is even more pronounced, with a difference of 18.9 years separating the life expectancy in high-income countries (82.0 years) and the life expectancy in low-income countries (63.1 years).

Almost eight hundred women die each day from complications during pregnancy or childbirth.

High-income countries have on average 90 nurses and midwives per 10,000 residents, whereas in certain low-income countries, the density of this type of personnel is less than 2 per 10,000 residents.

In Cuba, there are 6.7 doctors per 1,000 residents, compared with less than 0.3 per 1,000 in Afghanistan.

More than 1.2 billion people do not have access to electricity on a regular basis in the world.

The number of children not in school in the world went from 101 million in 1990 to 67 million in 2009.

SALT HARVEST, SALAR DE UYUNI, DANIEL CAMPOS, POTOSÍ, BOLIVIA 20°12′ S – 67°36′ W

Located on the Bolivian Altiplano, the Salar de Uyuni is the largest salt desert in the world. With an area of some 3,000 square miles (8,000 km²), it is located at an altitude of 12,000 feet (3,660 meters). The salt harvest is challenging work, carried out by a few mining families. Beneath this white gold are vast reserves of lithium, a component of batteries.

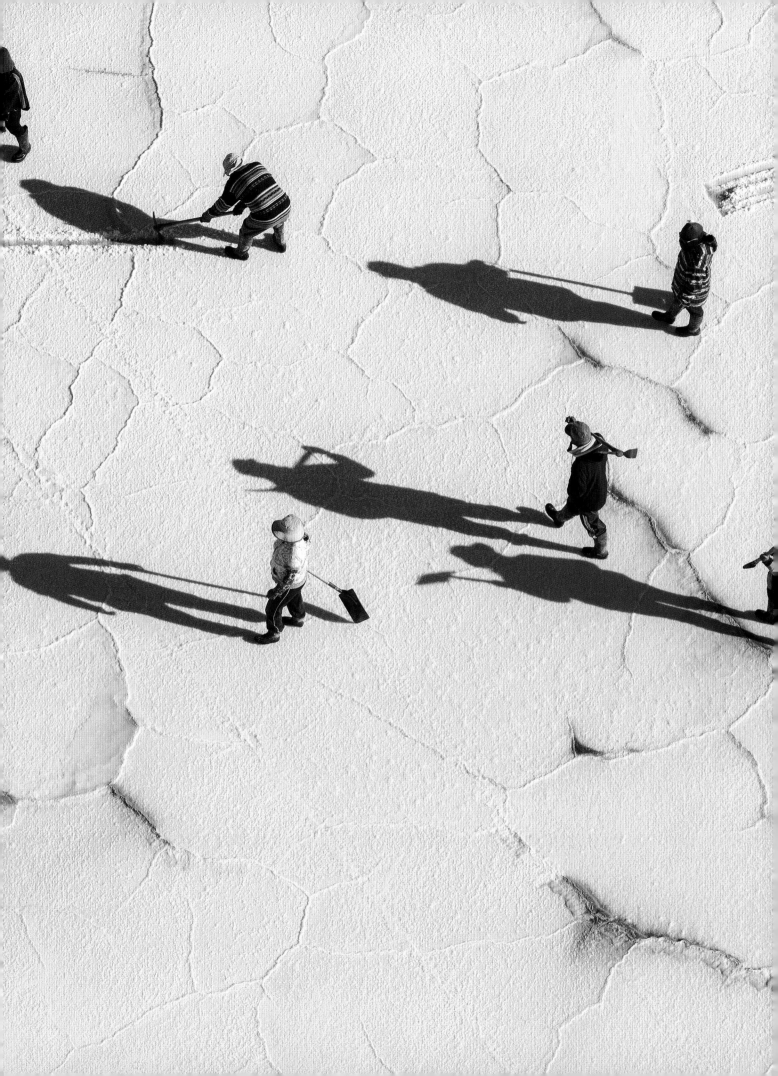

A FREE FILM

Human is a unique production that is the result of an exceptional collaboration.

For the first time, two esteemed nonprofit foundations have come together to enable an outstanding movie to emerge.

Fully funded by the Bettencourt Schueller Foundation and created by the GoodPlanet Foundation, *Human* is a not-for-profit feature film.

This partnership has enabled Yann Arthus-Bertrand to make a profoundly original work and to disseminate it as widely as possible.

Working without financial stress is obviously the dream of every artist.

With the support of the Bettencourt Schueller Foundation, *Human* is a free movie.

A FILM SUPPORTED BY THE BETTENCOURT SCHUELLER FOUNDATION

By funding Yann Arthus-Bertrand's film, the Bettencourt Schueller Foundation continues its commitment to the "value of images." The foundation believes that images can lead us to experience a collective renewal of our relationship with the environment, both natural and human. Central to this is the vision of great directors whose personal journey resonates with a desire to celebrate the beauty of the living world and to promote awareness of the fragility of our environment and present a humane vision of our future.

The Bettencourt Schueller Foundation's contribution to *Human* continues the foundation's tradition of supporting worthy films, such as *Le Syndrome du Titanic* (The Titanic Syndrome) directed by Nicolas Hulot and Jean-Albert Lièvre; *Winged Migration*, *Oceans*, and *Seasons* by Jacques Perrin; and *Ice and the Sky* by Luc Jacquet.

The support provided by the Bettencourt Schueller Foundation to the GoodPlanet Foundation ensured that this important film was made and shared by covering production costs and supporting international and multi-media distribution.

www.fondationbs.org

The first feature film from the partnership of these two nonprofit foundations

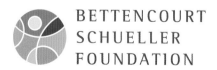

BETTENCOURT SCHUELLER FOUNDATION | GOODPLANET FOUNDATION

HUMAN, A GOODPLANET FOUNDATION PROJECT

Created in 2005 and chaired by Yann Arthus-Bertrand, the GoodPlanet Foundation educates and informs the public about issues related to our environment. It offers realistic, optimistic solutions, based on a series of programs aiming to bring greater awareness to ecology and living well together.

"I created the GoodPlanet Foundation to raise awareness, to inform and educate audiences of all ages and backgrounds. But also to take action and encourage that desire in everyone, to engage in projects which contribute to more respect for the planet and human rights."

—Yann Arthus-Bertrand,
president of the GoodPlanet Foundation.

GoodPlanet has designed all of the media (educational materials, web content, books, etc.) intended to accompany and ensure the dissemination of the film *Human.*

www.goodplanet.org

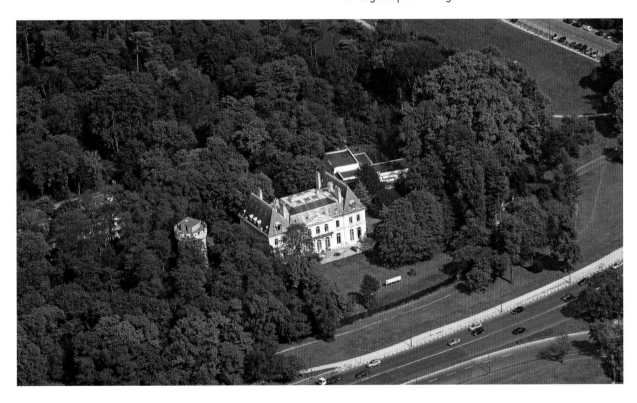

Human will have its home in the heart of the Bois de Boulogne in Paris. The Mayor of Paris has decided to entrust the GoodPlanet Foundation with about seven acres (three hectares) of the park and buildings of about 32,290 square feet (3,000 square meters), which will be intended to welcome all those who want to talk about the commitment to humanism in the context of major art exhibitions, cultural events, conferences, and more.

See you in Spring 2016.

CREDITS

Editor in chief:
Olivier Blond

Associate editor in chief:
Julien Leprovost

Coordination for GoodPlanet:
Galitt Kenan

Coordination for *Human*:
Florent Gilard

Journalists for *Human*:
Hervé Kern, Anastasia Mikova,
Anne Poiret, and Mia Sfeir

Reporting (selection and editing):
Catherine André and
Philippe Thureau-Dangin

Portraits
© HUMANKIND Production, unless
otherwise noted

Aerial photography
© Yann Arthus-Bertrand, unless
otherwise noted

Other photography credits
© Stéphane Azouze: p. 4 (photos 2,
4, and 6), p. 6 (photo 1), pp. 52–53,
pp. 66–67, pp. 86–87, pp. 218–219
© Emmanuel Cappellin, p. 6 (photo 5)
© Chloé Henry Biabaud, p. 6
(photo 3)
© Yoko Saido, p. 6 (photo 4)
© Yazid Tizi and Bruno Cusa, pp. 174-
175, pp. 180–181

Film excerpts
© HUMANKIND Production p. 4
(photo 3), p. 6 (photo 6), p. 8 (photos
2 through 6), pp. 32–33, pp. 144–145

Photo research—aerial photography:
Françoise Jacquot

**Photo research and photoengraving—
photography for *Human*:**
Julian Bondroit

Manufacturing:
Morgane Sort

Layout:
Léa Chevrier, Marina Delranc, and
Philippe Marchand for Copyright

Infographics:
Bertrand Loquet

Illustrations:
Marina Delranc

Proofreading:
Claire Lemoine

Acknowledgments for *Human*:
Stephane Azouze, Françoise
Bernard, Bruno Cusa, Anne-
Claire Decaux, Mathilde Froget,
Sterenn Hall, Maeva Issico, Anne-
Marie Sangla, Éric Salemi, Yazid Tizi,
and Valentin Wattelet

**Acknowledgments for the
GoodPlanet Foundation:**
Roxanne Crossley, Caroline
Humbert, Sebastián Eyherabide,
Marie Rouvillois, and Véronique
Jaquet

Additional acknowledgments:
Jeanne Etiemble, Jocelyn Rigault,
and Erwan Sourget

REPORTING/MANIFESTO SOURCES

Page 21 Extract from "Reaching My Autistic
Son Through Disney," *New York Times*
magazine, March 7, 2014. This article is adapted
from *Life, Animated* by Ron Suskind, published by
Kingswell, an imprint of Disney Book Group, 2014.

Page 36 "Words from Chinese Workers,"
excerpt from a transcription of a talk by Leslie
Chang, for © TEDGlobal 2012, June 2012.

Page 40 Extract from "On the Phenomenon
of Bullshit Jobs" by David Graeber, © *Strike!*
magazine, summer 2013.

Page 60 Extract from *Half the Sky: Turning
Oppression into Opportunity for Women
Worldwide* by Nicholas D. Kristof and Sheryl
WuDunn, published by Knopf, 2009.

Page 72 "I Am Malala" © Malala Yousafzai,
extract from her Nobel prize lecture, 2014.

Page 94 Extract from "Whoever Saves a Life,"
© Matthieu Aikins, *Medium* (http://medium.com),
September 14, 2014.

Page 125 "A Country Where Only Crime
Is Organized," extract from "Temporada de
muertos: Carta desde guerrero," by Alejandro
Almazán, © *Gatopardo* (www.gatopardo.com),
Mexico, December 2014.

Page 136 "Let Africa Show the World
How to Forgive," adapted from Desmond
Tutu's speech at his acceptance of an honorary
Doctorate of Laws degree, University of Toronto,
2000. © Desmond Tutu.

Page 158 "The Dirty Business of Human
Trafficking," extract from "Lo, scafista della
morte," by Fabrizio Gatti, © Gruppo Editoriale
L'Espresso Spa (www.espressonline.it), Rome,
October 16, 2013.

Page 165 "Hunger Is a Political Problem,"
interview with Olivier De Schutter by Yann
Arthus-Bertrand from *20 ans après…La Terre?
Le bilan du développement durable [Twenty Years
After…The Earth? The Assessment of Sustainable
Development]*, Éditions de La Martinière, Paris,
2012.

Page 166 "Poor Economics," excerpt from
a transcription of a talk by Esther Duflo, for ©
TEDGlobal 2010, February 2010.

Page 188 Extract from "Why Africa Is the
Most Homophobic Continent" by David
Smith, © 2015 Guardian News and Media Limited
or its affiliated companies (www.theguardian.com),
London, February 23, 2014.

INFOGRAPHIC AND DATA SOURCES

Page 22 Autism Early Signs in Infants:
http://www.ucdmc.ucdavis.edu//news/pdf/autism-in-infants.pdf

Page 24 "Up to $21,000...":
http://www.cdc.gov/ncbddd/autism/data.html

Page 26 Difficult Treatment: http://www.autismeurope.org

Pages 46–47 Happiness Map: http://unsdsn.org/wp-content/
uploads/2014/02/WorldHappinessReport2013_online.pdf
Love in Text Messages: mercialfred.com, www.tx.to
Key Figures: http://www.who.int/gho/urban_health/situation_trends/
urban_population_growth_text/en/, http://adage.com/article/media/
marketers-boost-global-ad-spending-540-billion/297737/,
http://www.oecd.org/newsroom/aid-to-developing-countries-rebounds-
in-2013-to-reach-an-all-time-high.htm

Page 63 Educating Women: http://www.uis.unesco.org,
http://unesdoc.unesco.org

Page 64 "31 million...": http://www.unesco.org

Pages 76–77 Women's Rights: http://www.uis.unesco.org/literacy/
Documents/fs-29-2014-literacy-en.pdf, http://www.who.int/
mediacentre/factsheets/fs241/en/, http://www.unwomen.org/en/what-
we-do/ending-violence-against-women/facts-and-figures

Page 89 "fifty thousand people..." https://www.prio.org/Data/
Armed-Conflict/Battle-Deaths/The-Battle-Deaths-Dataset-version-30

Page 98 Map of the Conflict in Syria:
http://www.bbc.com/news/worldmiddle-east-22798391

Pages 110–111 Refugees Worldwide: UNHCR – The UN Refugee Agency
Key Figures: http://www.theatlantic.com/international/
archive/2014/11/countries-without-militaries/382606/,
http://www.amnesty.org.au/armstrade/comments/28098/,
www.un.org/events/smallarms2006/pdf/backgrounder.pdf

Page 128 Principal Areas of Cartel Influence: Reports from the
United States Congress and Drug Enforcement Administration

Pages 140–141 Death Penalty Across the World:
http://www.amnestyusa.org
Prison Population: www.prisonstudies.org
Key Figures: http://www.unodc.org/toc/en/facts/factsheets/
index.html, rsf.org/files/bilan-2014-EN.pdf

Page 153 "Poverty is in decline...":
http://www.worldbank.org/en/topic/poverty/overview

Pages 170–171 Poverty in Numbers and Key Figures:
United Nations Millennium Development Goals Report 2014

Page 190 36 countries: http://www.loc.gov/law/help/criminal-laws-on-
homosexuality/african-nations-laws.php

Pages 198–199 Everyone Is Different: http://www.refworld.org/
pdfid/519b6ca24.pdf
Key Figures: http://www.bls.gov/news.release/pdf/wkyeng.pdf,
http://www.npr.org/sections/health-shots/2011/06/09/137084239/
nearly-1-in-7-people-on-earth-are-disabled-survey-finds

Pages 212–213 World Human Population: http://www.census.gov
Concentration of Greenhouse Gases: http://mapserver.
gsfc.nasa.gov/gcmd-open/mmorahan/Conentrations_Greenhouse_
Gases0to2005.png
Global Temperature Anomalies: http://www.wmo.int/pages/prog/
wcp/wcdmp/GCDS_3.php
Key Figures: http://www.epa.gov/climatechange/science/indicators/
ghg/global-ghg-emissions.html, http://www.iea.org/topics/coal/,
http://www.fao.org/3/a-i3720e.pdf, http://www.sciencemag.org/
content/347/6223/768, http://www.popsci.com/environment/
article/2012-10/daily-infographic-if-everyone-lived-american-how-
many-earths-would-we-need, http://www.wbcsd.org/changing-pace/
current-context/materials.aspx
Fresh Water Diverted for Human Use: United Nations
Environment Programme http://www.unep.org

Pages 214–215 Prevalence of Malnutrition:
http://www.fao.org/3/a-i4033e.pdf
Prevalence of Obesity: http://apps.who.int/iris/
bitstream/10665/148114/1/9789241564854_eng.pdf
Maps: http://www.fao.org/hunger
Key Figures: http://www.fao.org/docrep/005/y4252e/y4252e05b.
htm, http://www.fao.org/docrep/015/i2490e/i2490e01b.pdf, http://
www.epa.gov/climatechange/ghgemissions/global.html, http://www.
aboutmcdonalds.com/mcd/our_company.html, http://www.who.int/
mediacentre/factsheets/fs311/en/

Pages 216–217 Income Inequality: http://upload.wikimedia.org/
wikipedia/commons/1/11/World_Income_Gini_Map_%282013%29.svg
Share of National Income: https://www.oxfam.org/sites/www.
oxfam.org/files/bp-working-for-few-political-capture-economic-
inequality-200114-summ-en.pd
International Human Development Indicators: http://hdr.undp.
org/en/data/map
Key Figures: https://www.cia.gov/library/publications/the-world-
factbook/fields/2226.html, http://www.uis.unesco.org/FactSheets/
Documents/FS12_2011_OOSC_EN.pdf

INSIDE FRONT COVER: TEXTILES DRYING IN BAHAWALPUR, PUNJAB, PAKISTAN 29° 24' N – 71° 40' E

The Punjab region is the economic heart of Pakistan. The textile industry accounts for more than half of exports and 20 percent of the workforce. This sector, however, faces challenges: an unstable rupee, competition from neighboring countries, and power supply shortages that prevent factories from producing at full capacity.

INSIDE BACK COVER: HORSES AND RIVERBED IN THE ORKHON VALLEY, ÖVÖRKHANGAI, MONGOLIA 47° 03' N – 102° 42' E

The Orkhon Valley is included in UNESCO's World Heritage List. Its first known populations date back to 62,000 B.C. What's more, the valley was inhabited and traversed by several nomadic peoples who found an environment favorable to raising horses and herds: Huns, a Turkish people, Uyghurs, Khitans, and finally Mongols. Genghis Khan, founder of the Mongol Empire and a famed conqueror, established his base there, on the site of Karakorum, where his son would build the empire's capital.

ABRAMS EDITION

Editor: Laura Dozier
Designer: Shawn Dahl, dahlimama inc.
Production Manager: Denise LaCongo
Translation from the French: Hanna Hannah, Alan G. Paddle, Molly Stevens, The Art of Translation

Library of Congress Control Number: 2015941804

ISBN: 978-1-4197-1937-0

Copyright © 2015 Éditions de La Martinière, La Martinière Groupe, Paris

English translation copyright © 2015 Abrams Image, New York, and Thames & Hudson, London

Simultaneously published in French as *Human* by Éditions de La Martinère

Printed and bound in France
10 9 8 7 6 5 4 3 2 1

Abrams books are available at special discounts when purchased in quantity for premiums and promotions as well as fundraising or educational use. Special editions can also be created to specification. For details, contact specialsales@abramsbooks.com or the address below.

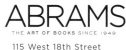

THE ART OF BOOKS SINCE 1949

115 West 18th Street
New York, NY 10011
www.abramsbooks.com